D0554645

THE CENTER FOR CHINESE STUDIES

at the University of California, Berkeley, supported by the Ford Foundation, the Institute of International Studies (University of California, Berkeley), and the State of California, is the unifying organization for social science and interdisciplinary research on contemporary China.

PUBLICATIONS

Wakeman, Frederic, Jr. *Strangers at the Gate: Social Disorder in South China, 1839–1861* (1966)

Townsend, James. *Political Participation in Communist China* (1967)

Potter, J. M. *Capitalism and the Chinese Peasant: Social and Economic Change in a Hong Kong Village* (1968)

Schiffrin, Harold Z. *Sun Yat-sen and the Origin of the Chinese Revolution* (1968)

Schurmann, Franz. *Ideology and Organization in Communist China* (Second Edition, 1968)

Van Ness, Peter. *Revolution and Chinese Foreign Policy: Peking's Support for Wars of National Liberation* (1970)

CHINA AND AFRICA
1949-1970

This volume is sponsored by the
Center for Chinese Studies,
University of California, Berkeley

CHINA AND AFRICA 1949-1970

THE FOREIGN POLICY OF THE PEOPLE'S REPUBLIC OF CHINA

BRUCE D. LARKIN

UNIVERSITY OF CALIFORNIA PRESS
BERKELEY, LOS ANGELES, LONDON

University of California Press
Berkeley and Los Angeles, California
University of California Press, Ltd.
London, England

Second Printing, 1973
First Paperback Edition, 1973
ISBN: 0-520-01761-7 cloth
0-520-02357-9 paper

Library of Congress Catalog Card Number: 78-123624

Printed in the United States of America

Designed by Dave Comstock

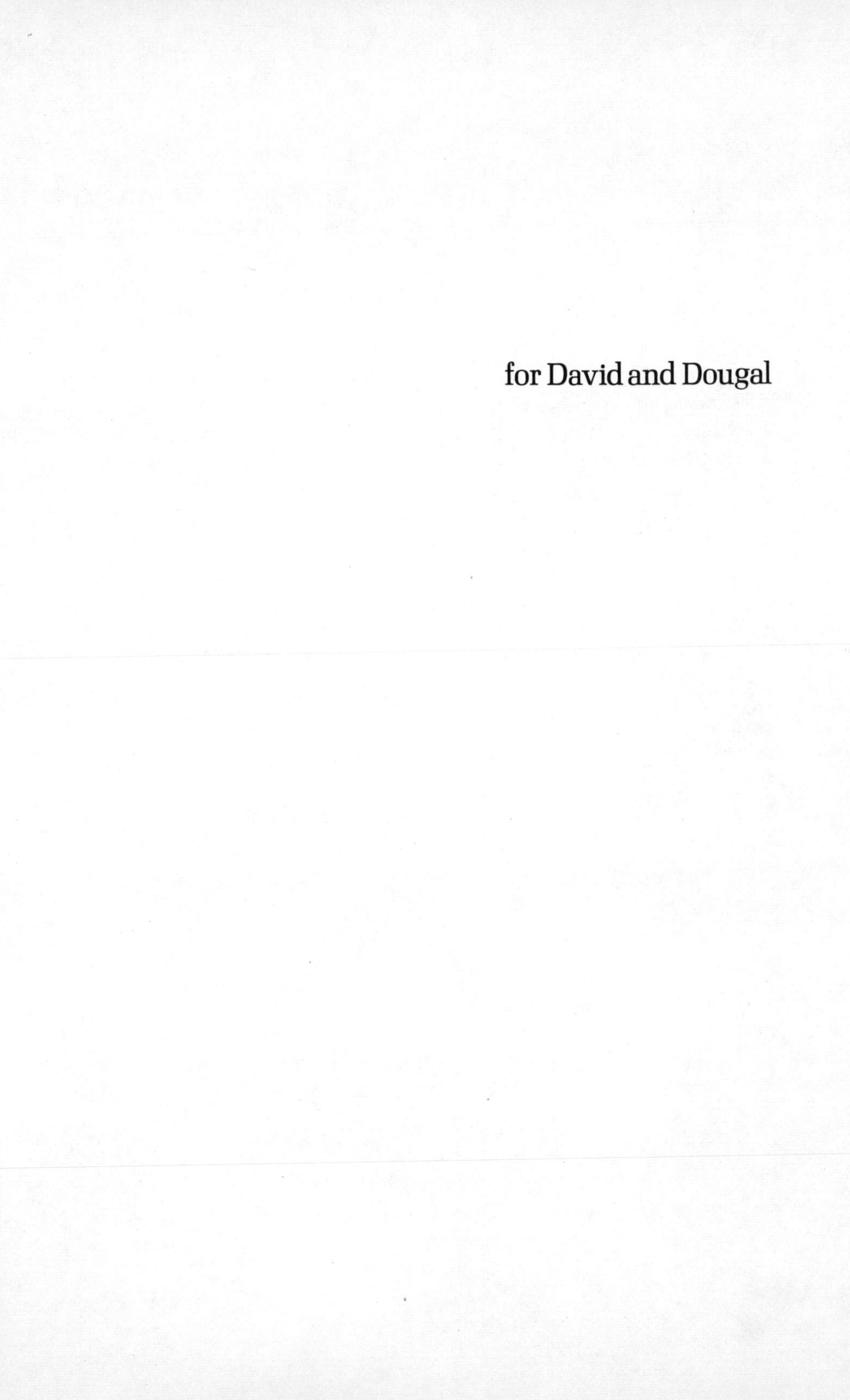

for David and Dougal

Preface

The casual reader who begins at the beginning deserves a word of warning. This study describes Chinese activities in Africa, but it is also an effort to explain how facets of Chinese foreign policy which appear to be contradictory to the outside observer may have been judged quite consistent by policy makers in Peking.

Because a basis must be laid to achieve the second objective, Chapter 1 centers on a statement of hypotheses concerning Chinese foreign-policy processes. The reader who is interested only in the tale of China's adventures in Africa could readily begin at Chapter 2, and continue with Chapters 3, 4, 6, and 8. If he were concerned with the policy consequences of an assessment of China's activities he might also read Chapter 9, the concluding chapter. The material is presented as it is because I believe that the activities described make little sense without two kinds of theoretical material: the first, Peking's acknowledged doctrine of revolutionary action, described in Chapters 5 and 7; the second, some preliminary ordering notions following from the premise that Chinese policy is accessible to systematic inquiry, since it is neither random nor uncontrolled. A detailed account of Chinese institutions concerned with Africa and the names of some persons conducting Chinese African policy have been placed in the Appendix.

This study was written in the belief that it might prove useful to persons with rather diverse interests: students of international politics and contemporary Chinese affairs, policy planners (in Africa and elsewhere) concerned with Sino-African relations, and members of the public who wish a more detailed and analytical rendering of this subject than is otherwise available. The reader who is not completely familiar with post-1949 Chinese politics and the more important Chinese figures, or who finds the names of some African states unfamiliar, may experience a little discomfort but will not find that any of the narrative or argument is difficult to follow.

Some students of international politics may find China's concern for Africa relevant to their studies because it is a new element in the international system, one change among many associated with decolonization and China's post-1949 coherence. Others may be struck by the way ideology — China's revolutionary commitment, in this case — guides Chinese policy, and yet is limited and confined by immediate Chinese needs and African realities. All readers will share a concern for these issues: Can China, with virtually no contacts and the disadvantage of distance, create an influential position for herself in African affairs? What are China's ambitions? And are there limits on the influence she may be able to attain?

The first twenty years of the People's Republic of China have now ended. This interval is sufficiently long to permit us to see regularities in Chinese policies toward specific countries and regions. We can speak with more confidence about the bases of policy. We can identify discontinuities in both domestic and foreign policy and view these discontinuities against the persistent trends of this period. Henceforth China's place in the world system, which may turn on military capabilities and the illogic of deterrence, will be increasingly disputed. Men will look to the first two decades for some insight into Chinese intentions and actions. It is desirable that the record be available to them.

I have tried to present this fragment of the record in detail and to analyze it with due care, although some pertinent material has been omitted in order to keep the narrative within bounds. The omissions do not, in my judgment, alter the main thrust of the accompanying argument. As time passes those who have been involved in Sino-African exchanges may tell more about them: the recent revelations of the Pan-Africanist Congress (see Chapter 8, note 53) are a case in point. Such material is fascinating and gives texture to our understanding of the political encounters related here, but the main lines of the encounters are already well defined.

I am responsible for the faults of this work. Whatever merit it has is the result of the contributions, direct and indirect, of countless others. I owe an important though diffuse debt to my teachers. Hans Morgenthau, Quincy Wright, and Philip Wagner introduced me to international politics and economic geography at the University of Chicago. John Fairbank, Benjamin Schwartz, and Rupert Emerson guided my study and research at Harvard University.

Valuable editorial suggestions were made by my parents and by Judy and Terry Ball, who read the entire manuscript with care. Patrick Cavendish, John Marcum, and members of the politics faculty of the University of California, Santa Cruz, read and commented upon portions of a draft. Don Klein, now at Columbia University, shared his painstakingly collected biographic files at a strategic time; his generosity sets a professional standard. William Foltz of Yale University made several substantive suggestions, which I have sought to follow. I am mindful of the contribution of Helen Kruse Williams, who prompted me to conceive this topic in November 1962.

Phyllis Killen of the University of California Press has been extraordinarily helpful in the final editing. Phyllis Halpin, Sharon Overgaard, and Barbara Chin of the staff of Cowell College have been kind and patient in their assistance.

Students have encouraged me throughout this work. I hold Victor Nee, Allen Hunter, Greg Herken, Don Goldstein, and Margaret Blades in special regard.

My greatest debts to institutions are due to libraries. I have relied on materials held by Harvard University (Harvard Yenching Library, East Asian Research Center Library, Widener Library); University of California, Los Angeles (a fine collection of African newspapers and an efficient research library); University of California, Berkeley (Center for Chinese Studies); Hoover Institution; Universities Service Center in Hong Kong; and the University of California, Santa Cruz.

Since September 1965, when the University of California, Santa Cruz, opened to its first students, I have enjoyed the fellowship of Cowell College. My colleagues, stimulating, acute, and humane, have supported me in work and in leisure.

Contents

Tables

Abbreviations

AAPSO	Afro-Asian People's Solidarity Organization	
CCP	Chinese Communist Party	
Congo (B)	Congo (Brazzaville)	
Congo (K)	Congo (Kinshasa)	The former Belgian Congo. In 1966
Congo (L)	Congo (Léopoldville)	the name Léopoldville was changed to Kinshasa.
CPSU	Communist Party of the Soviet Union	
FLN	Front de Libération Nationale (Algeria)	
PAFMECSA	Pan-African Freedom Movement for East, Central, and Southern Africa	

Periodicals

JMJP	*Jen-min Jih-pao* [People's Daily], Peking
KMJP	*Kuang-ming Jih-pao* [Enlightenment Daily], Peking
NCNA	New China News Agency. English Language Service. *Daily News Releases.*
NYT	*New York Times*
PR	*Peking Review*, Peking

Series Issued by the U.S. Consulate General, Hong Kong

CB	*Current Background*
ECMM	*Extracts from China Mainland Magazines*
SCMM	*Selections from China Mainland Magazines*
SCMP	*Survey of China Mainland Press*

For these last, the numbers represent issue and page numbers, and the original source is given in parentheses; when no original source is cited, the reader is to understand that the original was a Chinese publication or NCNA dispatch given public circulation. Note that the date is that of the original source, *not* that of the translation.

1 Introduction

The People's Republic of China, in the twenty-one years from 1949 to 1970, has come increasingly to act as an autonomous power. She conducts diplomacy with an enlarging number of states. She has declared independence from Soviet tutelage, and she has successfully developed nuclear weapons. In the 1950s China was a regional power in Asia, not a world power; by 1970 her actions had worldwide consequences, though her power was still limited.

This change took place as most African peoples moved from colonial status to political independence. Africa was no longer closed by European states. With some important exceptions, Africans could undertake diplomacy with whomever they chose. Moreover, even in the years prior to independence, indigenous political movements sought aid and recognition from outside Africa. Events created an opportunity for Chinese policy makers which barely existed in 1949. Peking's response to the new opportunity is the central content of this study. Starting with few political assets and hampered by scarcity, China attained distinctive political results.

Relations with Africa are surely less important to China than her affairs with some other states and regions: the Soviet Union, the adjacent Asian states, and the United States. Peking's creation and pursuit of an African policy represent an effort to alter some of the circumstances in which China finds herself and, by doing that, to gain leverage vis-à-vis the Soviet Union and the United States. In time Africa will probably become a more important political force in its own right than it is today; there are strong reasons to expect China will increase the share of her attention given to African policy.

China's actions in Africa already have a substance of their own. Peking had diplomatic relations with fifteen African states in 1970. Approximately 5.1 per cent of China's imports and exports were in African trade in 1966. By mid-1966 China had promised African countries $350,000,000 in aid, although the sums made available and actually drawn were much less. But these figures are dwarfed by her commitment to finance and build the Tanzania-Zambia railway; China could spend $280,000,000 or more for that project alone.

China has suffered disappointments. Five African states which once established diplomatic relations with her had broken them by 1969. Others refuse to enter into relations. On two occasions the men who conduct China's policy were forced to cut down their activities because of events inside China. In 1961 economic hardship led to drastic curtailment of political work in Africa; because of the Great Proletarian Cultural Revolution, almost all Chinese ambassadors were recalled to China for long stays during 1967 and 1968. China has aided a number of national liberation movements, but most of those that have received Chinese aid are far from winning power. China has severed ties with the permanent secretariat of the Afro-Asian People's Solidarity Organization. Even the governing nationalists who are friendly to China refuse to commit themselves to China's world view. No governing African leader has echoed Peking's assault on the Soviet leadership.

Disappointments are borne because they are unavoidable costs incurred in the pursuit of desired goals. If one looks at policies undertaken by China since 1949, when the Chinese Communist party (CCP) attained state power, one can discern the principal directions toward which policy has been aimed. Only to an extent are these like the aims of other states. The central end is that the Chinese state endure, and endure with continued CCP authority throughout China. Within the country, the CCP strives to attain economic development; without, it seeks identity and prestige. Within, it is attempting to recast the minds of China's people; without, it claims the place of leadership among Marxist-Leninists throughout the world. The CCP strives to establish and maintain Chinese freedom of choice. To attain that end fully it attempts nothing less than to restructure and to transform the world. China seeks not only the redistribution of power and the birth of a new world system, but it also seeks universal deference to a common interest defined by the CCP.

Today Africa contributes only modestly to these aims. China must rely on other strengths for security, but, if she were threatened in a showdown, African states would more likely extend political assistance to her if they had had a prior relationship. China might also dilute a threat to her own borders by involving her enemies in a revolutionary war in Africa. If United States troops were fighting a limited war in Africa, the United States would be less likely to risk war with China herself. In addition, Africa may prove a source of strategic materials. Lastly, the internal authority of the CCP gains a bit from foreign praise for Chairman Mao and visits by foreign dignitaries.

Trade opportunities benefit China's internal economy. An African market is attractive to China because her trade with the Soviet Union has shrunk. Trade also has a political effect. Since some states make a point of limiting trade with China, alternative trade ties enhance Chinese prestige.

China's aim to lead the world's Marxists-Leninists can be attained only if she goes into the world and practices politics. Verbal attacks on Soviet leaders, for example, would be pointless if Peking did not challenge Soviet political initiatives in foreign countries. Soviet capabilities in Africa are limited and internal African political life is certainly not fixed. Revolutionary warfare is being openly undertaken in several African countries. China's claim to be the vanguard of world revolution would be disbelieved if Peking stood aloof from African politics. By acting in Africa, China contributes to her own strategic, economic, and ideological aims.

Major changes in the world context since 1949 have created new opportunities and incentives for China, and they have altered in an important way the limits on Chinese action. France sloughed off her colonies and passed through the trauma of the Algerian War (1954–1962), but she sought to create a sphere of influence in her former African colonies and to forge links with other states, including China, outside the Anglo-Saxon sphere. By 1969 Great Britain, too, had shed her major colonies, with the painful exception of Rhodesia; she was obliged by economic necessity to withdraw from major foreign commitments not justified by home-island security or profitable trade. Belgium left the Congo in 1960, and her departure was followed by violence, bred in part by her failure to encourage political life among the Congolese at an earlier time and in part by centrifugal forces which she abetted. Britain, France, and Belgium all maintained important economic ties to Africa. Other West European countries increased trade and granted some aid. Portugal's efforts to retain Angola, Mozambique, and Guinea were an important exception to the principal trend.

The United States, assuming a global role, established diplomatic missions, gave aid, contacted members of political elites, and sought support for her policies in Africa. Like China, however, the United States viewed Africa as a tertiary concern. She was more concerned to reach a preliminary and partial understanding with the Soviet Union that nuclear war would be a disaster for all, and that massive spending on war preparations was shortsighted. War and defense spending, above all on the costly and misconceived Vietnam War, hampered Washington's activities in Africa. In certain respects the United States was deferential to British and French priority on the African continent.

The Soviet Union also drafted and undertook an African policy. To an extent it came to reflect Moscow's differences with Peking. Moscow championed some African causes — Egyptian armament in the mid-1950s and thereafter, the Algerian War (though at a late date), and opposition to Ian Smith's rule in Rhodesia — but she carefully avoided threatening war with the United States or assuming burdens as she did in Cuba in the 1960s.

A number of other states pressed themselves on Africa too. From Eastern Europe, Czechoslovakia, the German Democratic Republic, and Yugoslavia were especially active. Their vigor, as the Sino-Soviet relationship worsened dramatically, multiplied the assault on onetime Soviet claims to speak authoritatively for a scientific Marxism. Israel and Japan were also active. Israel gave some aid, gaining favor to offset her isolation from surrounding Arab states. Japan sought trade.

Africa is heterogeneous, but its states share a political culture. Independence has now been achieved in all but a few territories. Though most African states give evidence of attaining economic development, African leaders identify with those of Asia and Latin America who fear perpetual underdevelopment. The new elites have chosen to build nation-states and encourage greater political sophistication. In some cases they have enjoyed an uninterrupted tenure, but sporadic and usually localized political breakdowns have occurred, and in some instances — Congo (K), Sudan, and Nigeria — violence has taken place on a massive scale.

Africa's new political culture stems from independence, which in turn was evoked by a growing conviction that imperialism was wrong: African leaders rose and translated convictions into political action against the colonizers. One legacy of anticolonialism is a deep reserve about obligations to foreigners. Moreover, with independence came a turning inward, a preoccupation with domestic affairs. Foreign states can now engage in political and trade relations with Africa which once were impossible. African leadership judges these relations by the contribution they make to the individual African nations. The world outside Africa is not seen as a stage on which Africans can play major roles, but as a threat to security and an inevitable partner in economic relations. African states have neither the military strength nor economic wealth to act as brokers in world politics. They have taken seats in the United Nations and made common cause with other less developed states in Asia and Latin America on selected issues. Some aided United Nations peace-keeping forces and others pressed for arms limitation and control. African states played active parts in the United Nations Conference on Trade and Development; they hope to win economic concessions from the advanced industrialized countries. Multistate African organizations have shown modest success in some kinds of practical cooperation; moreover, elaborate plans to pool resources against continuing colonial and apartheid rule have been laid. Even on these issues, however, African states have found it hard to work together, or to give effective support to plans which promise no clear and demonstrable domestic return. The relations of African states with outsiders and interstate relations among Africans are both marked by the ambivalence of those who are drawn together but remain suspicious and distrustful.

The patchwork of separate states is a fundamental reality which offsets common characteristics and experiences. Many neighboring states, for example, have dealt with different foreign partners for the bulk of aid and trade. The states are endowed unequally with resources for development. In internal politics, a change of government in any one state—unless it sets a pattern copied in others—alters political life in only a small part of the continent. Bizarre politics can be practiced in small states without important consequences for the continent as a whole. In foreign relations, outsiders have a better chance of finding an African leadership willing to make common cause with them simply because the array of states is so large. By the same argument, though an outsider succeeds in establishing very close ties with one government, the range of his influence will still be confined.

The nation-state is the effective political unit. Chinese opportunities to influence political events expand and contract, conforming to patterns of political life in each individual state. China is forced to act differently toward the various African countries: her overall policy at any moment is expressed in many different ways. She must adapt to the particularities of each individual case, choosing whom to contact (other than those with whom she conducts formal intergovernmental affairs) and choosing goals to be sought in both official and unofficial dealings. Whom should China support? Whom should she oppose or threaten? The persistent dilemma of Leninist revolutionaries, well illustrated by Soviet uncertainty in China in the 1920s, persists.

Arguments and Problems

One conclusion of this study is that China's aims in Africa include revolutionary aims which are not important for the short term and are unlikely, in any case, to be achieved. There is no convincing evidence that Peking's revolutionists are a major threat to indigenous African political life. To succeed they would have to sustain their active involvement over an extended period, something uncommon in international politics. They must cope with an unreceptive socio-political environment and whatever countermeasures Africans take against them. Even if they were successful in one African country, there would be no guarantee that a Chinese-style regime could be maintained once it were in power, or that it would prove an attractive model for other countries.

The possibility remains that China may succeed. More important is the certainty that China will contribute to thoughts about proper world order circulating in Africa and to the repertoire of revolutionary expectations and techniques. Confronted by Chinese models and exhortations, African governments and independence movements can respond by attempting to insulate Africans from China or by finding ways to make Chinese interests tolerable or even useful. A further view developed in this study is that African leaders can devise their own strategies to manage collaborative relations with China which will not require unwise risks to autonomous African politics. Some African governments have already done that. The alternative, building a wall against Chinese influence, is no guarantee against risk; every government has opponents, and some of them might be drawn to the Chinese model as a means of turning the table.

China's actions include some direct support to revolutionary groups. For the most part, however, her moves which appear to be guided by revolutionary strategy are preparatory acts: circulating stories and reports of revolutions, gathering and processing information, making personal contacts, and establishing her presence. China contacts leaders of national liberation movements and, in some cases, leaders of factions within independent governments. She has given some subventions to persons not yet engaged in armed struggle and has proclaimed that a "revolutionary wave" will sweep through Africa. These actions could be put to revolutionary use at a future time, though many of them also enhance China's capacity to conduct short-term evolutionary policies.

The distinction between anti-imperialist revolution and social revolution clarifies the link between present actions and future hopes. Discussions of revolution in the colonies since the time of Lenin have assumed that foreign control must be ended before social revolution can be conducted, although strategists have differed on the part which non-Communist nationalists should play in the first period. China can advocate an end to colonial domination and apartheid regimes now because Africa's principal leaders hold the same view. Similarly, China can urge an end to neocolonialism. It does not disrupt the mainstream of African politics to profess these policies. Social revolution, replacing existing social structures of independent African states with structures designed and directed by "proletarian" Maoist parties, would require disruption in this sense.

The CCP does not describe the future in detail. What is pictured is roughly sketched in bold strokes. The future, as the CCP pictures it, will only be reached after thoroughgoing social revolution. Despite terrible struggle and the pain of failures and disappointments, men will make revolution. They will in turn remake society. Power will be pervasively reorganized by men of vision and a Maoist style of work. Ultimately they will universalize a profound and self-sustaining change of mental set ("cultural revolution"). Radicalism will be institutionalized. This future is not near but distant, probably many decades hence.

Direct Chinese support to revolutionary movements is intended to bring about anti-imperialist revolutions. Nonetheless, groups hardened in struggle against imperialism are more likely to train men for social revolution than groups which did not struggle, according to CCP doctrine. Therefore concrete aid to movements such as the Algerian Front de Libération Nationale (FLN) is a step toward later social revolution. Two anomalies, however, must be explained. One must explain why China has given some aid to groups and individuals who intend simply to oust existing governments of independent African states, and do not adhere to the Chinese world view in any orthodox sense. One must also explain why China has not yet attempted to create Communist parties in Africa which would adhere to a Chinese position. The apparent anomalies disappear if one accepts the view that China imagines true social revolution will come to Africa only in a future far removed from the present.

If China is preparing for a revolutionary future, rather than simply pursuing short-term goals, that also helps to account for the large scale of some Chinese commitments. Peking has created larger embassy staffs than trade or normal political relations required. Some Chinese aid commitments evidence either an extraordinary altruism or a strong wish for greater prestige and more political opportunities. She spends heavily on radio broadcasts and printed propaganda. Steps such as these might bring short-term benefits, but trade and immediate political gains could be promoted more readily by other kinds of action, such as direct encouragement of commerce and more care to court local political leaders. CCP leaders evidently believe that the stakes are much higher.

If China really did not expect a Maoist revolution in Africa, Peking's professions of revolution might be dismissed as empty deference to CCP tradition or manipulation of ideology for practical gain. Evolutionists in Peking, it could be argued, support limited assertive acts just to maintain their own intraparty political standing. Revolutionary movements might be supported today, too, to ensure future practical transactions. In this view, preparatory steps are taken for practical benefit in the future, not to shape revolution.

It is not impossible that such considerations contribute to some Chinese acts, but they are inadequate to account for the size of Chinese commitments in Africa, and those commitments have been made even though they jeopardize evolutionary goals. The propositions that a constituency within China believes that a Chinese-style revolution will be conducted in Africa at some point in the future and that China should act to help prepare that revolution are very strong.

Some argue that China's African policy is little more than a by-product of Sino-Soviet disagreements. Since China's concern for the Soviet Union is an undeniable factor in Chinese foreign policy, there are many respects in which Chinese choices do appear to respond to Soviet initiatives. It can be argued, however, that CCP assessments of Africa and other underdeveloped regions have been an important source, rather than consequence, of China's arguments with the Soviet Union. Each antagonist has cited African evidence to support the position she has taken and then has become more rigid. There is a real sense in which the first move does not matter now — except to students of historical process — because the two parties are deeply committed to the positions they have taken, whatever the sources might have been. Like all Chinese foreign policy, Peking's policy in Africa illustrates worsening relations with Moscow. It is more than a mere reaction to Soviet hostility, however, and demands a more complex understanding.

Finally, some find it useful to view Peking's activities in Africa as a foil to policies of the Republic of China. Taipei maintains diplomatic relations with African states — more numerous than those of Peking in 1970 — and conducts a modest aid program. She seeks support for the view that the Republic of China is not only a legitimate government, but the legitimate authority of all China. Her efforts have probably been encouraged, and indirectly funded, by the United States. Peking does not appear to have directed any significant proportion of her resources against Taipei's activities, either by threatening governments which recognize Taipei or offering inducements to switch recognition. The only major exception was a $4,000,000 credit offered to the Central African Republic at the time of recognition. China has supported antigovernment groups in some states recognizing Taipei, but there are quite convincing reasons for that support unrelated to the issue of recognition. Peking may well calculate that, in the long run, governments which profess that the People's Republic of China is not the government of China will appear foolish. Certainly the future significance of Taiwan for Africa will be limited to modest amounts of trade and aid. This study is directed to the policies of the People's Republic of China and does not include a description of the activities undertaken by the authorities on Taiwan.

In summary, to account for Peking's actions in Africa, it is not enough to cite the issue of Taiwan, the Sino-Soviet dispute, short-term economic and political gains which China may obtain, internal posturing, or any combination of immediate motives. The impetus for much of China's present activity is commitment to world revolution. Actions now speed the anti-imperialist revolution and create preconditions for social revolution, though the latter may not be undertaken for a long time.

Analytic Hypotheses

It is convenient to write of China's aims or the CCP's goals, but only a complex notion can picture the simultaneous quest for competing and conflicting objectives. In the chapters which follow, China's goals are discerned in statements and actions. Those goals are not strict complements of one another. For example, material support for African radicals diverts resources from economic development, and stress on revolutionary doctrine imperils the economic advantages of normal trade.

We do not have access to internal workings of Chinese policy-making bodies, but they undoubtedly function like such bodies elsewhere in many respects. The members of Chinese decision-making groups concerned with Africa are probably not of one mind, and they come to their work stressing different aims and concerns. The individual policy maker is equally subject to internal strain: one can assume he hopes for several goals which compete for resources and cannot all be attained at once. The individual's commitment to one goal may detract from another he also values. The group's policy choices require that some members are only partially satisfied, at best.

Those who make policy have many motives and speak for different constituencies within the party and bureaucracy. For example, neither a foreign trade specialist nor a party ideologist would be expected to think only about his formal responsibility. At the same time, we would expect the trade specialist to stress Africa's utility for Chinese economic development, and the ideologist to focus on disproof of Soviet contentions about the course of history. These thoughts lead to the hypothesis that policies which promise to contribute to several goals are more likely to be adopted than those which do not. Refined to take account of the grouping of several policies and the promise of success, the hypothesis takes this form: if the chances are similar that two policies (or sets of policies) will work, a policy (or set of policies) appealing to several constituencies is more likely to be adopted than a narrow, particular policy. Similarly, a policy (or set of policies) which appeals to several motives within the minds of those choosing is more likely to be adopted than one which does not.

To compare one policy with another, however, some salient distinctions must be developed. A familiar and central distinction is that between short-term and long-term policies. Another useful distinction separates policies which have their principal consequences in China from those with principal consequences outside China. A policy — for example, trade promotion — may involve foreign countries but be undertaken for internal ends. It is also useful to distinguish policies of substance from policies of expression. Some actions are limited, or largely limited, to expressions of comment and doctrine, but are not accompanied by important substantive commitments. Views are expressed for polemical purposes or to educate, to persuade, or to maintain an image.

Policies also differ according to whether they require a sustained sequence of gradual steps which provide benefits throughout or yield results only at a revolutionary moment. Finally, policies which assume that existing governments will be the units with which China deals are distinct from those which assume the existing government must be replaced during the policy's duration. Where a people is not now considered politically independent, a similar distinction can be made concerning the acknowledged nationalist movement(s) of the region. In the following hypotheses, these five pairs of distinctions will be employed:

(1) short term / long term
(2) domestic / foreign
(3) substantive / expressive
(4) evolutionary / revolutionary
(5) nondisruptive / disruptive

These are not distinctions made in CCP literature, but they aid in the portrayal of CCP policy making.

Typical short-term goals must be attained again and again; long-term goals do not have to be attained until a future time. A second hypothesis is that, with the passage of time, long-term goals tend to recede. Short-term goals may be achieved and replaced by new sets of short-term goals in such a way that long-term goals are always beyond reach.

A strategy to attain a goal is more likely to be favored if it includes several steps congenial to other strategies aimed at other goals. Similarly, strategies which include steps uncongenial to other strategies are less likely to be adopted. A strategy to attain a short-term goal is more likely to be favored if it is believed to contribute to the attainment of long-term goals. By the same symmetry, a strategy of the short term is at a disadvantage if it includes moves believed uncongenial to long-term goals. These can be summarized in the third hypothesis: steps which reinforce one another tend to be adopted, whereas those which clash with one another are less likely to be adopted.

An example of a major Chinese policy choice which appears unsound unless these distinctions are made is her insistence on doctrinal independence from the Soviet Union. The choice costs China development aid, markets, and probably some irreplaceable security guarantees. On the other hand, it was almost certainly argued in Peking that long-term security and development, as well as freedom of choice, required a break from the Soviet Union. A strategy antagonistic to some short-term goals could be said to be sound in the long term.

If elements of China's African policy were labeled according to the five distinctions just suggested, they would tend to fall into two groups. For the short term, strategies tend to be evolutionary, substantive, nondisruptive, and intended to achieve domestic results. There is an important strand in China's policy which is directed toward revolutionary action in Africa, but it is more expressive than substantive, and China does not expect it to yield results in the short term. The second group of strategies is therefore long term, revolutionary, expressive, disruptive, and intended primarily to achieve a result outside China. A fourth hypothesis is that Chinese African policy can be built of components which appear contradictory because the two groups of goals are not to be realized simultaneously: the expressive long-term revolutionary strategy need not interfere with substantive short-term policies.

In practice the distinction is hard to maintain. Some African leaders have wondered aloud whether China's revolutionary intentions include designs for their own ouster. If China practices a disruptive policy toward one African state, she finds it difficult to deny a disruptive intention toward another. It is not only in the minds of African leaders, however, that the two groups of goals are hard to reconcile. When resources are particularly short, CCP leaders are pressed to justify all policies even more than usual by demonstrating their utility for short-term goals. A fifth hypothesis is that economic strictures draw resources from long-term to short-term goals, although only the most severe disruption of evolutionary policies would demand suspension of revolutionary strategies or bar the possibility of brief spurts of revolutionary action. Even when resources are short, intense but brief action can be undertaken, reduced commitments to revolutionary strategies can be sustained, and some activities (such as training limited numbers of foreign guerrillas) can be performed as before.

Resources for ambitious and sustained action can be assured only if China's economic and social development succeeds. Shifting resources from short-term evolutionary goals to revolutionary action could jeopardize attainment of development and, therefore, ultimate attainment of revolutionary goals. The revolutionary drive would also flag, however, if it received scant attention for several years. Among the CCP leaders there are certainly some who argue that revolutionary action merits some resources from the budget and personnel rosters. To win allocations they must create a broader base of support. A sixth hypothesis is that advocates of revolutionary policies are more likely to obtain resources if they argue that withholding resources from revolutionary policies (in current allocations) will endanger other short-term goals. Evolutionists must be shown that there are objective threats to attainment of evolutionary goals which can be countered only by acts in a revolutionary style. For example, advocates of aid to African guerrilla movements might argue that postindependence trade was at stake; the Soviet Union could deny China access to exports after independence if China did not earn a decisive place by giving aid to the independence movement.

Internal and external policy are linked in times of domestic convulsion. When the CCP stressed radical organizational and ideological views—during the Great Leap Forward (begun in 1958) and the Great Proletarian Cultural Revolution (begun in 1966)—concern for domestic affairs did not lead to isolationist withdrawal. Instead, what had before been kept somewhat separate as long-term revolutionary goals were converted, to a degree, into short-term objectives. Feverish internal political activity diverted some resources from foreign policy to domestic action, and of that which remained for foreign policy more was allocated to revolutionary short-term and middle-term ends. Objective opportunities to make revolution are, however, in short supply. Outlets for revolutionary ambition are largely restricted to expression.

If the CCP were confident that slow-but-sure strategies of an evolutionary kind would lead China to the position it envisions for her, it would not turn to policies which interrupt evolutionary continuity. The CCP has, however, no such confidence. Its leaders seem especially fearful of permanent subordination to choices made by the Soviet Union and United States, whether in military affairs, the world economy, or the realm of belief. A seventh hypothesis is that the CCP leadership is more likely to doubt that evolutionary strategies are suitable if they do not improve China's freedom of choice in comparison with that of the Soviet Union,

United States, and other advanced industrial states. China is apt to be radical at home and disruptive abroad if her leaders believe that evolutionism promises only continuing subordination. She is more likely to urge revolutionary action in Africa if she believes that the Soviet Union and United States systematically frustrate Chinese efforts to win a fitting place in the world.

To Washington and Moscow, successful evolutionary policies increase China's capability to cause trouble. Success may also decrease the likelihood that China would act disruptively, but there is no way the observer can be sure. In quest of assurance the two major powers have pursued policies which frustrate China and provide arguments for Chinese policy makers who advocate revolutionary acts, now and later. If, instead, they made it easier for evolutionary policies to work within China, for example by sharing technology, they would have to take a chance that they could develop political relationships with China which would adequately prevent unacceptable disruption. This is the central dilemma of men who guide the relations which other states attempt to attain with China. For many reasons — fear of risk, prevalence of "realist" views, bureaucratic conservatism, preference for technical over political relations, and a profound unwillingness or inability to comprehend changing Chinese culture — most other countries will continue to assume that the safest China is a weak China. The eighth and final hypothesis in this series is that these processes repeatedly renew and strengthen the suspicions separating China from the other principal states. This reinforcing dynamic maintains Chinese frustrations and, in turn, guarantees a receptive audience for those within China who insist that world revolution is necessary.

The hypotheses introduced in the preceding paragraphs are not provable. Any study of Chinese foreign policy, however, must begin with views about the issues to be confronted. These eight hypotheses assume that consistence is required by a single policy-making body or its equivalent. In summary form, they are:

(1) Policies with broader appeal are more likely to be adopted.
(2) With the passage of time, long-term goals tend to recede.
(3) Steps which reinforce one another tend to be adopted.
(4) Consistent policy can be built of apparently contradictory goals provided the goals are not both to be realized in the short term.
(5) Austerity draws resources from long-term to short-term goals.
(6) Revolutionary steps are more likely to be supported by decision makers if their advocates argue that otherwise evolutionary goals are endangered.
(7) The CCP leadership is more likely to question or discard evolu-

tionary strategies if using such strategies does not improve China's freedom of choice.

(8) Other states can invoke strategies to limit Chinese attainment; they will act to damp Chinese evolutionary development if their governments perceive Peking's policy as a quest for disruptive capability. From (7), above, if they succeed in denying China improved freedom of choice, they may provoke the disruptive policies which they fear.

Overview

The text that follows describes China's actions in attaining short-term goals, her aid to revolutionary nationalist movements, and her preparations to sustain the long-term commitment to social revolution. Since the CCP can succeed only if it maintains its revolutionary intention for a long time, persistence is a central concept in Chinese doctrine and teaching. However, the CCP suffers failures and disappointments; doctrine therefore exists by which setbacks are explained and their damage to morale minimized. The text turns next to the Chinese revolutionary model and the conduct of her relations with specific states and movements. In the final chapter likely alternative trends are weighed. The study concludes with the proposition that African governments which choose to create relations with China may generate useful opportunities for themselves and lessen, rather than enhance, the likelihood that they will be disrupted by China's pursuit of world revolution.

2 Beginnings

In 1954 China enjoyed her first war-free year in almost three decades. CCP control was effectively consolidated. Agricultural producers cooperatives were being created in the countryside in significant numbers. Khrushchev and Bulganin paid a visit to Peking in the autumn, praising the CCP, extending a $130,000,000 loan, and endorsing a number of Peking's aims, including the recovery of Taiwan. The Geneva conference brought a favorable negotiated settlement to the warfare in Vietnam, and Chinese troops fought the United States to a stalemate in Korea. Despite the hostility of the United States toward China, and the wariness of other Asian countries, the CCP was better placed than ever before to launch domestic construction and broaden China's foreign relations.

Until the Bandung conference, CCP contacts with Africans were few and scattered. Key figures who later held important posts in the apparatus of Chinese foreign relations, notably Liao Ch'eng-chih and Liu Ning-i, met with African delegates in Soviet-financed international organizations, in some cases even before the CCP had attained victory in the civil war.[1] A handful of Africans, including Walter Sisulu, paid early visits to China.[2]

1. Liao and Liu had been vice-presidents of the World Federation of Trade Unions. The continuity of their service in foreign political affairs, from the late 1940s to the mid-1960s, is approached by three others: Ch'en Chia-k'ang, Wu Han, and Ou T'ang-liang. Ch'en and Wu attended the World Youth Festival in Berlin in 1951; in 1965 Ch'en was ambassador in Cairo and Wu was vice-mayor of Peking. Ou represented China at the 1948 council meeting of the International Union of Students; in 1965 she was secretary of the Chinese People's Committee for World Peace.

2. When Sisulu visited China after the World Youth Festival in 1953 he was secretary general of the African National Congress of South Africa. Sisulu remained active until his conviction at the Rivonia Trial of 1964; he was subsequently imprisoned. Another early visitor to China, though not an African, played an important role disseminating Chinese views in Africa. Jacques Vergès, son of a leader of the Communist Party of Réunion, represented Réunion at the International Union of Students executive committee meeting in Peking in 1951. He figured prominently as defense attorney for Algerian nationalists in France in the late 1950s. After Algerian independence, as editor of the journal *Révolution*, he published articles friendly to the

Africa was virtually closed to Chinese visitors. None of the four independent African states — Egypt, Ethiopia, Liberia, and South Africa — recognized China[3] and, with one exception, no representative of Peking visited African soil.[4]

Chinese comment on African affairs was also scanty. However, as early as June 1950, a *Jen-min Jih-pao* commentator damned the Malan government of South Africa and an anti-Communist measure it proposed. A month later Mao Tse-tung, observing that the proposed apartheid legislation would discriminate against the Chinese minority in South Africa, joined in protest against the legislation.[5] In late 1951 speakers at a meeting of the Chinese People's Institute of Foreign Affairs supported the Arab peoples and denounced imperialism. But Chinese commentary was neither persistent nor clamorous. Frequent Chinese references to Africa did not begin until the time of the Bandung conference.

Bandung Conference

The Asian-African Conference met in Bandung, Indonesia, 18–24 April 1955. Six of the twenty-nine states represented were African: Egypt, Ethiopia, Gold Coast (later Ghana), Liberia, Libya, and Sudan. Chou En-lai and Ch'en I[6] led the Chinese delegation. Among the delegation's advisers were two men, Ch'en Chia-k'ang and Huang Hua,[7] who would later hold

---

Chinese position. For a brief biography of Vergès, see [31]. (Numbers in brackets refer to items in the Bibliography.)

3. Egypt and South Africa reportedly considered recognition. *NYT*, 28 June 1950 and 6 January 1950. Haile Selassie had sentimental and political reasons for withholding recognition. He once said that the refusal of some governments, including Nanking, to recognize Italy's seizure of Ethiopia in 1936 had been of inestimable value to Ethiopia. Cited in [40], p. 249. Ethiopia's dispatch of a contingent to join the United Nations forces in Korea further impeded relations with China, though it strengthened the principle of collective security that the League of Nations had evaded fifteen years earlier. In February 1964 Ethiopia and China noted "agreement on taking of measures to strengthen relations," including "the normalization of relations between the two governments in the near future." [198], p. 259. But agreement to establish relations was delayed until November 1970. *PR*, 11 December 1970, p. 7. Egypt, alone of the four to experience a domestic revolution, was also the first to recognize China.

4. Three Chinese postal representatives attended a joint meeting of the International Air Transport Association and Universal Postal Union in Cairo in 1951. NCNA, no. 609, 27 January 1951. For a brief time the People's Republic of China also enjoyed the allegiance of the staff of the Chinese consulate in the French colony of Madagascar, but this was not of political moment. NCNA, no. 249, 7 January 1950.

5. NCNA, no. 408; NCNA, no. 447. Mao acted in reply to a cable from the Transvaal Indian Congress.

6. Chou was premier and foreign minister; Ch'en was a vice-premier. Chou yielded the portfolio of foreign minister to Ch'en in 1958.

7. China's delegates were: Chou En-lai; Ch'en I; the foreign trade minister, Yeh

key Chinese ambassadorial posts in Africa. Egypt's Gamal Abdul Nasser was the sole major African figure to attend; Kwame Nkrumah, who was leading a Gold Coast government well on the way to independence, and Haile Selassie of Ethiopia stayed home.

The first Chinese diplomatic contacts with Africans took place at the Bandung conference. Chou En-lai and Nasser, who had met socially in Rangoon en route to Bandung, talked together at the conference, and there were frequent contacts between the Chinese and Egyptian delegations.[8] Although steps toward diplomatic relations with African countries were not mentioned, discussions of Sino-Egyptian trade and cultural ties were initiated and the groundwork for China's opening of a trade office in Cairo eight months later was laid. Chou En-lai extended a blanket invitation to all Bandung delegates to visit China,[9] but it was accepted only by two Egyptians who continued the discussions on trade begun at Bandung and initialed a transcript of talks on cultural cooperation.[10] China welcomed their visit and voiced the hope that economic and cultural cooperation, a contribution to "safeguarding peace in the Asian-African region and the whole world," would soon be realized. A trade agreement was signed soon thereafter.

Chinese encounters with African national liberation movements also began at Bandung. Moses Kotane, who ten years later headed the African National Congress office in Dar es Salaam, was among the three South African observers.[11] A Maghreb delegation included Salah ben Youssef and Mohammed Yazid—the former a leading Tunisian figure and the latter an Algerian spokesman before and after independence.[12] Both ob-

---

Chi-chuang; the foreign affairs vice-minister, Chang Han-fu; and the ambassador to Indonesia, Huang Chen. The advisers were Ch'en Chia-k'ang; Huang Hua; Liao Ch'eng-chih; foreign affairs official Ch'iao Kuan-hua; the public security vice-minister, Yang Ch'i-ch'ing; Muslim leader Ta P'u-sheng; and protocol officer Wang Cho-ju.

8. NCNA, 3 June 1955. One report suggests that Chou came to Bandung resolved to court Nasser. Their paths crossed in Rangoon while they were en route to Bandung. Minutes after Nasser's arrival, Chou took the initiative to urge him to visit "all Asian countries." At a banquet that evening he pressed the subject again. *NYT*, 16 April 1955.

9. [60].

10. NCNA, 18 May 1955. The Egyptians were Sheikh Ahmed Hassan el Bakhouri, a cabinet minister, and Mustafa Kamal, a Cairo University professor. The transcript of talks was submitted to the Egyptian government for its approval. NCNA, 31 May 1955.

11. [60]. They represented the African National Congress and the South African Indian Congress. Their statements are in [58], no. 7, 22 April 1955.

12. Maghreb namelist in [47]. Ben Youssef later broke with Bourguiba and left Tunisia. Yazid became minister of information in the provisional government of pre-independent Algeria, and he remained a cabinet member after independence. A joint statement by Maghreb observers is in [58], no. 7, 22 April 1955.

observer delegations were intimately involved in the conference.[13] However, despite some references to the North African and South African situations in the Chinese press and a brief comment by Chou En-lai,[14] there is no evidence to suggest that the Chinese delegation made a special point of concerning itself with them. The Bandung conference was a meeting of governmental representatives in which China, while maintaining an anticolonialist position, sought to reassure her Asian neighbors and establish a reputation for reasonableness. Chou even offered to negotiate certain differences with the United States. Acknowledging but not stressing anticolonial and antiapartheid issues in Africa was consistent with China's general demeanor at Bandung.

Bandung became a symbol of Afro-Asia as a viable political concept. China could more plausibly and readily concern herself with African affairs if Chinese and Africans were joined by political ties. The vision of Afro-Asia — that Asians and Africans share common political and social tasks which can be better performed jointly than by any single isolated country — was powerful rhetoric, but it was never translated into broadly effective institutions. The Bandung conference itself did not create any machinery of continuation. Plans to hold a Second Asian-African Conference foundered in 1965. The chief institutional embodiment of Afro-Asia was the Afro-Asian People's Solidarity Organization (AAPSO), in which China took a major role; it came into being through initiatives quite separate from the Bandung Conference.

Institutions aside, China invoked the Bandung spirit to encourage Asians and Africans to join in initiatives which China favored. It stood for an aura of benignity. Guided by the *Panch Sheela* and the Bandung Ten Principles, on a platform of anticolonialism and mutual respect, countries as dissimilar as China and India could peaceably coexist and prosper. Real arguments aired at Bandung[15] were muted. African leaders, prompted to do so in the proper context, readily affirmed their attachment to the spirit of Bandung. Even after concrete disagreements divided the powers at

13. They lived at a hotel reserved for delegates. In the plenary session, their desks were next in order after those of the delegates. Ben Youssef was extended the privileges of an Iraqi delegate, though he was not actually listed as a member of the delegation. [60]; [47].

14. As early as November 1954, Peking knew that anticolonial issues concerning North Africa would probably be raised in Bandung. NCNA, 28 November 1954, 30 December 1954, and 5 January 1955. Chou En-lai's report on Bandung, however, merely touched on Africa. [199].

15. On the fate of a Turkish proposal, supported by three African states, to condemn "all types of colonialism, including international doctrines resorting to the methods of force, infiltration and subversion," see [61], pp. 18–31.

Bandung, Peking insisted that the spirit was alive and that she strove to realize it in Afro-Asian solidarity.

In the conference itself, few specifically African issues were dealt with, and China played no special part in bringing those issues forward. The Arab League, India (concerned for Indian minorities in Africa), and the two observer delegations from South Africa and the Maghreb pressed most strongly for discussion of African issues.[16] The African states did not evince special cooperation among themselves; they were not a bloc with which China could have dealt.[17] In the final communiqué, the conference supported the right of Algeria, Morocco, and Tunisia to self-determination and independence, urging France to effect a peaceful settlement without delay. In a paragraph devoted to racism the conference voiced sympathy and support for victims of racial discrimination and applauded those who helped sustain their cause, but it took no specific steps to aid antiapartheid activities. Chou En-lai stated China's position before the conference's political committee: "We have always regarded that different races are equal. New China has not practiced any discrimination."[18]

It does not appear that Africa was important to China at Bandung. Although Bandung marked the beginning of significant Chinese initiatives in Africa, there is no evidence that China foresaw this with clarity. And China's overtures to Nasser can be amply explained without postulating the existence of an African policy at this time. Egypt was a large state, increasingly independent of the West, and the leading state of the Arab League. Egypt's position at Bandung was enhanced by the fact that eleven of the twenty-nine participating states were predominantly Muslim, eight were Arab League members at the time of the conference, and the secretary general of the league was an Egyptian delegate.[19]

Even less was the conference a Chinese creature, nor did China take a part in its planning. Certainly Chou En-lai and Jawaharlal Nehru emerged as the most visible and effective statesmen present. But the measure of China's part in bringing the conference about is that she was not even envisaged as a participant in the original proposal.[20] Her part in the Asian Countries Conference, on the other hand, was considerable.

16. [47], pp. 20–21, 25; [61].

17. An Arab League analysis placed Ethiopia, Liberia, and the Gold Coast in the "Western camp," distinguishing them from Libya, Egypt, and Sudan. [47], p. 41.

18. [61], p. 60.

19. [47], p. 46.

20. Ali Sastroamidjojo of Indonesia proposed the conference to four states (India, Ceylon, Burma, and Pakistan), which then joined Indonesia as sponsors.

Asian Countries Conference

The lineage of the Afro-Asian People's Solidarity Organization, which was the chief institution embodying the Bandung spirit, runs back not to the Asian-African Conference but to a very different event which took place a few days earlier, the Asian Countries Conference. The first public step to organize this event occurred at a meeting sponsored by the World Peace Council.[21] China took a hand in organizing the event and sent a large delegation when this conference met in New Delhi 6–10 April 1955.[22]

Despite its primary concern for Asia, the conference anticipated positions taken at Bandung on South African and North African issues, and these decisions were disseminated by the New China News Agency.[23] Moreover, a gesture was made to broaden the geographic scope of the Asian Solidarity Committee, a liaison group created in the wake of the conference, by including representatives of the Arab countries. The gesture was made more concrete when four spokesmen for the committee went to Cairo in January 1957 to persuade Nasser that Egypt should host a major Afro-Asian solidarity conference. Among the four was Chinese representative Yang Shuo. Their mission was successful: it led to the first Afro-Asian People's Solidarity Conference and the installation of a permanent secretariat of the Afro-Asian People's Solidarity Organization in Cairo.[24]

Commencement of Trade with Egypt

Before 1955 China traded on a small scale with Africa, principally exports of green tea to Egypt and the Maghreb.[25] Egypt's commercial inter-

21. The International Conference for Relaxation of International Tension, Stockholm, June 1954.

22. Though not represented at an initial preparatory meeting, China soon thereafter volunteered "full support" and dispatched a man to New Delhi to work in the secretariat. NCNA, 20 and 24 February 1955. China's delegations at Stockholm and New Delhi were led by Kuo Mo-jo, who in 1970 remained among the most prominent Chinese greeting foreign visitors, and represented China at the funeral of Gamal Abdul Nasser in Cairo.

23. NCNA, 10 April 1955. But the conferees in New Delhi did not shape the Bandung decisions, which were largely consistent with declared policies of the Colombo states. Both government-sponsored and nongovernment delegates attended the Asian Countries Conference.

24. In addition to China, the Asian Solidarity Committee was to consist of representatives of the Soviet Union, six designated Asian countries, and "the Arab countries." NCNA, 13 April 1955. Establishment of a secretariat was entrusted to the Indian Association for Afro-Asian Solidarity. In 1957 it published the *Afro-Asian Quarterly*, which in turn passed to the control of the Afro-Asian People's Solidarity Organization in 1959.

25. [200], April 1955, p. 13.

est began in 1955 with the failure of traditional Western markets to buy Egyptian cotton at an acceptable price; this failure was especially grave because cotton provided 80 percent of Egypt's export revenue. China and the Soviet Union stepped in to buy. In July the conversations began at Bandung and continued in Peking yielded tangible results when Chinese representatives went to Cairo and contracted to buy 13,000 tons of cotton; 2,000 additional tons were bought later. In August an Egyptian delegation came to Peking and negotiated China's first trade agreement with an African country. At the same time it was agreed to set up a Chinese trade office in Cairo and Egyptian trade office in Peking.[26]

China appointed high-ranking personnel to Cairo, which suggests that she judged it an important political post. Egypt's purchase of arms from Czechoslovakia in 1955 and growing economic relations between Egypt and "Soviet-bloc" states may have been the basis for such a judgment. China sent deputy representative Chang Yüeh to the trade office, which opened in January 1956; he was a man with political rather than commercial credentials.[27] When diplomatic relations were announced,[28] Chang was named second-ranking diplomat in the new Cairo embassy. His chief was Ch'en Chia-k'ang. Ch'en was assistant minister of foreign affairs when he was appointed to Cairo.

Ch'en Chia-k'ang's long tenure in Cairo — he remained ambassador until late 1965 — provided an important continuity in China's African affairs. Cairo was not only the first site of a Chinese mission in Africa, but it was also a crossroads of political traffic — a natural port of entry and exit for persons traveling to and from the East. Moreover, by reason of President Nasser's political ventures, Cairo became a political center of the Arab world, headquarters of the Afro-Asian People's Solidarity Organization, and host to some African liberation movements which posted representatives there.

Khrushchev, the Third World, and an Independent Chinese Position

The events of 1954 and 1955 reflected vast changes in the world political scene: Stalin's death, the end of warfare in Korea and Vietnam, and China's own consolidation. Nikita Khrushchev's secret speech to the Twentieth Congress of the Communist Party of the Soviet Union in February

26. [200], December 1955, p. 12. The first-year protocol provided that China would buy 15,000 tons of Egyptian cotton and Egypt would buy 60,000 tons of Chinese rolled steel.

27. Chang Yüeh had been deputy director of the West European and African Affairs Division of the Ministry of Foreign Affairs since 1951.

28. NCNA, 17 May 1956.

1956 laid bare the worst features of Stalin's rule, and it was an event with consequences far beyond the revision of history. It seemed to provoke Polish and Hungarian moves toward independence from Moscow and the subsequent erosion of Soviet control over her allies. Khrushchev put forward other theses which, though intended to resolve some of the uncertainties in Soviet policy since Stalin's death, were also directed to questions of the third world. Khrushchev's initiative coincided with China's first comments on a number of African situations. Together these formed a backdrop to the more dramatic events of 1956 and 1957, including the Suez crisis.

Khrushchev argued, first, that "parliamentary roads to socialism" were possible. The working class, having won a parliamentary majority, could create in "a number of capitalist and former colonial countries" the conditions needed to secure "fundamental social changes." But whatever form of transition was followed, only a Communist party could supply "the decisive and indispensable factor."[29] Communist parties were important, but they could content themselves with winning elections and exercising constitutional rights. Nationalist leaders who feared to accept anticolonial aid from indigenous Communist parties might be mollified.

Khrushchev's second argument was that a "vast zone of peace" existed in which the socialist states were linked with newly-independent nonaligned states. The "imperialist colonial system" was disintegrating; a "complete abolition of the infamous system of colonialism" was in prospect.[30] The new states were invited, in effect, to stop comforting imperialism, to join in common foreign policy positions with the Soviet Union, and to tie their economies to the "socialist states." Khrushchev believed that time was on the Soviet side. Only a few weeks earlier he had returned from a triumphant tour of India. His first visit to an ex-colony must have encouraged him to think that the new states—and India was chief among them—could come to be counted on the "socialist" side in assessing the balance of forces. Egypt's acceptance of Czech arms must have reinforced that view.

China could accept the fact that colonialism was foundering and that nationalists could help steer it onto the rocks, but the "parliamentary road" was more than she could endorse.[31] She sidestepped that prong of Khrush-

29. [55], pp. 42–46.

30. [189], no. 4, contains the report of the Central Committee of the Communist Party of the Soviet Union to the Twentieth Party Congress, 14 February 1956.

31. [207], 2 June 1956. Roderick MacFarquhar has noted that the Moscow Declaration of late 1957, signed by China and the Soviet Union, mentions "peaceful transition" for capitalist countries but not for former colonies. [55], p. 41. Perhaps Mao

chev's argument and emphasized instead the anticolonial formulas pronounced at Bandung. Bandung was quite consistent with the "vast zone"—except that the Soviet Union and her East European allies were not present at Bandung. The states represented at Bandung had attacked colonialism, taken positions paralleling Soviet and Chinese views on certain issues, and even urged expanded trade with China. But what was to become of those nationalists who contributed to the "vast zone"? In declining to acknowledge the "parliamentary road," China hinted at future arguments with the Soviets and nationalists alike. If the "parliamentary road" was inadmissible, there was no route for non-Communist nationalists to follow. The issue was hardly a new one.

In Chinese eyes the peace zone was an instrument, a means, to be used in building Chinese prosperity. That, at least, was the point of a report which Ch'en I delivered to the Eighth Congress of the CCP in September 1956.

> All the endeavors of the Chinese people are bent toward building China into a prosperous, happy, socialist, industrial country. We need a peaceful international environment for our peaceful labour. This is the essential fact that determines our policy of peace in foreign relations.[32]

This is a baldly stated nationalist appeal. It appeared from the rest of his speech that the environment with which Ch'en I was concerned was primarily an Asian one.

Although mainly concerned with Asian issues, China was beginning to acknowledge the existence of a range of African questions and to assert that developments in Africa were favorable. Even before Khrushchev's speech, a Chinese commentator claimed that the growth of friendly relations between the "socialist camp" and the countries of Asia and Africa had dealt a serious blow to colonialism.[33] A few weeks later the Chinese press editorialized:

> The people of Egypt and the Sudan, countries in what used to be considered "dark Africa," have achieved independence. The people of Algeria, Morocco, Tunisia, Kenya, Rhodesia and many other countries of Africa have awakened. Their heroic struggle against colonial oppression has shaken the whole world.[34]

Tse-tung, who attended the Moscow meeting, quarreled with Khrushchev's views of the year before.

32. [205], vol. 2, p. 340.

33. [228], 20 January 1956, mentions Tunisia, Algeria, and Egypt.

34. *SCMP*, no. 1235, p. 27; *JMJP*, 21 February 1956.

Nonetheless, these comments had the flavor of ritual. They did not deal with specific issues. When Ch'en I spoke to the party congress in September 1956 he automatically coupled Asia and Africa together. His only explicit assertions on African affairs concerned Suez, and the Egyptians and other Arabs enjoyed "the full support of the Chinese people" in that imbroglio. In fact, Suez drew comment from Ch'en I at three different points in his speech;[35] at that stage the outcome was very much in doubt and Egypt's face-off with France, England, and Israel was to alter profoundly Peking's sense of what might occur in Africa.

Suez Crisis

President Nasser nationalized the Suez Canal on 26 July 1956, just a week after China's newly-appointed ambassador arrived in Cairo. China promptly endorsed Nasser's action[36] and, as Western reaction hardened, offered general support and said her trade with Egypt would continue. Peking declared that the West would be "burnt" if it did not stop threatening Egypt.[37] When Egypt called for canal pilots to replace those who had abandoned the canal, some Chinese volunteered — though they do not seem to have served.[38]

During September and October China maintained her criticism of British and French policy.[39] Hints that Britain and France might use force were met by Chinese warnings that "colonialists" should abandon their war plans. But China's full fury was reserved for the Anglo-French-Israeli invasion, which was condemned in the Chinese press, in a formal government statement, and by a special committee created to support Egypt.[40] On 9 November China began registering volunteers, who would presumably be transported to Egypt to fight as Chinese volunteers had fought in Korea.[41] However, the Egyptian ambassador in Peking denied that volunteers had been requested; the crisis gradually faded and nothing more was heard of the scheme.

China was one of many states from which Egypt sought diplomatic

35. [205], vol. 2, pp. 333, 338, and 342.

36. *SCMP*, no. 1341, p. 28 (28 July 1956); *SCMP*, no. 1342, p. 19 (30 July 1956).

37. *SCMP*, no. 1355, p. 26 (*JMJP*, 18 August 1956).

38. *SCMP*, no. 1367, p. 37 (1 September 1956); *SCMP*, no. 1366, p. 33 (5 September 1956); *SCMP*, no. 1368, p. 30 (9 September 1956). Western press accounts emphasized work on the canal by Soviet pilots, but they did not mention Chinese pilots.

39. For example, Chou En-lai. *SCMP*, no. 1376, p. 40 (20 September 1956).

40. *SCMP*, no. 1375, p. 29; *SCMP*, no. 1404, p. 33; *SCMP*, no. 1405, p. 24; *SCMP*, no. 1410, p. 27; *SCMP*, no. 1411, p. 37.

41. *SCMP*, no. 1411, p. 42; *SCMP*, no. 1411, p. 44 (9 November 1956); *NYT*, 11 November 1956.

support during the Suez crisis. China's response was substantive, and it earned Egyptian thanks. Shortly after the invasion began Cairo's ambassador in Peking paid a call on Chou En-lai. China's aid, the ambassador later said, was "prompt and generous."[42] President Nasser expressed his gratitude for Chinese support in a message to Chou.[43] The most concrete support was a $5,000,000 loan — China's first credit of the kind[44] — although China's suggestions that she send columns of volunteers may have been symbolically more evocative. In retrospect, the possibility that China might actually have sent volunteers seems virtually nil, if only because China did not have the capacity to transport many men to the Middle East. On the other hand, if the fighting had persisted and if Nasser had imagined any political advantage in the presence of a Chinese contingent, China might have found herself under pressure to dispatch a token force.

China continued to secure ties with Egypt and attack Western political initiatives into December, as the crisis ebbed.[45] When Egypt recovered Port Said on 25 December it was celebrated in Peking as a victory.

The Suez affair was more than a convenient vessel for Chinese influence. In one interpretation, it was confirmation that anticolonialism was a powerful force, "the peak of the movement for national independence of the Asian and African people in 1956."[46] An even stronger view is suggested by Chou En-lai, who reported in March 1957:

> [Suez was] a great revelation to us, showing that although the Asian and African countries are not yet powerful in material strength, all aggression by the colonialists can be frustrated, as long as we maintain our solidarity and firmly unite with all peace-loving forces of the world and wage a resolute struggle.[47]

In other words, the CCP had not anticipated that Western control of the strategic waterway could be ended so abruptly. But it was ended. Military action by France and Britain was not enough to force Egypt from the

42. *SCMP*, no. 1405, p. 24 (1 November 1956); *SCMP*, no. 1415, p. 32; *SCMP*, no. 1421, p. 33.

43. *SCMP*, no. 1418, p. 28 (22 November 1956).

44. *SCMP*, no. 1411, p. 44 (12 November 1956). Some term it a grant, but they appear to be wrong.

45. *SCMP*, no. 1429, p. 35; *SCMP*, no. 1430, p. 36.

46. *ECMM*, no. 68, p. 1; [228], 20 December 1956.

47. "Report on Visit to Eleven Countries in Asia and Europe," *CB*, no. 439, p. 16 (*JMJP*, 6 March 1957). Presumably those newly enlightened are "the people of Asia and Africa," including Chou and his colleagues.

canal. This union of "peace-loving forces," therefore, was stronger than the CCP had thought. If Chou En-lai's phrasing was carefully planned, if the sense of Chinese surprise which it conveys was accurate, Egypt's ultimate possession of the canal after a vigil of five months must have left an extraordinary impression on the makers of Chinese foreign policy.

Department of West Asian and African Affairs

In September 1956 China's Ministry of Foreign Affairs assigned African responsibilities of the West European and African Affairs Department to a newly created office, the West Asian and African Affairs Department. As long as Britain, France, and the other metropolitan powers controlled all but a small part of Africa, the earlier institutional arrangement made sense. The change recognized that colonialism was ending. The pivotal position of Cairo in Africa and in the Arab world may have suggested placing concern for both under one institutional roof. The practice of keeping many staff members for rather long terms in the department, of filling key African posts from department personnel, and of reclaiming many of those for Peking assignments after their tours of duty in Africa ensured gradually-increasing experience and coherence for the new department. These practices and some career patterns are considered in the Appendix. As an example, it is useful to look at the cases of two men appointed to the new department in September 1956. Director K'o Hua had headed the Protocol Department in the ministry. His new duties took him on visits to Ghana (1957) and to North Africa (1958). In 1960 he was named first ambassador to Guinea, a post he held until August 1964. In late 1964 the West Asian and African Affairs Department was further divided: K'o Hua assumed directorship of the new African Affairs Department, and Arab concerns were delegated to a separate West Asian and North African Affairs Department.

Ho Kung-k'ai first came to notice in 1953 when he was appointed director of the Alien Affairs Department of a regional administrative committee. In early 1956, when he traveled to Egypt as a member of a trade mission, he was a deputy director of the West European and African Affairs Department. In September 1956 he switched to the new department, where he remained as deputy director until he was appointed counselor of the Cairo embassy in 1963. When Ch'en Chia-k'ang was absent, Ho served as chargé d'affaires.[48]

These are thumbnail sketches of official titles, but they show that continuity was maintained. They also indicate how successive departments

48. [65]; [129]; [133].

dealing with African affairs were important contributors to the creation of Chinese policy, or became that in time. Key ambassadors had experience in Peking and often they had long tenure in the field. They could speak with unparalleled authority, and their superiors, at least until 1964, helped to perpetuate their expertise and authority by assigning them to African duties in Peking. It cannot be inferred that their views were decisive; neither is it known what their views may have been in crucial matters.

Algerian War

From 1957 until 1962, when France acceded to FLN demands for Algerian independence, the Algerian War was an important subject of Chinese policy. The FLN sought aid from China and aid was granted. Moreover, after the FLN success, China cited the successful FLN guerrilla struggle as an inspiration for other colonial peoples.

Until February 1957, neither the French Communist party nor the Soviet Union had been willing to endorse the minimum FLN demand that France acknowledge Algeria's right to self-determination prior to any negotiations.[49] Both the USSR and the French Communist party felt constrained by other hopes and commitments in metropolitan France itself. China deferred to them and issued weak statements of support that fell shy of the FLN position. When the French Communist party aligned itself with the FLN view, China took up the call. Statements in support of Algerian independence were issued in quick succession.[50] China respected Moscow's restraint while it lasted. When the Soviet Union gave way to FLN insistence, China hastened to outdo the Soviet Union in promises of moral support.

The tenacity of the FLN posed an unmanageable problem for France. The CCP, which had come to power through guerrilla war, respected the FLN and believed that it had a good chance of success. The proven military capability of the FLN's armed forces was a fact which CCP leaders could observe. Like Egypt's perseverance through the Suez crisis, it showed

49. Consider the curious Soviet claim that Algerian Communists acted in total independence of the FLN leadership in seeking to rally all the forces opposed to colonialism, a claim which may have been true but merely reflected the isolation of Algerian Communists. [170], December 1956, pp. 122–126.

50. As early as August 1956, a Chinese group voiced support for the Algerian struggle. *SCMP*, no. 1360, p. 55. In October, *JMJP* delicately sidestepped the issue, saying differences "could only be settled by peaceful negotiation based on respect for Algerian independence and sovereignty." *SCMP*, no. 1403, p. 33. The French party finally acted in March. [153], March 1957, pp. 454–455. See also *SCMP*, no. 1468, p. 33 (*JMJP*, 7 February 1957); *SCMP*, no. 1508, p. 23 (6 April 1957); *SCMP*, no. 1516, p. 55 (22 April 1957).

that paths which had not previously been traveled by independence movements in Africa were being opened. China's ideological propensity for struggle, her belief that struggle is a great educator, intensified her attraction to the FLN cause. Peking did not immediately extend aid to the FLN. But Algeria's importance became evident early in 1957 as one sign that the African political scene was on the verge of immense change. China perceived some dimensions of the change which would follow.

First Steps Toward Decolonization

It cannot be assumed that China saw more clearly than the United States or the Soviet Union did how quickly Africa would become a continent of independent states, for there is no such evidence. However, both France and Britain were visibly moving toward fundamental changes in their colonial domains in Africa.

Pressed by African demands and the modest scale of her own resources, France invented successive plans which led to the independence of her African holdings. Tunisia and Morocco were shed in 1956. The *loi-cadre* of 1956 presaged further change, but the French did not yield sub-Saharan territory until September 1958.

The indications that British territories would be granted independence were more insistent. Britain's actions in Asia were a precedent. The quickening pace of Gold Coast self-government was accented at Bandung, where the Gold Coast was represented despite Britain's retention of control of Gold Coast foreign affairs at the time.[51] The Gold Coast case also illustrated the pattern, much remarked upon since, of Britain's use of force to subdue champions of independence and then, at a later point, yielding power swiftly to those same individuals. Kwame Nkrumah, for example, was released from jail in 1951 to take up the chief post under self-government. The CCP was surely sensitive to the precedents and signs that Britain would yield. In that sense, China's repeated references to independence gained by "struggle" are merited, though they also seem strangely exaggerated.

Nieh Jung-chen, a member of the CCP Central Committee, led China's delegation to Ghanaian independence celebrations in March 1957. He was the first Central Committee member to visit sub-Saharan Africa.[52] His visit dramatized China's new interest in Africa and the new opportunities

51. The official list of participants includes Gold Coast, though some report that she was an observer.

52. Foreign trade minister Yeh Chi-chuang, a Central Committee member, visited Egypt and Sudan in 1956.

for contact which independence created. China may also have dispatched Nieh in the belief that he could persuade Ghana to establish diplomatic relations. Despite the air of friendship, however, relations were not established until 1960.

China took other action aimed at making contacts with African states, and, in some instances, establishing diplomatic relations. It was common for China to congratulate a newly independent state and voice the hope that close relations would be established, a hint to prompt recognition.[53] In 1956 and 1957 Chinese delegations visited Ethiopia, Morocco, Sudan, and Tunisia in addition to Egypt and Ghana. Visitors from Libya, Nigeria, Senegal, and South Africa also came to China. Yet these scattered contacts and approaches do not suggest that either recognition or an increase in United Nations votes was the chief concern.

China gave attention to some dramatic issues — Suez and the Algerian War — and there is sufficient evidence to conclude that she was aware of a trend toward political independence in Africa; but by mid-1957 there was still no evidence of a major Chinese drive to extend her contacts or foreign policy concerns which would make Africa more important to her. The final months of 1957 and the eventful year 1958, however, were a time of internal tumult in China; she made a far-reaching reassessment of her foreign policy. Her changing requirements and growing self-assertiveness coincided with changes in Africa which opened new opportunities for Chinese action. This was a decisive period that merits close attention.

The East Wind Prevails Over the West Wind

At the beginning of 1956 Soviet military power was principally important to China as a defensive shield behind which China could accomplish domestic construction and consolidate her position. The power of the "socialist camp" was not great enough to give the Soviet Union a clear advantage; it was "as strong as the imperialist bloc, if not stronger."[54] The Soviet Union could not undertake adventures far from her borders without hazard at home and, in turn, hazard to her capacity to protect China. Therefore Soviet-American relations and the growing military capability of Western Europe overshadowed any expectations of gain in peripheral areas, including Africa.

On 24 August 1957 Moscow achieved its first successful ICBM test. That was one key which led Mao Tse-tung, in November, to advance

53. On Morocco, *SCMP*, no. 1247, p. 35 (9 March 1956). On Tunisia, *SCMP*, no. 1245, p. 40 (23 March 1956); *SCMP*, no. 1586, p. 28 (2 August 1957).

54. [207], 2 January 1956.

the now familiar assessment that "the East Wind prevailed over the West Wind." The main lines of China's new view were detailed by Chou En-lai in a report to the National People's Congress in February 1958.

> A decisive change has taken place in the international situation that favors our socialist construction, the socialist camp, the cause of world peace and the progress of mankind. As all the world knows, in October and November 1957 the Soviet Union launched two artificial earth-satellites, while on the occasion of celebrating the 40th anniversary of the great October Socialist Revolution, representatives of the Communist and Workers' Parties of the socialist and other countries met in Moscow and issued two statements of great historic significance demonstrating the unity of the Communist and Workers' Parties of various countries.
>
> This has brought about a new change in the long-standing superiority of the forces of socialism over those of imperialism, and of the forces of peace over those of war, a new turning point in the international situation. As Chairman Mao Tse-tung has said, in the present international situation it is not the West Wind which prevails over the East Wind but the East Wind which prevails over the West Wind.
>
> Everybody can now see that, compared with the imperialist camp, our socialist camp has definitely gained supremacy in population and popular support, in the rate of industrial and agricultural development and in a number of important fields in science and technology. Even the imperialist aggressors cannot but admit that they stand before an invincible socialist camp headed by the Soviet Union, stronger and more united than ever before.[55]

China's new assessment came as China was also asking the Soviet Union to share her technological advantage. China's population exceeded that of the other states of the "socialist camp" taken together. But, above all, China had backed Soviet efforts to reestablish authority over East European Communist parties at the end of 1956 and the beginning of 1957. Chou En-lai had interrupted a tour of Asian countries to go to East Europe, where he insisted on the need to maintain the bloc's integrity. Soviet leadership had turned to China for political aid. Would the Soviet Union be willing to share some of the true instruments of modern power? Chou En-lai's speech can be understood only if one considers how the Soviet Union and China were dealing with each other at the time.

China has claimed that a Sino-Soviet agreement on "new technology

55. *CB*, no. 492.

for national defense" was entered into on 15 October 1957.[56] A month later, while Mao Tse-tung was in Moscow to attend the meeting of Communist parties, concurrent talks on military and scientific questions were held by Soviet and Chinese representatives. In Alice Hsieh's view, the membership of the military mission strongly suggests it sought to discuss China's acquisition of a nuclear capability,[57] and subsequent revelation of the October agreement lends credence to her view. It is reasonable to conclude that when Mao talked with Khrushchev he had in mind the new Soviet missile capability and the prospect that China might adapt it to her own purposes.

Soviet and Chinese statements have been studied, especially by Alice Hsieh, in an effort to determine the views and hopes of the two parties.[58] A good deal of byplay took place in public; its purpose was not always clear. However, a letter from Khrushchev to Chou En-lai on 4 April 1958 mentioned that the Soviet Union would maintain its nuclear arsenal but that states which did not yet have nuclear weapons should not be aided in attaining them.

> Today only three powers possess nuclear weapons — the USSR, the United States, and Britain — and therefore agreement to end their tests is comparatively easy to achieve. If the tests are not terminated now, other countries may develop nuclear weapons within a certain space of time and then it will, of course, be more difficult to reach agreement on ending tests thereof.[59]

After sifting the evidence, Alice Hsieh concludes that the CCP probably conducted a policy review that lasted well into May 1958. Aware that the Soviet Union would not grant nuclear capability immediately, China could only create it herself. In the meantime, she continued to adhere to a transitional strategy based on acceptance of her own military weakness.[60]

It may be that Khrushchev agreed to help China design nuclear weapons, but not very speedily, and to give her a sample atomic bomb,

56. *PR*, 16 August 1963, p. 14.

57. Kuo Mo-jo, who led China's delegation at the Asian Countries Conference, was also chief spokesman in the discussions with the Soviet Union on scientific and technological assistance. The talks lasted three months. Defense minister P'eng Te-huai met his Soviet counterpart, Marshal Malinovsky, while the talks were taking place. He was soon joined by Marshal Yeh Chien-ying and Su Yü, chief of the general staff. [54], p. 72.

58. See also [34].

59. *SCMP*, no. 1753, pp. 44–46 (14 April 1958), cited in [54], p. 107; text from [184], 6 April 1958, cited in [34], p. 165.

60. [54], p. 111.

but not right away; that is one fair reading of China's later disclosure of the October 1957 agreement.[61] China probably asked for much more. She may have sought nuclear weapons on sites controlled by Soviet or Chinese crews, complete technical instructions on production, key components China could not easily produce, or substantive technical assistance. Apparently Khrushchev's ploy was to promise assistance toward future development, and much of that deliverable only in the future.

If Mao Tse-tung, P'eng Te-huai, and Kuo Mo-jo had returned from Moscow disappointed, why did Chou En-lai in February press the idea that the "socialist camp" was unprecedentedly strong? To the Soviets, Chou may have been saying that the CCP was a loyal party, deferential to the Soviet Union which headed the "socialist camp"; if the Communist Party of the Soviet Union (CPSU) was less sanguine than the CCP, or perhaps distrusted the CCP, it should reconsider. Domestically, the new assessment readied Chinese party cadres to take important foreign policy steps without Soviet concurrence.[62]

In internal discussions and to make arguments to Moscow, CCP leaders placed a premium on evidence that the world situation was indeed changing abruptly. In fact, they interpreted two African conferences in just that light.

Afro-Asian People's Solidarity Conference

It was noted earlier that the Afro-Asian People's Solidarity Conference could be traced back to the Asian Countries Conference held in New

61. "As far back as June 20, 1959 . . . the Soviet government unilaterally tore up the agreement on new technology for national defense concluded between China and the Soviet Union on October 15, 1957, and refused to provide China with a sample of an atomic bomb and technical data concerning its manufacture." See note 56.

62. Two arguments are implicit, assuming China was correct about the strength of the "socialist camp." If Peking were ready to act, but Moscow hesitated, only unilateral action by Peking would prove that she was correct. The second argument is that "imperialists," knowing the "socialist camp's" strength, would be afraid to provoke China and the Soviet Union, and thus the risks to China would be lowered. This second argument was valid only as long as Western powers judged China and the Soviet Union to be acting in concert, or at least that Moscow would use her technology to deter or retaliate against an attack on China. Both were still widely believed in the West in 1958. The arguments, that China could be proved right by action and that action was less risky than before, tip the balance toward a judgment favoring action. Furthermore, an episode forcing Moscow to decide to act might encourage men in Eastern Europe and the Soviet Union who were more sanguine than Khrushchev and who could press him to act. Peking's leadership may have argued that, if China faced a confrontation and Khrushchev allowed China to be sacrificed, Soviet power and prestige would suffer. The Taiwan Straits affair of 1958 was designed in such a way to force Soviet guarantees. It did not have that result, but neither did its failure dampen China's desire for a more active and independent foreign policy.

Delhi in 1955. Not only was a Chinese representative among the four who obtained President Nasser's consent to hold the first solidarity conference in Cairo, but China was one of the states contributing a secretary to the permanent secretariat created after the Cairo conference. Therefore three questions should be considered. How great was China's influence on the conference? What new opportunities did it open to China? And what conclusions did the CCP leadership profess to draw from it?

Although China had a seat on the preparatory committee and dispatched a twenty-five man delegation to Cairo,[63] whatever influence China attempted to exercise was overshadowed by Egypt and the Soviet Union. A Soviet representative was also among the four. The Soviet Union, far more than China, was an important source of political and economic support for Egypt. Colin Legum believes Nasser consented to have the conference in Cairo because he felt obligated to the Soviet Union, which had shortly before agreed to build the Aswan dam.[64] Like China, the Soviet Union named one of the secretaries.

Egypt's role was even more central. As if to underscore his uncertainty about sponsorship of the conference, Nasser did not open it himself; instead he sent a spokesman who struck a neutralist note.[65] The conservative Sudanese and Ethiopian governments were strongly represented. And when the permanent secretariat was created, the secretary general was to be an Egyptian.[66] Legum concludes:

> Whatever success the Russians might have had at Cairo, they failed to capture the conference. . . . A communist-inspired resolution advocating nationalization as an instrument of policy for African and Asian countries was killed in the committee stages. To represent the Cairo Conference as a "communist front" is to misinterpret what happened there.[67]

China's place was clearly a subordinate one.

The permanent secretariat offered China contacts and information,

63. *SCMP*, no. 1681, p. 25 (22 December 1957). The conference ran from late December 1957 into January. China's delegation was led by Kuo Mo-jo and two others; Kuo came to Cairo fresh from the scientific and technological talks in Moscow, where a strategy for Cairo was probably also discussed.

64. [76], p. 40.

65. *Ibid.* Anwar el-Sadat said: "The neutralism in which we believe means that we should keep aloof from international blocs and at the same time make efforts to bring about a rapprochement between those blocs." See also [73], pp. 6–9.

66. China and the Soviet Union were each allotted an ordinary secretary, as were Cameroon, Ghana, India, Indonesia, Iraq, Japan, Sudan, and Syria. Presumably the Afro-Asian Solidarity Committee of each country named its secretary.

67. [73], p. 9.

an opportunity for the Chinese secretary to meet African representatives of national solidarity committees and liberation movements which had dealings with the Cairo office. In that sense, his work supplemented that of embassy officials and New China News Agency representatives. He could also monitor the secretariat itself; by the 1960s, if not before, that included keeping track of Soviet moves. The first of China's secretaries was dispatched to Cairo in April 1958.[68]

Despite whatever concealed disappointment he may have felt for Egyptian moderation, Kuo Mo-jo was evidently struck by the extent and quality of African participation.

> More African delegates attended the Cairo Conference than any previous international conference. It marked the first time in recent history that the oppressed African nations had played an important role on the stage of international affairs. Delegates from Algeria, Kenya, Cyprus, Oman, Cameroon, Uganda, Somaliland, Zanzibar, Chad and Palestine, now in the forefront of the anti-colonialist struggles, received particular welcome and respect from the conference.[69]

Even before the conference, Peking had staged a rally at which Kuo Mo-jo voiced Chinese support for national liberation movements in Algeria, Kenya, Cameroon, Uganda, and Ifni.[70] Mao Tse-tung's awareness of the conference is suggested by greetings sent to it over his name.[71]

Chou En-lai's treatment of the conference is doubly revealing. On the one hand, he underscored the new situation of Africans. "The masses of the African people," he said, had entered the arena of international politics for "most of the countries taking part in the conference were African." On the other hand, socialist unity and support for decolonization promised new victories.

> The existence of this mighty socialist camp and its powerful support to national independence movements has inspired all those peoples striving to win or preserve their freedom and independence, and pro-

68. *SCMP*, no. 1762, p. 59 (28 April 1958).

69. *SCMP*, no. 1711, p. 39 (9 February 1958), adapted from NCNA. A few weeks earlier Africans had also participated in a more specialized event, the Asian-African Lawyers' Conference, Damascus, 7–11 November 1957. Eight of twenty countries represented were African. The Chinese delegation declared, "We are facing a new type of colonialist, the American bloc, who are carrying out the Eisenhower doctrine in Africa and in the Near and Middle East." One resolution argued that China's seat in the United Nations should be filled by the People's Republic. *SCMP*, no. 1651, pp. 43–44; *SCMP*, no. 1685, pp. 35; *SCMP*, no. 1652, p. 44.

70. *SCMP*, no. 1674, p. 27 (14 December 1957).

71. *SCMP*, no. 1681, p. 28 (26 December 1957).

> vides increasingly favorable conditions for them to wage successfully their heroic struggle against imperialism and colonialism. . . . So long as all the peace-loving countries and peoples maintain their solidarity and persevere in the struggle, as they have up till now, they will be able to cause the international situation to continue to develop in a direction favorable to peace and compel the imperialist aggressive forces to accept peaceful coexistence.[72]

With hindsight, one might imagine these words were directed as much to the Soviet Union as to Chou's Chinese audience. A breakdown of "bloc" unity, which is just what Soviet hoarding of nuclear capability and economic wealth subsequently induced or aggravated, would slow favorable development in the colonial world.

First Conference of Independent African States

The new assessment of Africa's significance is succinctly stated in a *Jen-min Jih-pao* editorial at the close of the First Conference of Independent African States, held in Accra, 15–22 April 1958.

> The awakened African people are concerned not only with African affairs but also with the destiny of the whole world. Events in Africa once again show that the anti-imperialist national independence movement is a force of peace. The African peoples have emerged in the international political arena as a new factor of peace. . . . No matter what obstructions and interference the colonialists vainly resort to, the torchlight of independence and freedom in the hands of the African peoples will illumine their broad future. The bright future of Africa knows no bounds.[73]

There was an objective basis for this reaction. Eight of Africa's nine independent states — all except South Africa — had committed themselves to anticolonialism and, even more concretely, to the Algerian revolution. On the other hand, much about the conference must have displeased China, though the polemical nature of her comment prevents mention of it. China took no public cognizance of the profoundly moderate preoccupations of the conference. Nor did she acknowledge the first fundamental principle of foreign policy to which the eight subscribed: "Unswerving loyalty to and support of the Charter of the United Nations and respect for decisions of the United Nations."[74]

72. *CB*, no. 492 (11 February 1958).
73. *SCMP*, no. 1760, p. 52 (25 April 1958).
74. Resolutions in [76], pp. 139–148. Youssef el-Sebai, AAPSO secretary general,

Turning to an Assertive Policy

In the first months of 1958 the CCP declared that African peoples were a newly-important factor in world politics. This was not yet the view — which China advanced in the 1960s — that Asia, Africa, and Latin America constitute the decisive arena of world struggle. It did identify forces just coming into play, however, which could reinforce the Soviet technological and military advantage.

But as November 1957 receded it became increasingly clear that Soviet nuclear weaponry would not be put at China's disposal. China then took the position that the Chinese army must rely on conventional strengths and that China would build her own nuclear weapons and delivery systems.

Internally, in May 1958, Liu Shao-ch'i proclaimed the general line of socialist construction.[75] The Great Leap Forward, which convulsed planning and production under the slogan "let politics take command," was begun; the people's communes were created; the militia movement was revived. The Great Leap Forward did not come into being all at once in May, but it brought together and extended moves toward decentralization, self-reliance, and agricultural consolidation which had been suggested during the latter part of 1957. Its extension throughout China was the major item of her economic business during 1958.

Africa first assumed major importance on Peking's agenda at this time. In retrospect, the reasons seem clear enough. Newly independent African governments met for the first time and issued radical proclamations. National liberation movements in dependent African territories were newly visible. China needed proof that the Soviet Union underestimated its opportunities — and events in Africa seemed to supply it. Moreover, processes set in motion months before, of which the most important was the holding of the solidarity conference, exposed African changes vividly and conveniently.

The seed of a deep flaw in Chinese policy was also formed at this time. Her emphasis on the prospects for new victories had depended on the solidarity of all "peace-loving countries and peoples." With the new weapons at her disposal, the Soviet Union could stand down the Western powers; China, with Soviet backing, could do so too. But the solidarity on which this new calculus of the balance of forces had been premised was illusory. China could *not* count on Soviet power to abet national liberation

---

termed the conference's resolutions "an extension to those of Bandung and Cairo." [7], pp. 14–17. Thus in China and elsewhere these public forums were pictured as related steps in a single political progression.

75. At the second session of the Eighth Congress of the CCP.

movements. China continued to encourage such movements with no suggestion that they should be cautious in the face of Soviet restraint.

Perhaps Peking still held the view that by maneuver, or a lucky consolidation of events, or the demonstrable vigor of the liberation movement, Khrushchev could be jerked from his cautious position. If so, she would not hold that view for long. The important point is that by May 1958 the key ingredients of a radical and assertive position in both foreign and domestic policy were advanced by China and utilized in the making of concrete decisions. Chief among the bases of such policy were reliance on the masses, disparagement of modern weapons (even as China sought to acquire them), and emphasis on independence movements in the balance of power.

In summary, between 1954 and the middle of 1958 China had acquired new entrées to Africa and, with them, contacts which she had not had before. She had an embassy in Cairo. She had made institutional innovations in the foreign ministry and solidarity committee.[76] Economically she had begun the Great Leap Forward with all it implied. In military affairs she turned to policies rooted in the guerrilla war period, most dramatically the "every man a soldier" movement for a massive militia. Internationally, Mao Tse-tung met with the Soviet leadership to discuss the whole trend and purpose of Soviet and Chinese foreign policy; and thereafter China acted abroad with an independence which, though only lightly discernible in 1958, became gradually more and more pronounced. As Stuart Schram has put it:

> [The winter of 1957–1958 constituted] a major watershed in the history of the contemporary world. Before it, China's economic and other policies appeared basically similar to those of the Soviet Union, and the monolithic unity of the Communist bloc was taken for granted by most observers, despite the Yugoslav precedent. After it, China was embarked on a series of policies radically different from those of the Soviets both in style and content, and an evolution was in progress that would soon lead to an open clash between Europe-centered and Asia-centered forms of Communism.[77]

An important arena in which China asserts herself, and in a mode which becomes clearly different from that of the Soviet Union, is Africa.

76. For example, the Chinese Asian Solidarity Committee was retitled the Chinese Committee for Afro-Asian Solidarity. The change was made in response to the Cairo conference and "with a view to further strengthening the friendship and solidarity of the peoples in the Asian and African countries." *SCMP*, no. 1766, p. 43 (4 May 1958).

77. [111], p. 283.

3 The Chinese Presence in Africa

Peking's prompt recognition of the Gouvernement Provisoire de la République Algérienne (GPRA) was one of the first signs of a Chinese position concerning Africa that was distinct from the position of the USSR. On the day the new government was formed, 20 September 1958, a Chinese diplomat met with GPRA ministers in Cairo, and Chinese recognition quickly followed.[1] The GPRA welcomed China's gesture, although relations were not formally established until December. Moscow did not extend recognition at this time.

China was optimistic about the turn of events in Africa in 1958, and the activities of Algerian revolutionaries probably further encouraged her. For example, an Algerian student, who was in Peking when the GPRA was formed, spoke at Peking University criticizing U.S. aid to France and asserting that China's recognition of the GPRA "once again shows that the Chinese government is always on the side of the just people and against imperialism and colonialism." He assured his hosts that Algerian youth were "firmly united" with Chinese youth in the struggle to liberate Taiwan.[2] Chou En-lai later told the visiting Algerian that "the present world situation is favorable to your struggle." Chou commended heightened African unity and urged isolation of the colonial powers.[3]

A high-level GPRA delegation visited China ten weeks later. The Algerians were aware that China might be persuaded to grant aid and

1. *SCMP*, no. 1861, p. 42 (22 September 1958); *SCMP*, no. 1860, p. 59 (20 September 1958).

2. Ait Cha'lal, chairman of the Union Générale des Etudiants Musulmans Algériens (UGEMA), later Algerian ambassador to Rome. With Cha'lal was Reda Malek, director of the FLN newspaper *El Moudjahid*. *SCMP*, no. 1862, p. 38 (23 September 1958). Malek was later Algerian ambassador to Belgrade and Paris. The late Mohammed Khemisti, named independent Algeria's first foreign minister in 1962, visited China in 1957 as head of a student delegation. Statements by UGEMA spokesmen, who were closely linked to the FLN leadership, were considered authoritative.

3. *SCMP*, no. 1864, p. 49. For Chinese messages to Algerian organizations, see *SCMP*, no. 1862, pp. 40–41.

that the talks might lead to material support "if need be."[4] Although the only public hint that they sought material aid was Ben Youssef Ben Khedda's description of the Algerian people "with but feeble means" facing "a true coalition of the imperialist forces," the final communiqué recorded China's resolute support for the Algerian people and specified that both countries had studied concrete methods to strengthen their relationship. They also agreed to establish diplomatic relations.[5] Although the leaders of China were involved in the touchy Sixth Plenum of the CCP Central Committee in Wuhan, the GPRA visitors were flown there to meet with Mao Tse-tung, Chou En-lai, Ch'en I, and others.

Peking greeted the delegation and called upon other independence movements to emulate the guerrilla warfare of the FLN. The heroic struggle of the Algerian people and their success proved "that all oppressed nations are unconquerable so long as they rise and struggle."[6] China was probably also attracted by the bold challenge to France embodied in the GPRA claim to be a government. The claim made unwanted compromise with France difficult; and it facilitated aid from abroad. Indeed, Chinese aid was forthcoming: an Algerian military mission visited China in the spring of 1959, reportedly securing a credit for the purchase of arms and other supplies having an estimated value of $10,000,000.[7]

China's commitment to the FLN was her first involvement in an anticolonial war on African soil.

Guinea

A few days after the GPRA was proclaimed, Guinea attained independence by voting no on a French constitutional referendum. China promptly recognized Guinea and was, in turn, granted recognition,[8] but

4. Information Minister Mohammed Yazid, *NYT*, 1 December 1958. In April 1958 three Chinese organizations donated $172,000 to the FLN, using the secretariat of the AAPSO as an intermediary. *SCMP*, no. 1749, p. 46; *NYT*, 8 May 1958.

5. *SCMP*, no. 1911, p. 48 (7 December 1958); *SCMP*, no. 1921, p. 38 (20 December 1958). The delegation was in China 3–13 and 16–21 December 1958, and China dates diplomatic relations with Algeria from 20 December 1958. *JMJP*, 22 November 1964, p. 4.

6. *SCMP*, no. 1864, p. 49.

7. Harold Hinton reports the agreement and ventures the $10,000,000 sum, but cites no source. [50], p. 185. The delegation announced no agreement, much less any terms. Subsequent Algerian statements, however, leave little doubt that Chinese material support during the three remaining years of the Algerian War was substantial. For example, see Algerian statements during Chou En-lai's visit to Algeria of December 1963 in [198].

8. *SCMP*, no. 1873, p. 67 (8 October 1958).

China did not hasten to endorse Sékou Touré's administration or its policies. Guinea was not cited at the time as an anticolonial model for other African states to emulate. When China did make a gesture toward Guinea, dispatching her ambassador in Morocco on a mission to Conakry in June, she underwrote the mission with a modest grant of 5,000 tons of rice.[9] China's hesitation was likely motivated by the desire to wait and see how the government of Sékou Touré would develop.

Early Diplomatic Relations

When a Chinese embassy opened in Conakry in December 1959 it was the fourth Chinese mission in Africa. Morocco and China had established diplomatic relations in November 1958. Richard Lowenthal, following Fritz Schatten, believes that Morocco recognized China in order to facilitate aid to the FLN. In that sense, the move was a consequence of forces within Moroccan political life which placed a high value on proof of solidarity with Algerian nationalism.[10] The first Chinese ambassador to Morocco was a former assistant minister of foreign trade, Pai Jen. China's third mission was in Khartoum, where Sino-Sudanese relations were formally established in February 1959. Thus, at the end of 1959 China had embassies in Cairo, Rabat, Khartoum, and Conakry, as well as relations with the GPRA.

Imperialists Quit Africa Day, 1 December 1958

On 1 December 1958 a full page of *Jen-min Jih-pao* was devoted to Africa. An editorial cited the Bandung conference, the Afro-Asian People's Solidarity Conference, and the Conference of Independent African States as having given great impetus to the African national independence movement.[11] A statement by the Chinese Afro-Asian Solidarity Committee, issued to mark the day, was typical of Chinese comment on Africa in 1958. "The imperialists will not leave Africa of their own accord," the statement averred, but "the Chinese people always sympathize with and support the African people in their just struggle for national independence and against colonialism and racial discrimination."[12] Such comments were not, of course, a full statement of China's considered view. Optimism was offset by a characteristic pessimism, and by a sensitivity to real obstacles

9. [230], 1961, p. 408.
10. [83], p. 165.
11. *JMJP*, 1 December 1958. Through much of December 1958 there were frequent articles on the visiting Algerian delegation too. For example, *SCMP*, no. 1911, pp. 39 ff.; *SCMP*, no. 1915, p. 30; *SCMP*, no. 1921, p. 38 (joint communiqué).
12. *SCMP*, no. 1907, p. 37.

which blocked a prompt end to imperialism. In discussing the events of 1956, we suggested that China had doubts and misgivings about nationalist leadership. In 1959, whether prompted by the studied moderation of a leader like Bourguiba or by Nasser's pressure on local Communists—which had strained relations between Cairo and Moscow as well—Kuo Mo-jo told a Peking rally that "some statesmen in certain Asian and African countries have come to the conclusion that the task against imperialism has come to an end and [that they] can now point their sword to the people."[13]

Other comment stressed unity, with the implication that unity was endangered. This meant that China's aim, which was "to drive all the imperialists out of the continent of Africa," was also in danger or liable to delay.[14] Still, the moderation of African nationalists and threats to unity were not judged to be so severe as to stem the favorable trend of developments. The lessons already learned—Suez, Algeria, and Guinea—were reinforced by political violence in the Belgian Congo on 4 January 1959. Outside Africa, but with profound implications for guerrilla war and popular anti-imperialism, Fidel Castro won state power in Cuba on 1 January 1959. A Chinese overview, issued in mid-April 1959, claimed more for the development of revolution in Africa than had been claimed at any prior time. The current situation in Africa showed "that by their own practical experience in struggle, the African people have come [to] maturity step-by-step, politically and organizationally."[15]

China and the Soviet Union Draw Apart

Soviet distrust of China had grown so deep that Moscow withdrew aid to the Chinese nuclear development program on 20 June 1959,[16] and in August 1960 all Soviet technicians aiding Chinese economic development were withdrawn. These moves forced China to rely increasingly on her own resources. It is quite plain what this meant in the military and economic spheres. In external policy, China could choose to placate the Soviet Union in an effort to restore the lost benefits, to seek political advantage elsewhere without regard for the Soviet Union, or to evolve a combination of conciliatory and independent policies. China elected an independent position which generated mutually reinforcing reasons for

13. *SCMP*, no. 2001, p. 43.
14. *SCMP*, no. 1995, pp. 44–45, including comment marking annual Africa Freedom Day.
15. *SCMP*, no. 1995, p. 45.
16. *PR*, 16 August 1963, p. 14.

proclaiming China's interest in Africa. In doing so, she clashed directly with the USSR both in Africa itself and in the AAPSO.

China's wish to acquire nuclear weapons displeased Moscow because, once she had them, China might provoke a nuclear confrontation that Moscow did not want, and she could, moreover, threaten the Soviet Union directly. The USSR wanted *military superiority over China*, and she did not trust China to limit the use of nuclear weapons to the ways Moscow approved.

To China, the Soviet refusals made a lie of Khrushchev's protestations about fraternal relations in the "socialist camp." Moscow sought to perpetuate her military advantage by depriving China, for as long as possible, of great power status. We may speculate that the CCP feared that Khrushchev would take further steps to arrest or to delay China's development of nuclear weapons. For example, the CCP probably suspected anti-Chinese collusion between the United States and the USSR when Khrushchev and Eisenhower talked in the United States in September 1959.

What conditions would cause Moscow to come to Peking's defense? We do not know the guarantees that existed before June 1959, much less afterward, but we can guess that more optimistic members of the Chinese leadership were shaken by Soviet withdrawal. Before June 1959 CCP leaders may have felt sure that Moscow would be forced to reply to an unprovoked nuclear attack on China; after June they must have doubted any Soviet guarantee, although in an actual encounter the USSR might still have been obliged to help. In September 1959 Lin Piao was placed in charge of the Chinese military and stepped-up politicization of the army was undertaken, a sign of the decision to be self-reliant.

The Soviet Union also used economic aid policy as a coercive device. Although production began on a large number of Soviet-supported projects in 1958 and 1959, Soviet aid provided for only a few of China's needs. In fact, one of China's criticisms was that non-Communist states received Soviet aid at China's expense. From his advantageous position, Khrushchev could offer aid as a reward for moderation,[17] threaten to withdraw aid if China was obstreperous, or, ultimately, end technical assistance. That final step, when he took it in August 1960, made clear the grave objections that

17. Khrushchev announced in February 1959 that a major aid package would be granted China. A few weeks earlier China had decided to slow the Great Leap Forward. See [146], pp. 127–128. Still, she had not foresworn assertiveness. Chou En-lai told the Twenty-First Party Congress of the CPSU in January 1959 that acts of imperialists would force the people to "cast away their illusions and take the road of struggle and revolution." *Ibid.*, p. 239. The Soviet aid offer was not implemented, as the chasm between Soviet and Chinese views deepened.

the Soviet Union harbored against Chinese policy. Moreover, it made the point publicly. China's leaders, coming to grips with economic difficulties which were to become even more serious in the ensuing months, must have concluded that Moscow sought either permanent deference from China or her permanent impoverishment. Neither prospect was tolerable.

What was the driving mechanism? Did China, judging Soviet policy for the third world frightfully wrong, press her own claim to leadership? Or was her assessment of the balance of forces merely facile language behind which China could exact revenge for Soviet refusals of support?

A. M. Halpern observes that the main points of China's revised view of the significance of underdeveloped countries had already been outlined by April 1959: colonialism's decline was envisaged as bringing Asia, Africa, and Latin America to the forefront of the anti-imperialist struggle, and the third world was no longer a mere contributor to the "peace zone" of socialist and underdeveloped countries. He notes, however, that China did not revive the model of her own revolutionary experience as a guide to be followed in attaining independence—a challenging step—until 1 October 1959, after Moscow's decisive action and after CCP consideration of it.[18] It is likely that China drew conclusions from the world situation that Moscow would not accept. Khrushchev, disgruntled by China's unorthodox world view and her claims for the communes, and irritated that Peking was not more receptive to his conciliatory gestures, forced China across a threshold in June 1959. The die was cast.

Until September 1958 the CCP may well have believed it could force Khrushchev to be more assertive. But Khrushchev refused to abet China's move in the Taiwan Straits. Peking did not make a doctrinal adjustment; no new strategic doctrine, no substitute for the "transitional" doctrine of May 1958, was set forth. Instead, the People's Liberation Army (PLA) took solace in the advice to "despise the enemy strategically but respect him tactically."[19] In the summer of 1959 a new policy was worked out, probably at the Eighth Plenum of the CCP Central Committee.[20] In Sep-

18. [45], pp. 8–9. Halpern observes that, using hindsight, one can discern the Sino-Soviet differences about underdeveloped countries in a discussion between Soviet and Chinese foreign affairs writers; see [170], March 1959.

19. [54], p. 165.

20. At this meeting, held in Lushan from 2–16 August 1959, the effective unit of agricultural production was decreased from the commune to the production brigade. The move followed revelations that 1958 production statistics in agriculture and industry had been extremely overoptimistic. Zagoria reconstructs a conflict among three factions in the Lushan plenum. According to his analysis, a center group defeated rightists, who would have abandoned communes altogether, and leftists, who sought to press on without respite. [146], pp. 134–141. From his materials, it appears that

tember, newly-appointed minister of national defense Lin Piao stressed the primacy of party over army, the political over the purely military, and the need for restraint while China developed the capacity to supply her own arms requirements.[21] His remarks forecast the intensification of "transitionalism." He undertook a political program within the army to strip it of remnants of bourgeois ideology. Soviet policy and Chinese economic setbacks obliged the PLA to rely on the "man over weapons" doctrine.

At the celebrations marking the tenth anniversary of the founding of the People's Republic on 1 October 1959, Chinese spokesmen expressed views about the underdeveloped world which were distinct from those of the Soviet Union. As previously noted, they pressed the claim that China's revolutionary experience was valid as a model for backward areas.[22] The Chinese path to power was a typical example for underdeveloped countries.[23] Furthermore, the Chinese revolution was an example "for transforming a backward, agricultural country into an advanced, industrial country."[24]

Rather than conciliate the Soviet Union, China chose to challenge Moscow for leadership of the "socialist camp." The challenge was a gradual one, qualified until July 1963, but it did not attempt to placate Khrushchev.

"Once bitten, twice shy," the CCP leaders felt that they would have had to pay dearly for Soviet military or economic guarantees which, even at a high price, could never be reliable. China's alternative was to make her own guarantees, even if they were marginal, partial, temporary, and imperfect. This implied action both at home — indigenous nuclear production, politicization of the army, bootstrap economic construction — and abroad. But China's very size and the singularity of her position meant that no important ally was available. Since she had decided not to soften her political stance — had she done so she might well have repaired relations with Moscow — the alternatives left open to her were limited. For Africa, this meant:

(1) China sought friends where she had not sought them before, probably believing that political pressure could be mustered if needed against threats or an attack.

---

between 2 June and 18 July 1959 the Soviet Union abandoned cautiously favorable references to the communes and began to reject them outright.

21. [232], cited in [54], p. 178.

22. [146], pp. 266–267; [45], pp. 8–9.

23. [232], pp. 276 ff.

24. Teng Hsiao-p'ing, CCP secretary general. [184], 2 October 1959.

(2) China still needed evidence that her assessment of the prospect of revolution was correct. If it was, she might win allies, in Eastern Europe and within the Soviet Union itself, capable of restraining the use of Soviet power against her. And she might contribute to unseating Khrushchev and to replacing him by someone more friendly.
(3) China could strengthen her political position vis-à-vis the Soviet Union if she had influence on African leaders from whom Moscow sought favor.
(4) China would prefer moves which embroiled the United States (or even the Soviet Union) in an African conflict. A draining guerrilla war, to relieve U.S. (or Soviet) pressure on China's own borders, would be best of all.
(5) China could compete with the United States and Soviet Union for African resources.
(6) China would try to buy and sell more vigorously in Africa.
(7) China would increasingly take a position at odds with that of the Soviet Union — more reliant on struggle, mass action, and calls for concerted anti-imperialist action.
(8) China would attempt to bar Soviet countermoves and Soviet efforts to extend Moscow's influence in Africa.

In 1959 China was doing little more than making contacts, conducting trade, and publicizing evidence of Africa's revolutionary potential. The other implications for Africa could only follow after China had acquired the necessary entrée.

Sino-African Contacts, 1958–1960

Between 1958 and 1960 Chinese contacts with Africans increased rapidly. African delegations visiting China numbered eighteen in 1958, thirty-nine in 1959, but they reached eighty-eight in 1960. This pattern suggests that the CCP was trying to strengthen its hand for the November 1960 Moscow conference of Communist parties. Moreover, visitors from a greater number of African countries came to China each year: eight in 1958, thirteen in 1959, and twenty-nine in 1960. China was broadening as well as intensifying her activities.

The number of contacts with specific states and movements is closely correlated with political relations. Sino-Egyptian relations soured in 1959, and almost all delegation contact vanished. On the other hand, China's attraction to revolutionary movements in Algeria and Cameroon is demonstrated by the fact that thirteen of the thirty-nine African groups visiting

China in 1959 came from those two countries.[25] China also continued to meet Africans at Moscow-guided meetings and at Afro-Asian conferences held under various sponsorships.[26]

Growth of Afro-Asian Groups

Where China lacked diplomatic missions, she used alternative means to make new contacts and to express her policies to African audiences. A variety of small-scale conferences, the secretariat formed by the Afro-Asian People's Solidarity Conference, and later the second solidarity conference itself were vehicles for the development of new relations. At the second conference some proposals were made which would have equipped the solidarity movement with potentially significant machinery — including an armed volunteer corps — had they been put into effect. But China's capacity to utilize Afro-Asian initiatives to expand her scope of action did not mean that she could control the Afro-Asian bodies which sponsored them. Sometimes Chinese wishes were stubbornly and effectively resisted; some ideas which China favored, including the plan for a volunteer corps, fell by the wayside.

The conferences included meetings of women,[27] ophthalmologists,[28] youth,[29] and writers. The latter created a Permanent Bureau of Asian and African Writers, in which China had disproportionate influence.[30] On

25. Country-by-country totals and monthly figures for arrivals reveal quite strikingly the foci of Chinese attention at specific times. Specialists may wish to consult [70].

26. China's sustained interest in these avenues is best illustrated by the Eighth World Youth Festival, Vienna, July–August 1959. Four hundred Chinese attended, and the delegation held a reception for African participants from twenty-eight countries. *SCMP*, no. 2068, p. 20.

27. Afro-Asian Women's Conference, Colombo, 15–24 February 1958. It was sponsored by women's groups of the Colombo states and achieved token African participation from Egypt, Tunisia, and Uganda. *SCMP*, no. 1716, p. 43. Arrangements were not in keeping with Chinese sensitivities. Observers from United Nations agencies were present, and the Chinese delegation temporarily withdrew while an International Labor Organization observer spoke. *SCMP*, no. 1686, p. 35; *SCMP*, no. 1719, p. 44.

28. Afro-Asian Congress of Ophthalmology, Cairo, March 1958. Two Chinese professors attended. *SCMP*, no. 1724, p. 51.

29. Afro-Asian Youth Conference, Cairo, February 1959. China's delegation was led by the chairman of the All-China Youth Federation, Liu Hsi-yüan, who also led the Chinese group at the World Youth Festival in the summer (see note 26). Chinese newspapers praised the conference. *SCMP*, no. 1945, p. 44; [171], no. 5–6 (1959), pp. 18–21; *JMJP*, 10 February 1959; [203], 11 February 1959; *SCMP*, no. 1953, p. 50. At its close, the AAPSO council met in Cairo and claimed that participants from forty countries had attended. [180], no. 8 (1959), p. 32.

30. China helped to plan and organize the First Afro-Asian Writers' Conference, Tashkent, 7–13 October 1958. In June 1958 Chinese endorsed the event and then

the other hand, one of the clearest examples of resistance to Chinese maneuvers occurred at the First Afro-Asian Economic Conference. Its Egyptian patrons maintained a tight grip on the conference and quashed Chinese efforts to politicize the meeting through changes in organization.[31] The Chinese delegate also voiced distress at Philippine efforts to introduce the issue of representation for Taiwan.

China's use of the permanent secretariat to gain further contacts is illustrated by Yang Shuo's attendance at the All-African People's Conference, 5–13 December 1958, in Accra. As an observer for the solidarity movement, he saw a number of key personalities who were to head movements for independence as this was a meeting of political parties, not governments. In attendance were Patrice Lumumba, subsequently premier of the Congo (L); Holden Roberto, head of the Union of the Peoples of Angola; and Dr. Félix Moumié, leader of the Union des Populations du Cameroun to which China subsequently gave extensive moral support.[32] The permanent secretariat also dispatched a delegation to the tenth anniversary celebrations of the People's Republic of China.[33]

The Second Afro-Asian People's Solidarity Conference, 11–15 April 1960, in Conakry, met in the wake of signs indicating fiscal, political, and administrative strains within the organization.[34] Nonetheless, as the first truly major Afro-Asian event since the original solidarity conference in

---

attended, with representatives of Algeria, Cameroon, and the United Arab Republic, meetings of the preparatory committee in Tashkent. [180], no. 40 (1958). Chinese participants in the conference included Yang Shuo, AAPSO secretary in Cairo, and Chou Yang, principal CCP spokesman on the tasks of intellectuals. Chou Yang's speech is excerpted in *SCMP*, no. 1876, p. 52, and *SCMP*, no. 1880, p. 59. The permanent bureau included members from China, Cameroon, Ghana, Sudan, and the United Arab Republic, and the conference was a staging point for visits to China by Angolan, Ghanaian, Nigerian, Senegalese, Somali, and Ugandan writers.

31. Cairo, 8–11 December 1958. As in the cases of the Afro-Asian Women's Conference of 1958 and the Afro-Asian Congress of Ophthalmology, this event was not sponsored by AAPSO. Delegates were representatives of trade and industry. Nan Han-ch'en, board chairman of the Bank of China, represented Peking. After the event he reported efforts at "disruption." *SCMP*, no. 1933, p. 22. But the *Proceedings* reveal repeated vain efforts by China to change the conference's organization. [6].

32. [76], p. 44. UPC vice president Ernest Ouandie had visited Peking three months earlier, but this was almost certainly China's first introduction to Lumumba and Roberto.

33. Led by Youssef el-Sebai, AAPSO secretary general, it included two leaders of African organizations: Majmout Diop, of the Parti Africain de l'Indépendence (Senegal), and Abubakr Hamud Socorro, president of the Somali National Union. On these men, see [33] and [123].

34. For example, the permanent secretariat denied responsibility for holding an Afro-Asian Women's Conference mandated by the First Afro-Asian Solidarity Conference and complained of financial hardship. [9].

Cairo, it received close Chinese attention. Chinese personnel in three distinct roles were positioned to exert influence on the delegates and the proceedings: Chu Tzu-ch'i in the secretariat,[35] K'o Hua as newly-appointed Chinese ambassador, and fifteen delegates—including Liao Ch'eng-chih and Liu Ning-i. A forty-seven-member Chinese acrobatic troupe arrived in Conakry on the day the conference opened.

This meeting also exposed China to an array of African leaders and movements. The executive committee it elected included—in addition to Liao Ch'eng-chih—Ouandie (Cameroon), Oginga Odinga (Kenya), Joshua Nkomo (Rhodesia), J. Kozonguizi (South-West Africa), Ahmed Tlili (Tunisia), and Patrice Lumumba (Congo), each familiar to students of African affairs. Other regions and organizations were also represented.[36]

These rich possibilities for political encounter and the concentration of Chinese personnel at the meeting should not imply that China exercised any more control at Conakry than she had at Cairo twenty-eight months before. In language reminiscent of Egyptian speeches at that meeting, Secretary-General Youssef el-Sebai warned:

> We are not at all worried about the form taken by the domestic systems of other countries, but we are categorically opposed to the imposition of any system by force or pressure. We do not tolerate interference in the internal affairs of other nations, just as we do not consent to the use of the Afro-Asian movement for the advantage of a single country or a single group of countries.[37]

Whether his words were directed at China and the Soviet Union together, or to either one alone, they were a bold rejection of interference.

The solidarity movement's limitations sprang from its nongovernmental character and its inability to act forcefully or to command attention between conferences. To overcome these handicaps, the Conakry meeting resolved that a second Bandung conference should be convened, "grouping around the Asian and African chiefs of state the effective forces of two continents: political organizations, trade unions, women's movements, movements of youth and scholars, and so forth."[38]

35. Chu Tzu-ch'i, who replaced Yang Shuo as China's member of the permanent secretariat, began work on preparations in Conakry more than two months before the conference. *SCMP*, no. 2235, p. 37.

36. Including: Algeria (FLN), Angola, Basutoland, Niger (Sawaba); various Congolese and Somali political parties; the Fédération des Etudiants d'Afrique Noire en France (Paris); and the Committee of African Organisations (London). [8], pp. 7–8, p. 124.

37. *Ibid.*, pp. 34–35.

38. *Ibid.*, p. 66.

Only governments had enjoyed full privileges at Bandung; at the proposed conference the unofficial world of national liberation movements and the official world of independent states would commingle. Moreover, Bandung had not created any institutions. The Conakry meeting envisioned the establishment of the following executive machinery at the second Bandung conference:

(1) A body charged with responsibility to disseminate complete and objective information on the anti-imperialist struggle.

(2) A corps of Afro-Asian volunteers to aid all Asian and African peoples who struggle for liberation against the imperialists.

(3) A solidarity fund to aid all Afro-Asian peoples struggling against imperialism.[39]

In fact, the move to combine governments and liberation movements had little real effect, although some AAPSO participation was always sponsored by governments. The idea of a solidarity fund was implemented within AAPSO, while the volunteer corps was not. Had it been approved, contingents would most likely have been recruited from all Afro-Asian states, and China's skill, experience, and commitment would have assured her of influence far exceeding the share of personnel she would have been called upon to contribute. In 1960 China may have expected that this proposal, or one like it, would be realized.

The solidarity movement reached its zenith at Conakry. By April 1960 few African states had attained independence, and the nationalist movements in dependent territories wanted the political gains offered in a nongovernmental forum. Furthermore, their energies were not yet turned to domestic construction and mundane governmental affairs.

For the most part, the institutional proposals made at Conakry were attempts by movements to embrace the prestige and treasuries of sovereign states. But in late 1960 a host of African states suddenly achieved independence, and the growing momentum of decolonization was everywhere evident. Incentives to make AAPSO more powerful were on the decline. Moreover, Peking would soon discern forces at work which would eventually lead her to denounce AAPSO and withdraw from its secretariat.

Moscow Conference of Communist and Workers' Parties, November 1960

Like China, the Soviet Union began to pay increased attention to Africa in 1958. Alexander Dallin observes that the late Soviet specialist Academician I. I. Potekhin's reports on the First All-African People's

39. *Ibid.*

Conference were "a landmark, indicating (despite unmistakable reservations) a strong desire to associate the Soviet Union with the African upheavals."[40] Additional Soviet efforts were planned in the summer and fall of 1959. The quarterly *African Communist* first appeared in October 1959, "clearly designed," in the words of Richard Lowenthal, "as a policy-making organ and a 'collective organizer' for the whole of tropical Africa."[41]

Both Moscow and Peking sought an advantageous footing for their forthcoming encounter at the Moscow conference. China believed that the Soviet Union was too willing to compromise with the United States and only halfhearted in its support of national liberation movements. The nucleus of the forthcoming widespread Chinese attack on Soviet policies was contained in an article issued to mark the ninetieth birthday of Lenin in April 1960. This document became a position paper advancing China's views for the Moscow conference. In addition to contending that the "socialist camp" had achieved an advantage over imperialism at the end of 1957, it maintained:

> The socialist camp headed by the Soviet Union has grown more powerful; the Soviet Union has gone even more markedly ahead of the United States militarily and in the most important aspects of science and technology. . . . At the same time the national independence movements in Asia, Africa and Latin America and the struggles of the people in the capitalist countries for democracy and socialism have also shown important new developments. . . . The east wind prevails over the west wind.[42]

"Whether or not one dares to expose imperialism" was the touchstone proving whether or not one wished the "complete emancipation of the oppressed nations" and other revolutionary goals. National liberation for colonies and semicolonies required struggle against United States imperialism:

> In order to oppose the aggressive policy of US imperialism, it is necessary to unite all the world's revolutionary forces and peace-loving forces. World peace can be further defended and effectively defended only by linking up the struggle of the people of the socialist countries, the national liberation struggle of the people of the colonies and semi-colonies, the revolutionary struggle of the proletariat in the capitalist countries and the struggle of all peoples for peace,

40. [27], p. 30.
41. [85].
42. [204], pp. 65–66.

> forming them into a mighty anti-imperialist front and dealing firm blows at the US imperialist policies of aggression and war.[43]

In further preparation for the Moscow conference and to broaden the range of her activities in Africa, China created the China-Africa People's Friendship Association (CAPFA) in April 1960. Kuo Mo-jo, speaking in Peking on the occasion, said that the "billowing national independence movement" had compelled imperialism to consent to independence for more new states in 1960. In Nyasaland, the Rhodesias, Tanganyika, Uganda, Kenya, Congo, Ruanda-Urundi, Somaliland, Zanzibar, and Angola the people were intensifying their struggle against colonialism and for national independence. Algeria, he contended, was a major center of struggle.[44]

Other Chinese spokesmen took up related themes during April. Chou En-lai, noting changes in Africa, told a Rangoon audience:

> In the past five years, under the inspiration of the Bandung spirit, a tremendous change has taken place in the face of Asia and Africa. . . . The African people [like the Asians before them] have awakened more and more, and the flames of the struggle against colonialism and racial discrimination are raging throughout the African continent. The influence of the Bandung Conference is continuing to spread and penetrate deeper into the minds of the people.[45]

Chou's remarks help us to understand Chinese impatience. Not only was the objective situation changing, but there were complementary and reinforcing changes in the subjective situation. The African people were attaining political consciousness. Without heightened consciousness, Chou implied, African states would not gain political independence. If one follows his reasoning further, Chou appears to imply that China and other "progressive" forces should help to widen consciousness as well as take specific steps which would alter the objective situation if they wished to hasten revolution.

Liao Ch'eng-chih echoed the assertion that tremendous changes had taken place in the preceding two years when he spoke to the Second Afro-

43. *Ibid.*, p. 103.

44. *SCMP*, no. 2247, p. 28; *JMJP*, 18 April 1960. He cited three post-Bandung events, each of which had dealt a heavy blow to imperialism: the 1956 Suez affair, the Iraqi revolution that overthrew Nuri es-Said, and the frustration of "armed intervention by the United States and British imperialism" in the Middle East. These cases were probably adduced in internal discussions to demonstrate the wisdom of activist policies.

45. *SCMP*, no. 2242, p. 37 (16 April 1960).

Asian People's Solidarity Conference in Conakry. He noted that imperialists had met defeat in Iraq, Lebanon, Jordan, the Taiwan Straits, and Cuba. Then, invoking two themes central to China's professed view of Africa — the man over weapons doctrine and the assertion that China and Africa both suffered imperialist repression — he remarked:

> We pay special homage to the heroic Algerian people and their gallant National Liberation Army. They are standing at the forefront of the struggle against imperialism. They have won admiration and support from the Afro-Asian peoples and the whole world. . . . The imperialists dream they can crush the struggle of the Algerian people by "superior weapons" and save their colonial empire by means of armed suppression. But they are digging their own graves for history has shown that justice always prevails over injustice, the weak over the strong and the new-born forces over the decaying one. The people of Vietnam have shown this in Dien Bien Phu and the experience of long years of struggle of the Chinese people has proved that "millet plus rifles" can defeat "airplanes plus tanks." The decisive factor in the struggle against imperialism is the people and so long as the people are determined and persist in their heroic fight they are invincible.
>
> The Chinese people entertain especially close warm feelings for the African people in their struggle against the colonial rule and for national independence. We were regarded by the imperialist aggressors as a so-called "inferior race" and our people suffered the same bitterness of slaughter, plundering and enslavement at the hands of foreign colonialists.[46]

In Liao's view there was no shortage of opportunity. With Chinese moral support and relying on the decisive superiority of men over weapons, the African people were fully capable of taking up the arms available to them and beginning a successful struggle against imperialism.

By August 1960 China faced Soviet threats to her military, economic, and ideological positions. Chinese security had never been so severely imperiled.[47] The concurrent withdrawal of Soviet experts from China emphasized the gravity of the situation.

The Soviets miscalculated in mid-1960 if they believed that threats

46. Liao added: "In the past two years since the First Afro-Asian People's Solidarity Conference, the world situation has undergone a tremendous change. The forces against imperialism and colonialism are forging ahead from victory to victory while the imperialist bloc headed by the United States is tumbling down and nearing its doom." *SCMP*, no. 2242, p. 26 (14 April 1960).

47. [146], p. 335.

would subdue China; they were correct, however, in predicting that China would not risk the blame for splitting the world Communist movement. According to one reconstruction of the secret Moscow discussions in November, the Chinese did press their views and openly attacked Khrushchev's policies in both preliminary committee meetings and the conference itself.[48] But in the end, while insisting on its right to pursue policies with which most of the attending parties did not agree, the CCP did sign a long communiqué. Ambivalencies, omissions, and evasions in the communiqué masked the real differences that separated the CCP and CPSU. It is therefore hardly surprising that after the conference each proceeded to emphasize those portions of the text most congenial to its own positions. Nevertheless, a public showdown was avoided.

Organization was the key issue in the Moscow talks. When fraternal parties disagreed, how were their differences to be adjudicated? Was "factionalism"—one party's claiming to be correct after another leading party, or a group of parties, had decided to the contrary—to be condoned? But the organizational problem would not have been significant had Peking and Moscow not differed on matters of substance—on what was sound policy. Although some disagreements had nothing to do with Africa, a surprising number did: What was to be expected from governing nationalists? How could risks and opportunities in small-scale wars be compared? Where might Communist energies best be spent to hasten world revolution?

The Soviet Union believed that communism could triumph through economic competition with the West; she also feared escalation of local wars; above all, she feared the prospect of a nuclear holocaust. China neither expected victory from economic competition nor thought that nuclear war was likely to follow from local war. If nuclear war were forced by the imperialists, the people would make the best of it. For these reasons, she did not consider the governing nationalists to be as useful as did the Soviets.

The Moscow conference offered a plan which the governing nationalists were invited to adopt if they wished to be counted among progressive forces: any state conforming to the conditions laid down in the communiqué earned the title of national democratic state.

China ignored the proposed plan for national democratic states. A brief look at its main elements will show why. Moscow proposed that governing nationalists be enlisted to lead the state while local Communists organized and joined in national policy formation. The process would

48. [42], especially pp. 38–39, note 3.

endure for an indefinite period during which trade and aid relations with Communist states would be established and domestic land reform undertaken. China's hostility to this scheme was rooted in these convictions: temporary gains in trade and ad hoc political advantage would be risky while the nationalists maintained hegemony; backsliding might occur; and, even if it did not, national democratic states would slow rather than hasten global revolution.

Some African nationalists had already prompted Chinese suspicion. Moreover, the Chinese revolution itself was so much a tale of suspicious cooperation with the national bourgeoisie that any such scheme would have been distrusted. In urging China's experience on Africa, the national democratic state was hardly what the CCP had in mind.

China hoped that African events before and after the Moscow meeting would demonstrate that her assessment was sound. These pressures put a premium on information about critical situations in Africa and the ability to guide events. When Ch'en Chia-k'ang made a hurried trip to Léopoldville in August 1960, shortly before Kasavubu ousted Lumumba as premier, he was probably in search of both. On the other hand, the very indecisiveness of the Moscow communiqué might have provoked China to a new round of ventures in Africa. Nevertheless, soon after the conference China's level of activity in Africa dropped dramatically and precipitously. Economic dislocation at home had derailed her drive for an assertive role abroad.

Economic Retrenchment

In January 1961, faced by serious economic disarray, the CCP ordered the redirection of resources.[49] Many Chinese activities abroad were cut severely. Until this retrenchment, Chinese programs directed toward Africa had been unprecedentedly large in scale; afterwards aid and visitor traffic were dramatically curtailed.

In September 1960 China made her first significant economic gesture in sub-Saharan Africa, a credit of 100,000,000 (old) rubles granted to Guinea.[50] However, large credits extended to Ghana and to Mali in 1961, after retrenchment, included the curious proviso that they could not be drawn upon until July 1962. China's second significant aid was neither cash nor credit, but a grant of medical supplies, steel, and wheat (which may not have been grown in China, at that).[51] The evidence suggests that

49. At the Ninth Plenum of the Eighth Central Committee, 14–18 January 1961.
50. [80], p. 118.
51. To newly-independent Algeria, announced 13 August 1962. During this period China was buying wheat from Canada and Australia.

during 1961 and 1962 Chinese leadership felt the pressure of domestic claims and refused to divert to Africa more than minimum resources.

Two major Chinese delegations[52] were dispatched to Africa early in 1961, but their trips had probably been arranged before retrenchment. In sharp contrast to the previous year, only three Chinese visitors entered Africa between April and December 1961. The number of African delegations to China also fell sharply: eighty-eight in 1960; forty-three in 1961; and thirty-two in 1962.

Congo (Léopoldville), 1961

Just as economic strictures forced China to cease many forms of action abroad, the murder of Patrice Lumumba created new opportunities in the Congo (L). There was some prospect that a radical Congolese government would be formed to wrest power from Léopoldville. Displaying characteristic caution, and unable to assume large-scale economic commitments, China lent her support to the Gizenga government in Stanleyville but refrained from making costly commitments. Although events in the Congo did not yield results pleasing to China, the example of separatist action against Léopoldville was endorsed. Peking's posture toward the Congo in 1961 was even more significant when viewed as a prelude to decisive action in 1964.

Early in 1961 a secret Chinese analysis of the Congo situation was circulated in Peking; by chance it has fallen into Western hands.[53] This document reveals China's revolutionary concerns at the time and her specific hope that a revolutionary base might be constructed in the Congo (L). It also shows that China had only modest expectations for the Lumumba-Gizenga group:

> At present the national liberation movement of the Congo is mainly led by the capitalist [bourgeois] nationalist elements. Among them wavering and compromise prevail and so they cannot undertake correct and firm leadership. The strength of the nationalist party is also scattered and there is no single force which can unite the whole country. . . . [The] scope of activities [of political parties] is limited to one place and they are continuously in the process of splitting up.
>
> As a result of long colonial control, there exist in various places of the Congo the comprador class and the reactionary feudalistic tribal

52. A trade delegation led by Lu Hsü-chang, vice-minister of foreign trade, reached Africa on 7 February. A CAPFA delegation arrived in Africa on 2 March. Liu Ch'ang-sheng, a member of the CCP Central Committee and CAPFA chairman, led the second party.

53. [227].

> influence. . . . These feudalistic influences unite with the imperialistic and thus increase the difficulty of the revolutionary struggle of the Congo people.
>
> The struggle of the Congo people is extensive, severe and heroic, but at present there is no core guidance organized by the workers' class.

Written shortly before Lumumba's assassination, the speculation above takes on a sober tone, in marked contrast with China's public statements at the same time. The efforts at class analysis and an estimate of forces show China's concern for objective conditions.

The anonymous author goes on to speculate about three possible paths that the Congolese situation might follow. His most pessimistic scenario, from China's point of view, posits the persistence of many separate groups, each with ties to imperialists or internal comprador-feudalist elements, which might unite to form a weak central government. Less pessimistically, he speculated that imperialist and comprador-feudalist elements might maintain control for some time and might even entice Lumumba to conciliation. His optimum scenario is the one in which Lumumbists would cease wavering, internal and external revolutionary forces would be correctly deployed, and, with Oriental Province as a consolidated base, they would fight back from Stanleyville to unite the entire Congo.[54]

Publicly, China was committed to the legality of the Lumumba-Gizenga government and an optimistic assessment of events:

> The lawful Congolese government is still there; its Deputy Prime Minister, Antoine Gizenga, is acting on behalf of the Prime Minister [Lumumba] and the lawful Congolese government continues to exercise powers. . . . The people in the Oriental Province have mobilized themselves to resist the imperialist aggression. Patriotic soldiers in Kivu Province have risen to action and fought heroically against the forces of imperialism and its agents there.[55]

Privately, China's calculations were summed up in a single sentence: "The situation is favorable but the leadership is weak."[56]

Lumumba's death created a martyr for the Stanleyville government. China soon agreed to establish diplomatic relations with Stanleyville, but she waited five months before dispatching an envoy. China's last-minute

54. *Ibid.*, pp. 179–181.
55. *JMJP*, 3 January 1961; excerpts in *SCMP*, no. 2413, p. 22.
56. [227], p. 181.

action may have been an attempt to match Soviet moves, or it may have been a final effort to bolster Gizenga's sagging opposition to the central government of Adoula in Léopoldville. When the envoy arrived, the Gizenga group was already negotiating with Adoula. Peking could clearly see that a compromise might signal the end of the Stanleyville government, and, as it happened, China's worst fears were realized when Gizenga and Adoula stepped off an airplane in Léopoldville together after they had reconciled their differences at the First Conference of Non-Aligned States in Belgrade.[57] The Chinese mission in Stanleyville was closed less than two months after it had opened.[58] A calculated risk had been taken, but it had failed.[59]

International Committee for Aid to Algeria and the Congo

In early 1961 AAPSO created the International Committee for Aid to Algeria and the Congo, to which China named a vice-chairman. The committee met in Cairo. The practical effects of its work were few, but it considered questions which became important three years later when arms and supplies were shipped to Christophe Gbenye's forces around Stanleyville in December 1964. Of the four states — China, the United Arab Republic, Algeria, and the Soviet Union — which reportedly gave

57. [157], 12 September 1961.

58. Ch'en Chia-k'ang maintained contact with the Lumumbist-Gizengist group through its representative in Cairo. Prior to Lumumba's death, East European states had been unwilling to establish missions in Stanleyville unless African governments also agreed to do so. *NYT*, 16 January 1961, reports the remarks of André Mendi, minister of state in the Stanleyville government, who had talked with Ch'en Chia-k'ang and ambassadors of East European states in Cairo. Whether China, too, feared to oppose African states we do not know. In any case, on 19 February China cabled her readiness to establish relations with Stanleyville, and on the next day a joint communiqué announced that an exchange of ambassadors had been agreed upon. Pierre Mulele, a key figure in the Congo revolutions of 1964, then headed the Stanleyville mission in Cairo. *SCMP*, no. 2444, p. 25; *SCMP*, no. 2445, p. 21. A Congolese embassy was set up in Peking on 12 April. *SCMP*, no. 2478, p. 29. China presumably felt free to reciprocate; her delay therefore seems significant. Chang T'ung, a senior colonel who was appointed chargé d'affaires ad interim, arrived in Stanleyville on 31 July 1961. *SCMP*, no. 2554, p. 25. Soviet and United Arab Republic embassies had been established in Stanleyville before his arrival.

59. Chang T'ung left Stanleyville on 16 September 1961. *SCMP*, no. 2590, p. 24. The embassy was withdrawn "in view of the fact that the lawful government of the Republic of the Congo [Stanleyville] has announced its own termination" and because Léopoldville maintained diplomatic relations with Taiwan. *SCMP*, no. 2584, p. 29. This wording suggests that China hoped to maintain her mission in the Congo even after the Gizenga-Adoula reconciliation, but that Adoula would not agree. Chang T'ung was apparently not blamed for this; he has since held more important posts. [133], 1966.

logistic support to Gbenye, all but the Soviet Union were represented on the committee, which met weekly throughout much of 1961. Obstacles to supplying Stanleyville were many, and they were among the topics considered by the committee.[60]

Despite her role in the committee, China gave it no money. Of course, there were already direct ties between China and the GPRA. Moreover, China had reportedly put £1,000,000 at the disposal of Lumumbist Congolese prior to the committee's formation.[61] Perhaps China abstained to save money, but relying on direct grants, without an intermediary, assured Peking independent political leverage on the recipient Congolese and Algerians.[62]

60. El-Sebai termed its creation a "most important consequence" of the extraordinary session of the AAPSO council (21–22 January 1961). [150], vol. 3, no. 3 (supplement), May–June 1961, p. 22. The committee had thirteen members. [150], vol. 4, no. 1 (supplement), January–February 1962, p. 41. Soon after it was set up, the committee sent some members to Dar es Salaam "to participate in the work of the steering committee of the All-African People's Conference." The delegation was to contact African representatives and reach agreements on the best ways to collect aid and to channel it to the Congo. A second group stayed in Cairo to prepare lists of requirements, in cooperation with "the Congo Foreign Minister in Cairo" (representing Stanleyville) and the GPRA. "The Committee then proceeded to hold regular meetings in Cairo, and thanks to the assistance and cooperation of the Permanent Secretariat, the work has been carried out successfully. Regular weekly meetings were held, which studied the difficulties of dispatch of the aid to the Congo, in Stanleyville. Aid to Algeria did not present many difficulties, since that was being already sent via the governments." [150], vol. 4, no. 1 (supplement), January–February 1962, pp. 41 ff.

The original thirteen members were United Arab Republic (chairman), Algeria (vice-chairman), China (vice-chairman), Morocco (secretary), Congo, Ghana, Guinea, India, Indonesia, Japan, Mali, Sudan, and USSR. But, according to a complaint made at the AAPSO executive committee meeting in December 1961, five national committees — those of Ghana, Guinea, Mali, Morocco, and Sudan — did not name representatives. Of the African states named, only the host, the United Arab Republic, and the prospective recipients, Algeria and Congo (Stanleyville), took part. It is not known how actively China participated. One commentator, writing in October 1962, stated that the Chinese AAPSO secretary did not return to Cairo after the meeting of the fourth council in Bandung, April 1961. [25], p. 268. Another claims that in 1961, in a fit of pique, China withdrew her secretary from the permanent secretariat for six months and suspended financial contributions. [63], p. 439–440.

61. A letter of 12 September 1960, purportedly sent by the Chinese ambassador in Cairo, Ch'en Chia-k'ang, to Antoine Gizenga, promised "une premier aide d'un million de livres sterlings qu'il met à la disposition du gouvernement congolais." [53]. It is still not clear how the money was spent.

62. Though Chinese participation was a public demonstration of concern, the committee's activities were quite minor. By December 1961 it had obtained cash only from the United Arab Republic, USSR, and India (Indian Committee for Aid to Algeria), totaling about $20,000. The USSR, East Germany, and Hungary gave drugs, food, and clothing of approximately the same value.

Afro-Asian Solidarity Fund Committee

A second AAPSO group of similar character was the Afro-Asian Solidarity Fund Committee. Joint action to aid liberation movements had been considered for some time.[63] The solidarity movement's Conakry resolution on a second Bandung pointed toward a concerted effort; initial action was taken by AAPSO itself, and the fund first met in Conakry in February 1961.[64]

China was likewise prominent in the fund. The Chinese secretary in Cairo, Chu Tzu-ch'i, was a vice-chairman.[65] China promised materials worth $40,000, scholarships and medical facilities in China, and an unspecified cash contribution to the fund's budget. China apparently defaulted on her promise of cash.[66] Whether this was due to general economic retrenchment, or to disputes with the USSR and the United Arab Republic in AAPSO, we do not know. Internal inconsistencies in the fund's reports cause us to speculate that grants of weapons were made covertly; since three of the groups which received grants from the fund were engaged in armed conflict, it is possible that Chinese materials included weapons.[67]

63. The Pan-African Freedom Movement for East, Central, and Southern Africa (PAFMECSA), known as PAFMECA before embracing the problems of southern Africa as well as those of the eastern and central regions, was founded in September 1958. It effectively yielded to the Liberation Committee of the Organization of African Unity, when that committee was formed in May 1963. [23]. Meeting in Tunis, 26–31 January 1960, the Second All-African People's Conference urged the creation of a group to coordinate support and solidarity for African liberation movements; it also endorsed an Algerian request that African volunteers be recruited to fight in Algeria. International assistance would be sought. See its general resolution in [150], vol. 2, no. 9–10, p. 44. There is no evidence that recruitment actually took place, though the GPRA did threaten to enlist volunteers from time to time. The restriction of volunteers to Africans is significant.

64. At the Second Afro-Asian People's Solidarity Conference, el-Sebai offered a proposal for an Afro-Asian Solidarity Fund. [8], item 13 of the proposed program in the secretary general's report. However, the conference chose to bracket the fund with the proposal for a second Bandung conference. In November 1960 the AAPSO executive committee decided to proceed with the fund, to be sponsored by AAPSO rather than by the proposed second Bandung conference. The fund's creation was formally endorsed by the AAPSO council in April 1961. [150], vol. 3, no. 5–6, May–June 1961.

65. The chairman was Ismail Touré (Guinea), and the second vice-chairman was Mehdi ben Barka (Morocco). An Egyptian, two Indonesians, and the Soviet orientalist, Gafurov, completed the board. The statute specified that in urgent cases the chairman and two vice-chairmen could act to aid movements resisting armed imperialist aggression. [83], p. 177.

66. [150], vol. 3, no. 3 (supplement), May–June 1961; [150], vol. 4, no. 3–4, March–April 1962, pp. 47–48.

67. *Ibid.* The fund estimated its needs at $450,000 but granted a mere $8,500. The list of beneficiaries illustrates the fund's contacts: general secretariat of the All-African

More important is the fact that China probably became apprised of the internal affairs of a number of liberation movements through her role in this fund, since petitioners for assistance were likely to seek the support of Chu Tzu-ch'i, the Chinese vice-chairman. Long after the Liberation Committee of the Organization of African Unity undertook parallel tasks, the fund remained in existence; its Chinese representative was active at least until November 1963, and China made a contribution of £2,000 to the fund in 1964.[68]

Richard Lowenthal believes that Soviet consent to China's prominent place in the fund was secured before the fund's establishment. "This important concession," he suggests, "may have formed a part of the temporary Soviet-Chinese compromise reached in Moscow at the end of 1960."[69] But it is also possible that China bought her way into the fund by promising $40,000 in materials, and that she was able in conjunction with Guinea, whose effort to move the entire AAPSO secretariat to Conakry she had supported without success, to attain her position without Soviet approval.

China's Assessments, 1961–1963

At the start of 1961, commenting on the Casablanca conference of African heads of state, *Jen-min Jih-pao* defined the situation in Africa as one of rising struggle between nationalism and imperialism:

> The basic situation in Africa is: On the one hand, the flames of the national independence movement have spread to all parts of Africa and the scope of the struggle is growing continuously. . . . On the other hand, the imperialist group headed by the United States is still intensifying its brutal suppression of and aggression against the African countries.[70]

China maintained her optimism until Gizenga capitulated in late summer. But the growing success of "imperialism" had to be reckoned with.

People's Conference; MPLA (Angola); PAIGC (Portuguese Guinea); National Union of Ruanda; ANC (South Africa); South Africa United Front; United National Independence Party; UPC (Cameroon); Union of West African Women; and the Sawaba party of Niger. MPLA, PAIGC, and UPC were engaged in armed struggle.

68. Chu Tzu-ch'i attended the fund's fourth meeting in Conakry, November 1963. *SCMP*, no. 3097, p. 27. The Fourth Afro-Asian People's Solidarity Conference urged continuing support for the fund. [10], p. 74; *The Winneba Conference, Ghana, May 1965* (Cairo: Afro-Asian People's Solidarity Organization, n.d.), pp. 127–128.

69. [83], p. 177. He argues that China sought a "special relationship" with Guinea, to Soviet disadvantage, and that presumed Chinese support for electing Ismail Touré chairman of the fund may have been a quid pro quo.

70. *SCMP*, no. 2418, p. 24; NCNA, summary, 11 January 1961.

Five days after Adoula and Gizenga met in Belgrade, Peking commented on the meeting of nonaligned states and challenged, openly and vigorously, the Soviet notion of peaceful coexistence. The commentator stated that China remained faithful to peaceful coexistence nevertheless:

> Peaceful coexistence is [not] possible between the imperialist countries and the countries fighting for and upholding national independence. How can the oppressed co-exist peacefully with the oppressor? . . . How can the colonial peoples live in peace side by side with the colonialists? . . . Peace can only be won by fighting for it, not by begging. . . .
>
> In the last analysis, it is not the imperialist forces of war but the daily more awakened people of the world who decide the destiny of the world. The peoples of Asia, Africa and Latin America will hold still higher the anti-imperialist and anti-colonialist banner and will continue to win great victories in their struggle to win and uphold national independence and defend world peace.[71]

There are two implications. First, since Khrushchev had rendered aid and comfort to the oppressors, Moscow should bear some blame for failures of the national liberation movement. Second, "in the last analysis" that does not change the end result, for the people, becoming more conscious, will force the ultimate outcome. This formula anticipates Lin Piao's September 1965 assertion that the outcome of the world struggle "hinges on the revolutionary struggles of the Asian, African, and Latin American peoples."[72]

China's multiple interests required her to cope with an increasingly diverse assortment of African states. The power and growth of the national liberation movement was demonstrated by many discrete situations. For example, a survey early in 1962[73] professed to find the national liberation movement in some already-independent states (Ghana, Guinea, Mali); in the challenge posed by radical insurgents to some independent states

71. *SCMP*, no. 2578, p. 32 (9 September 1961). China had voiced reservations about peaceful coexistence earlier, but in more gentle terms. An article published soon after the Moscow conference quoted Mao Tse-tung's "On the People's Democratic Dictatorship": "As for the imperialist countries, we should also unite with their peoples and strive to coexist in peace with those countries, do business with them and prevent possible wars, but under no circumstances should we harbor any unrealistic notions about those countries." [228], 20 January 1961, cited in *SCMM*, 251, pp. 1 ff.

72. [216], p. 49.

73. "Hail the Great Victories of the National Liberation Movement," [209], 1 January 1962; widely distributed in *PR*, 5 and 12 January 1962.

(Cameroon); in straightforward anticolonialist guerrilla struggles; in the clash of African nationalism and Afrikaner racism; and even in the efforts of some African states to win independence by British fiat. The omissions are even more significant. The United Arab Republic, Tunisia, Morocco and Sudan pass without mention: an illegal and weak Communist party functioned in each, but there was no effective challenge to the government from any radical quarter. Ethiopia, Somalia, and French Somaliland were ignored, for they did not illustrate Peking's optimistic theses. Similarly, the French succession states of sub-Saharan Africa (except for the "progressive" among the Casablanca states) and former British colonies in the Monrovia group were unmentioned. Ignoring these omissions, the commentator lay stress instead on the Congo (L); he concluded that the United States and the United Nations were hostile to the national liberation movement in Africa.

The Algerian War ended in March 1962. Ch'en I spoke of the "correct use of the two tactics of armed struggle and struggle through negotiation." The revolutionary victories in Algeria and Cuba were two "great events of recent years" that would "exert a far-reaching influence all over the world."[74] Liao Ch'eng-chih said that the victory furnished "another proof that the Algerian people were right when they chose the road of armed struggle seven years ago."[75] And Liu Shao-ch'i affirmed this explicitly in a message to Ben Khedda:

> Algeria's independence . . . shows that the people of Algeria and those of the rest of Africa are invincible and that imperialism and colonialism, old and new, can be defeated. The brilliant example set by the heroic Algerian people is sure to help bring about a further upsurge in the national-independence struggle in Africa.[76]

The path of armed struggle was the correct one; any Soviet vacillation, the comments implied, sprang from an incorrect view of the world. The Central Committee of the CCP noted publicly that Algeria had won independence "through protracted armed struggle."[77]

China's delegation at the third solidarity conference, held in early 1963,[78] confronted the Soviet representatives on a spectrum of organiza-

74. *PR*, 30 March 1962, p. 22.
75. *PR*, 13 July 1962, p. 8.
76. *PR*, 6 July 1962, p. 9.
77. *PR*, 28 September 1962, p. 5.
78. The Third Afro-Asian People's Solidarity Conference was held in Moshi, Tanganyika, 4–11 February 1963. China's delegation, somewhat smaller than earlier ones, was led by Liu Ning-i. Although AAPSO's role was waning, the conference remained

tional and substantive issues, and thereafter her increasingly distinct arguments led to an outright political contest with the Soviet Union.

The Sino-Soviet Conflict

After 1960, both China and the USSR grew more and more quarrelsome. At the Twenty-Second Congress of the CPSU in October 1961, and during the Cuban missile crisis of October 1962, differences deepened rapidly. The Soviet Union had reacted to China's border war with India by taking steps antagonistic to Chinese interests. Thus, it was in keeping with a downward trend in Sino-Soviet relations that China sought to bar "representatives of international democratic organizations and the East European socialist states" from observer status at the third solidarity conference — a move that met with some success.[79] But, on the substantive points at issue at this conference, Chinese amendments to each paragraph of the general declaration were defeated, convincing the partisan and self-congratulating Indian delegation that an end had been reached to "Chinese influence (and even sometimes domination)" in AAPSO.[80]

Until the summer of 1963 China encouraged the view that she hoped to change the Soviet leadership's position by straightforward persuasion.[81] China had endeavored to reason, and the CCP openly undertook to split the parties only after the July 1963 talks with Moscow. However, the bases of a go-it-alone policy went back to 1959. Efforts to create new Afro-Asian groups dated from October 1962, when China and Indonesia began to discuss an Afro-Asian trade union conference independent of Soviet or World Federation of Trade Unions involvement.[82] Nor were all Chinese statements issued before the July 1963 meeting conciliatory; some made the Soviet negotiating position more difficult. Of course, China might have envisaged that the talks could be helpful to her. She would have been pleased to win over the Soviet leadership. By agreeing to talk, she avoided charges that she was provoking a split. By holding out some prospect of concessions, China won time for economic recovery at home

---

a useful meeting ground. African participants included Mario de Andrade (Angola); Oginga Odinga, Tom Mboya, and Joseph Murumbi (Kenya); Tunji Otegbeye (Nigeria); Ndabaningi Sithole (Rhodesia); Oliver Tambo, Robert Resha, Tennyson Makiwane, Duma Nokwe, and Moses Kotane (South Africa); Jariretundu Kozonguizi (South-West Africa); Mongi Kooli (Tunisia); and Abdoulaye Diallo (Guinea) as an observer for the All-African People's Congress. [229].

79. [180], 2 October 1963; [68], p. 10.

80. [68], p. 10. China fared better in May when she excluded the Soviet Union from the Afro-Asian Journalists Association, unrelated to AAPSO. Its formation in May 1963 is best understood as a joint Indonesian-Chinese initiative.

81. [124], p. 2.

82. [43], pp. 204–205.

and political work abroad. But Peking appears to have assumed that the Soviets would not yield and that China would go her own way.

Moscow's decision to join London and Washington in initiating the nuclear test ban treaty was made public on 25 July. China's reaction was prompt: with more hope than foresight, she declared that "manipulation of the destiny of more than one hundred nonnuclear countries by a few nuclear powers will not be tolerated." Her counterproposal, aimed understandably at the destruction of all nuclear weapons, included a call to keep Africa free of nuclear weapons.[83]

Embassies and New China News Agency Offices

Table 1 is a chronological record of the establishment of Chinese embassies in Africa. Only four — those in Cairo, Rabat, Khartoum, and Conakry — had been established by mid-1960. Thereafter the pace quickened.

In July 1960 diplomatic relations were established with Ghana, where the Chinese embassy became an important center under Ambassador Huang Hua. Envoys already in Africa were sent on missions to states with which China sought to establish relations. A week after Mali granted recognition to China, K'o Hua was in Bamako to discuss diplomatic relations; he was successful. Relations with Somalia followed Ch'en Chia-k'ang's delivery of a message from Chou En-lai to the president of her council of ministers, who was visiting Cairo; relations were established in December 1960.[84] Relations were established with Tanganyika late in 1961.[85] Ho Ying, then director of the West Asian and African Affairs Department, was named ambassador in February; he in turn visited Kampala a week after Uganda's independence and successfully established diplomatic ties.[86] On 10 September 1962, a Chinese embassy was opened in Algiers.

The ambassador to Algeria, Tseng T'ao, had been the New China News Agency (NCNA) bureau chief in Havana and later had served as secretary of the Office of Foreign Affairs. In fact, NCNA offices throughout Africa were important adjuncts to diplomatic missions from Peking.

83. "Statement of the Chinese Government Advocating the Complete, Thorough, Total and Resolute Prohibition and Destruction of Nuclear Weapons [and] Proposing a Conference of the Government Heads of All Countries of the World, July 31, 1963," in *PR*, 2 August 1963, pp. 7–8.

84. Peking had had contacts with Somali opposition leaders. Her prompt recognition of Somalia was not reciprocated. *SCMP*, no. 2288, p. 50 (25 June 1960). The Cairo message was more politic. Still, some weeks passed before relations were established. *SCMP*, no. 2403, p. 35.

85. *SCMP*, no. 2641, p. 36 (9 December 1961).

86. *SCMP*, no. 2845, p. 32 (18 October 1962).

Kao Liang, senior correspondent in Dar es Salaam, was regarded by Colin Legum as the key figure among Chinese in that city.[87] The NCNA has figured in other ways in the history of Chinese-African relations, even as employer of the man who later became foreign minister of the revolutionary Zanzibar government, Abdul Rahman Mohammed Babu.[88] Judging by their reports, NCNA correspondents in the key centers systematically canvass exile liberation movement representatives residing there and elicit their views on issues of current importance.

No additional Chinese embassies in Africa were opened between October 1962 and December 1963.

Chou En-lai Tours Africa

The decision to encourage radical dissidents to split from Communist parties and groups deferential to Moscow, which the CCP had made by October 1963,[89] was China's most open challenge of Soviet hegemony. In regions where parties were well developed, this decision had more important implications than it did in Africa. But, as we can see by Chou En-lai's

87. [183], 27 September 1964. Kao Liang is described by Legum as "the tough, ubiquitous correspondent of the NCNA, who carries out the exploratory probes for Ho Ying and who acts as a go-between for the diplomats and their African contacts." Like ambassadors, NCNA correspondents sometimes visited countries with which China had not established relations. See NCNA, 13 July 1962, a dispatch by Kao Liang entitled "Visit to Kingdom of Burundi."

The first African NCNA office was opened in Cairo, but not until 1958. In the summer of 1960 offices were opened in Conakry, Rabat, and Accra. [156], no. 4, p. 129. Richard Lowenthal says these branches opened "as soon as Chinese diplomats were accredited there." [83], p. 158. That seems to be overstating the case. But by the mid-1960s there were NCNA offices in almost all, if not all, African capitals where China maintained embassies. A further glimpse of NCNA's method of work is given in *PR*, 22 June 1962, p. 9. Working from Rabat, two correspondents, Wang Wei and Lu Ming-chu, had by mid-1962 spent more than two years in North Africa, among Algerians and Tunisians as well as Moroccans. Their assignment was thus comparable with that of the ambassador in Rabat, who was also in contact with Algerian and Tunisian officials.

88. [114].

89. Chou Yang, "The Fighting Task Confronting Workers in Philosophy and Social Sciences," speech of 26 October 1963, made public 26 December 1963. *PR*, 3 January 1964, pp. 10–27. Its publication in *PR* in this length was an index of China's wish that non-Chinese readers would find it relevant to their own concerns. Chou Yang's key remark on party legitimacy was: "If . . . a proletarian party fails to stand in the forefront of the people's revolutionary struggle, discards the banner of revolution, renounces the revolutionary tradition of its own country and adopts a passive or even negative attitude towards the cause of the proletarian revolution, then it is bound to become an opportunist, revisionist party and forfeit its place in the ranks of the vanguards of the international proletariat." *Ibid.*, p. 15.

Table 1

CHINESE DIPLOMATIC RELATIONS WITH AFRICA, 1956–1970

	State	Date of Independence	Diplomatic Relations Established	Date Embassy Opened	Ambassadors and Selected Chargés*	Date of Appointment	Date of Arrival	Chargé Noted in Press
(1)	United Arab Republic	1922	30 MAY 56	14 JUN 56	Ch'en Chia-k'ang	29 JUN 56	19 JUL 56	
					Huang Hua	JAN 66		
					*Yin Te-hsing			OCT 69
					Ch'ai Tse-min	JUN 70		
(2)	Morocco	2 MAR 56	1 NOV 58		Pai Jen	19 FEB 59		
					Yang Ch'i-liang	6 JUN 61	11 AUG 61	
					*Hsü Fan-yü			OCT 69
(3)	Algeria	21 SEP 58[a]	20 DEC 58	10 SEP 62	Tseng T'ao	13 NOV 62	28 NOV 62	
					Yang Ch'i-liang	1969	1969	
(4)	Sudan	1 JAN 56	4 FEB 59		Wang Yü-t'ien	7 JUN 59	15 JUL 59	
					Ku Hsiao-po	9 APR 59	2 JUL 62	
					Yü P'ei-wen	JAN 66		
					*Hsüeh Na			OCT 69
(5)	Guinea	2 OCT 58	4 OCT 59	23 DEC 59	K'o Hua	4 MAR 60	31 MAR 60	
					Ch'ai Tse-min		1964	
					Han K'e-hua	1969	1969	
(6)	Ghana[b]	6 MAR 57	5 JUL 60		Huang Hua		25 AUG 60	
					Ch'en Ch'u	JAN 66		
(7)	Mali	22 SEP 60	27 OCT 60	7 JAN 61	Lai Ya-li	3 JAN 61	8 MAR 61	
					*Feng Yüeh			OCT 69
(8)	Somalia	1 JUL 60	14 DEC 60		Chang Yüeh	17 MAR 61	14 MAR 61	
					Yang Shou-cheng		1964	
					*Chang Ching-fang			OCT 69
					Fan Tso-k'ai	20 SEP 70		
(9)	Congo (L)[c]	30 JUN 60	20 FEB 61	31 JUL 61	*Chang T'ung[d]		31 JUL 61	
(10)	Tanganyika	9 DEC 61	DEC 61		Ho Ying	27 FEB 62	31 MAR 62	
					Chung Hsi-tung	1969	1969	

(11)	Uganda	9 OCT 62	18 OCT 62	17 DEC 62	Ho Ying Ch'en Chih-fang *Mou P'ing	16 APR 63	. . .[e]	 OCT 69
(12)	Zanzibar[f]	10 DEC 63	11 DEC 63		Meng Ying[f]	25 MAR 64	4 APR 64	
(13)	Kenya	12 DEC 63	14 DEC 63		Wang Yü-t'ien *Kuo Chih-chiang	4 FEB 64	18 APR 64	 OCT 69
(14)	Burundi[g]	1 JUL 62	23 DEC 63	13 JAN 64	Liu Yü-feng	3 APR 64	1 JUN 64	
(15)	Tunisia[h]	20 MAR 56	10 JAN 64	20 APR 64	Yao Nien	3 MAY 64	22 MAY 64	
(16)	Congo (B)	15 AUG 60	22 FEB 64		Chou Ch'iu-yeh Wang Yü-t'ien	16 MAY 64 1969	8 JUN 64 1969	
(17)	Central African Republic[b]	13 AUG 60	29 SEP 64		Meng Ying			
(18)	Zambia	24 OCT 64	31 OCT 64	28 NOV 64	Ch'in Li-chen	12 FEB 65	14 MAR 65	
(19)	Dahomey[b]	1 AUG 60	12 NOV 64	19 DEC 64	Li Yün-ch'uan			
(20)	Mauritania	28 NOV 60	19 JUL 65	3 SEP 65	Lü Chih-hsien Feng Yü-chiu	SEP 65 1969	 1969	
(21)	Equatorial Guinea	12 OCT 68	15 OCT 70		. . .[i]			
(22)	Ethiopia		24 NOV 70		. . .[i]			

* From 1967 until 1969, and in many cases thereafter, embassies were headed by a chargé d'affaires. In some cases successive chargés were identified in October 1967, 1968, and 1969. This table cites all ambassadors, a chargé where no ambassador was named, and chargés identified in October 1969 if no new ambassador had been appointed to replace one recalled during the Great Proletarian Cultural Revolution. Each chargé is identified by an asterisk before his name.

a. Date of formation of the GPRA. China recognized the new Algerian Republic on 3 July 1962.
b. Diplomatic relations were suspended in 1966.
c. The Gizenga government in Stanleyville.
d. Withdrawn 16 September 1961.
e. Concurrently ambassador in Dar es Salaam.
f. Meng Ying withdrawn 11 July 1964. Embassy downgraded to consulate after Tanganyika-Zanzibar union.
g. Diplomatic relations suspended in early 1965.
h. Diplomatic relations suspended in 1967.
i. Embassy not yet opened.

speech to FLN cadres in Algeria in December, it was not without significance for Africa, too:

> The truths of revolution cannot be monopolized. The revolutionaries of all countries will find the way for revolution suitable to the realities of their own country, and earn the support and respect of the popular masses so long as they rely on the masses and persevere in revolution. Otherwise, they will be renounced, sooner or later, by the masses of the people.[90]

In other words, the FLN could "find the way." The Algerian Communist party, which had adhered to Moscow in the Sino-Soviet dispute, had no monopoly on the truths of revolution. Certainly, if the FLN did not "earn the support and respect of the popular masses," it would be outrun by some other organization yet unformed. Chou apparently believed the FLN could be persuaded to take up the mantle of a true Marxist-Leninist party, a party adhering generally to the Chinese rather than the Soviet world view. In turn, he may have imagined that a revolutionary tide would flow outward from Algeria, endowing African radicals with Algerian prestige in order to transform the character of struggle. On the other hand, his remarks implied a threat: if the FLN proved inadequate to the task — and at this juncture Ben Bella was treading a careful path between Moscow and Peking — China would lend her support to true revolutionaries.

The decision to dispatch Chou En-lai to Africa was probably made some months before his departure, perhaps in August or September. He had several objectives. He sought support for the projected second Bandung conference, and he probably also wished to discourage participation in the Second Conference of Non-Aligned States.[91] He explained China's stand on the test ban treaty. Because many African states planned to sign the treaty, China concluded that direct talks were needed to persuade

90. *PR*, 3 January 1964, p. 35.

91. His public position, however, was precisely that taken at the time of the First Conference of Non-Aligned States (Belgrade, 1–6 September 1961): that the two forums were compatible. But he must have been mindful of the consequences of the Belgrade meeting, which strengthened the "third force" notion at some cost to dichotomous world views. "Being a committed country," he told a press conference in Algiers, "China obviously will not participate in a conference of non-aligned countries. We support the result of the first conference of non-aligned countries in opposing imperialism, defending world peace, combating colonialism and supporting the national independence movement. I believe that the second conference of non-aligned countries, should it take place, would follow the policy of the previous conference; otherwise it would fail to play the progressive role of arousing the people of the world to struggle." [198], pp. 78–79.

African government leaders that China's intentions, even her intention of testing nuclear weapons, were peaceful. Chou also claimed that one object of his visit was to learn. Finally, he spoke of China's African interest in ways that placed the Soviet Union in a bad light. He urged "self-reliance" in discussing aid, implicitly recalling China's own failure to create a dependable aid relationship with the Soviet Union (although use of the term "self-reliance" also served to parry any expectations that China might subsidize African states as Moscow had subsidized Havana). China's terms, he stressed, fully respected the sensitivities of recipient countries.

The size and scope of Chou's mission was indicative of its importance. Chou was accompanied by foreign minister Ch'en I, ten important officials, and some forty others. The group visited the United Arab Republic, Algeria, Morocco, Tunisia, Ghana, Mali, Guinea, Sudan, Ethiopia, and Somalia.[92] Much of its itinerary was improvised.[93] Perhaps because of Chou's proximity, Tunisia received him and agreed to establish long-postponed diplomatic relations.[94] Despite its grand scale, the tour was a

92. As follows: United Arab Republic, 14–21 December 1963; Algeria, 21–27 December; Morocco, 27–30 December; Tunisia, 9–10 January 1964 (after a side trip to Albania); Ghana, 11–16 January; Mali, 16–21 January; Guinea, 21–26 January; Sudan, 27–30 January; Ethiopia, 30 January to 1 February; and Somalia, 1–4 February.

93. On 7 December 1963 China made the first announcement that Chou would visit the United Arab Republic, Algeria, and Morocco. *SCMP*, no. 3117, pp. 25, 33, and 35. Soon thereafter *JMJP* reported that the tour came at the invitation of the three African states and the West African countries which had diplomatic relations with China. [198], p. 423. While Chou was in Morocco, Tunisia was added to the itinerary. On 4 January 1964, the addition of Tanganyika was announced. Ho Ying went to Uganda and Kenya on 8 and 10 January; it was promptly announced that both were added to the itinerary. *SCMP*, no. 3141, p. 31; *SCMP*, no. 3138, pp. 43–44; *SCMP*, no. 3139, pp. 33–35. But Tanganyika, Uganda, and Kenya were struck from the list before Chou arrived. On 12 January a revolution took place on Zanzibar; then, in a move unrelated to the Zanzibar coup, on 20 January the Tanganyikan army mutinied. The Kenyan and Ugandan armies mutinied too. On 4 February, Chou's last day in Africa, "postponement" of the three East African visits was announced. *SCMP*, no. 3156, p. 17. No reason was given. Presumably China had tried to hold the itinerary together while the East African states considered whether the visit would be wise. In the meantime, China sought other invitations. It was announced only on 27 January, after Ch'en Chia-k'ang visited Addis Ababa and talked with Haile Selassie, that Chou would visit Ethiopia. *SCMP*, no. 3150, p. 15. Announcements that Chou was to visit Zanzibar and Burundi were made, respectively, on 4 and 6 February, though no dates were suggested. *SCMP*, no. 3156, p. 17; *SCMP*, no. 3158, p. 31. This was almost surely the result of Chinese diplomatic activity intended further to extend Chou's trip. In one view, the itinerary was hurriedly improvised; in another, Chou seized opportunities to visit additional states and created new opportunities in a flexible manner rare in formal diplomacy.

94. *SCMP*, no. 3130, p. 41 (27 December 1963).

mixed success. Several states did commit themselves to the second Bandung conference, but China's position on the test ban treaty received scant acknowledgment. Haile Selassie, critical of China's test ban refusal and her continued revolutionary clamor, lectured Chou publicly. There was widespread African interest in the tour, but journalistic assessments at the time suggested that public reaction was lukewarm.

Chou sought to advance both pragmatic and revolutionary goals. His speeches were highly rhetorical, yet he did not make any gratuitous public remark which would cast a shadow over practical cooperation. His much quoted statement, made in Somalia, that "an excellent revolutionary situation exists in Africa" was in keeping with earlier Chinese comment. Though Chou spoke of African peoples who had already won independence by "pushing the revolution forward" and he doubtless envisioned eventual transformation of Africa's nationalist governments, there was nothing in his remarks at Mogadishu to justify the interpretation that they were an assault on men presently in power.[95]

Chou's visit did impress on Africa — and on the West — that China now had a special interest in Africa. He was the most important statesman to have visited some capitals. We have seen that China's interest in Africa had been mounting for a decade, but to some casual observers China's concern seemed sudden, and therefore more attractive or anxiety-producing — as the case might be. Perhaps China erred in seeking sudden and conspicuous visibility. Popular diplomacy, of course, is practiced by all major states; they commonly circumvent a foreign government and appeal directly to its citizens. But the greater a foreign state's visibility within Africa, the more pressures there may be to limit its influence. This is not an iron law: visibility is necessary to some forms of influence, but visibility has costs, too.

Further Diplomatic Relations

Between December 1963 and February 1964, as shown in Table 1, Zanzibar, Kenya, Burundi, Tunisia, and Congo (Brazzaville) established diplomatic relations with China. Ho Ying, China's ambassador in Dar es Salaam, negotiated the agreement with Zanzibar's prime minister and sultan on 17 December 1963, a month before they were overthrown in a coup.[96] The new revolutionary government maintained relations, however. Ch'en I attended Kenya's independence celebrations, and diplomatic relations were announced on 14 December.[97] A few days later a "friend-

95. [198], pp. 284–285.
96. NCNA, 17 December 1963.
97. *JMJP*, 22 November 1964, p. 4.

ship visit" by Ho Ying to Burundi led to a similar announcement.[98] As for Tunisia, relations were established shortly before Chou's visit. In the case of the Congo (Brazzaville), Huang Hua traveled from Accra to secure diplomatic relations, which were formally instituted on 22 February 1964.[99]

Congo (Léopoldville), 1964

Much African comment about China during 1964 focused on the question of the Congo (L), where a set of semi-independent guerrilla movements seemed for a time to threaten the central government. China's views of the Congo and her actual role there are the keys to any account of the events of 1964; these, in turn, set the context for her subsequent relations with governing nationalists and hopeful revolutionaries.

China could take a major role in Congolese affairs only because three chains of events developed independently in 1964.

First, internal Congolese politics, which had been subject to sudden changes ever since independence, experienced another major shift at the end of June when the final contingent of United Nations troops left the Congo and Adoula's government resigned.[100]

Second, revolutionary bands—those led by the late Pierre Mulele were the most prominent at the beginning of 1964—posed an increasing threat to the Léopoldville government. From January, when Mulele's group undertook its first operations on a large scale, anti-Léopoldville forces gained momentum until, at year's end, the resistance was broken and the guerrilla bands were scattered or controlled. China watched this sequence of events very closely. On 2 May 1964, for example, a pitched battle between revolutionaries and Congolese troops prompted *Jen-min Jih-pao* to proclaim a "new upsurge in the Congolese national liberation movement." The commentator went on to insist—the consequence not only of an unquestioned assumption but of Gizenga's experience as well—that "it is impossible for the Congo to achieve national liberation through so-called parliamentary struggle, but only through armed struggle."[101] Two days before the exiled Moise Tshombe returned to the Congo, *Jen-min Jih-pao* commented again, saying that "an excellent revolutionary situation is emerging on the vast expanse of the Congo."[102]

Third, China was acquiring avenues through which to reach Congo-

98. NCNA, 23 December 1963.
99. NCNA, 18 February 1964; *JMJP*, 22 November 1964, p. 4.
100. See [147], August 1964, p. 16.
101. [147], June 1964, p. 14, citing *JMJP*, 6 May 1964.
102. [147], August 1964, p. 16, citing *JMJP*, 24 June 1964.

lese insurgents and to provide them with matériel. It has been widely reported that Mulele visited China, although Fox et al. believe his stay did not exceed two months.[103] There appears to be no evidence that Mulele maintained contact with China after his return to the Congo in the summer of 1963; neither is the body of doctrine he espoused distinctively Chinese in character, despite its emphasis on "struggle" and some vague and infrequent allusions to China herself.[104] China's diplomatic establishments in countries neighboring the Congo were very important. The missions with most bearing on the Congo were those opened in Usumbura in January 1964 (by chargé d'affaires Chiang Yen) and in Brazzaville in April 1964 (by chargé Kan Mai).[105] Tung Chi-p'ing, an assistant cultural attaché in Usumbura who defected almost immediately after arriving there, tells of attending a briefing session for Liu Yü-feng, the ambassador-designate, on 8 April 1964; Liu was told that most of the mission's attention should be given to the Congo, where "the revolutionary situation is very good for us." The official conducting the briefing quoted Mao Tse-tung as having said, "If we can take the Congo, we can have all of Africa."[106] But there is no independent verification of this.

Although China made strident statements about the guerrilla actions, persistently encouraged armed struggle, and devoted considerable emphasis to the part being taken by white mercenaries in suppressing the

103. [35], p. 89.

104. Time of return in *NYT*, 12 May 1964. Fox et al. put Mulele in Kikwit in July 1963, "about to begin his officially agreed upon service in the provincial government." [35], p. 94.

105. One careful journalist, Gavin Young, visited Brazzaville in mid-1964 and reported that he had found Western diplomats "doubtful that the Chinese were physically involved in training rebels." He quoted Bochley Davidson, spokesman of the principal Congolese exile group, as saying that "we do not need foreigners to teach us guerrilla warfare." [183], 2 August 1964. The staff of the Chinese embassy in Brazzaville numbered about twenty in August. Young quotes Congo (B) President Massamba-Debat as telling him: "Now that we have a Chinese embassy here, the Americans can't sleep. But that's ridiculous, absolutely idiotic. We are non-aligned." Young concludes: "It is at least clear that two tiny countries, Burundi in the east and Congo Brazzaville in the north, are providing shelter and a free hand to the rebel elements trying to seize power by violence in Léopoldville. In Burundi there is active Chinese support for the Congolese rebels in the interior." [183], 23 August 1964. Gaston Soumialot, a Congolese revolutionary leader, occupied a room in the Paguidas Hotel in Usumbura, where the Chinese diplomats were also installed; one journalist claims that he saw a Soumialot lieutenant, Laurent Kabila, with the Chinese staff. Ian Colvin, *Daily Telegraph* (London) correspondent, [178], 16 August 1964, p. 4. Another report tells of guerrilla training films being shown in the hotel, allegedly for visiting Congolese; *NYT*, 26 March 1965.

106. The briefing was given by Chou Erh-fu, secretary general of the Commission on Cultural Relations with Foreign Countries. [127], p. 223.

guerrillas, she gave every sign that she wished the extent of her actual assistance to remain secret. She stressed that "revolution cannot be exported."[107] "We never conceal our position and we regard it as our unshirkable and honorable internationalist duty to support the revolutionary struggle of all oppressed nations and peoples" said a formal Chinese statement of 1 September; this was joined to an angry denial that China was fomenting or intervening in the Congolese warfare.[108] Gaston Soumialot, reacting to similar charges, said China had not financed his movement.[109] Liu Shao-ch'i denounced charges of Chinese intervention as "slanderous."[110] Assuming that some aid was being given to Congolese at this time, China's posture served a twofold purpose: it spared her hosts in Usumbura and Brazzaville embarrassment, and it gave credence to the view that the revolution was dependent on internal sources rather than on foreign provocateurs.

Throughout the remainder of 1964 revolutionaries parried mercenaries. The Belgian-American airdrop on Stanleyville, timed to coincide with a mercenary-led drive to capture that city, elicited extravagant Chinese statements. The themes were familiar: the "consciousness of the Congolese people" was higher than ever; they had identified their enemy; if they would "close their ranks and persist in the struggle," they would drive imperialism from the Congo.[111] But even the movement of Algerian and Egyptian arms into the Congo through Sudan, and Chinese arms through Tanganyika, could not halt the disintegration of Gbenye's forces. Although anti-Léopoldville forces were not wholly destroyed, many key figures — including Gbenye and Soumialot — went into exile, and the Mulelist elements were contained within an ethnic region.

At their peak the revolutionary forces had effective freedom of movement in approximately half of Congolese territory. China might have made a still stronger commitment, recognizing Gbenye's government as she had Gizenga's, but she did not. The experience with Gizenga caused China's hesitation; Gbenye had been the go-between who twice in 1961 undertook to persuade Gizenga that he should join the Adoula government. The ideological naiveté of the Congolese insurgents — which the Chinese might dub a "low level of political education" — also cautioned

107. For example, "People of the Congo (L), Fight On!" *JMJP* editorial of 6 May 1964, in *PR*, 15 May 1964, pp. 13 ff, and "Hail the Triumphant Revolutionary Developments in the Congo (L)," *PR*, 3 July 1964, pp. 15–16, from *JMJP*, 24 June 1964.

108. *PR*, 4 September 1964, p. 10.

109. *NYT*, 14 August 1964.

110. *NYT*, 29 September 1964.

111. *PR*, 4 December 1964, pp. 8–9.

China. Recognition might have implied material commitments exceeding those China was willing to make, and, as pointed out in reviewing China's denial of intervention, China did not wish to appear unnecessarily threatening to African states. Harboring these doubts and weighing the risks of premature action, she waited to see if a guerrilla movement could successfully withstand attempts to suppress it. Two reports in July 1964 stated that China insisted the guerrillas win at least one province as a condition for additional Chinese aid.[112] It was the quality of guerrilla conduct that interested Peking. If these reports are accurate, they indicate that China wanted evidence that the guerrillas could accomplish a complex military and administrative task and not merely occupy territory for a time. China did not choose to link her prestige again to an ephemeral regime.

Additional Chinese Comment in 1964

With the virtual end of the Congo insurgency, the one episode so volatile and widespread that it seemed it might conform to China's hope for "armed struggle against imperialism" drew to a close. In Portuguese Guinea, Angola, and Mozambique armed struggle was also under way, but it was not as extensive or dramatic as the war in the Congo.

China also sought influence in less spectacular ways. In Zanzibar and in the Congo (Brazzaville) she attained some leverage, but her efforts were cramped and subject to counteraction, and she never actually acquired decisive influence. Immediately after the January 1964 coup in Zanzibar, it was fashionable for Western correspondents to say that China, though discreetly out of sight, exercised authority and great influence through Abdul Rahman Mohammed Babu. But with the federation of Zanzibar and Tanganyika, Babu moved to the mainland as a Tanzanian cabinet minister; Karume consolidated his leadership of Zanzibar, and Chinese influence was subsequently judged to be less than that of the Soviet Union or East Germany. Despite a report that Kan Mai attended "all of the Politburo's closed door deliberations" in the Congo (B), the representatives of other states carried more weight.[113] Because France un-

112. [182], 6 July 1964, p. 30: "Recently, government forces captured from a [CNL] courier near Coquilhatville a sheaf of Chinese guerrilla training documents translated into French. . . . Printed in capital letters was a warning that foreign military aid would not be forthcoming until the Congolese guerrillas had on their own captured at least one whole province." Gavin Young wrote that, "according to an apparently reliable report, China has indicated to Mr. Soumialot that recognition will be extended when his supporters succeed in controlling a considerable area of the country." It is possible that these were independent incidents, since Coquilhatville is far removed from the area in which Soumialot was operating. [183], 12 July 1964.

113. By 1970, however, China had again won a prominent place in Zanzibar. Chinese there were estimated to be 400 to 500. East Germans, once as numerous as

derwrote much of Brazzaville's budget, she retained a large part of her prior influence, and it was Cuban guards who successfully defended threatened government officials in Brazzaville during an attempted coup in June 1966.

Elsewhere China encouraged specific steps which were consistent with the emerging Chinese style in political life. Ben Bella's adherence to a middle way between China and the Soviet Union did not deter China from proclaiming Algeria as a good example, particularly when it appeared to follow a Chinese pattern. Commentary from Peking pointed to Algeria's decision to create militia units, and China signed an agreement to supply the militia with arms.[114] A succession of transactions concerned with technical cooperation between China and the United Arab Republic prompted observers to speculate that China would speed Egypt toward nuclear capability. This was an alarmist and exaggerated deduction, but it is probably warranted to conclude that China sought to trade technical cooperation for political support, with an eye to the planned Asian-African conference inter alia.[115]

The tone of Chinese policy statements on Africa in 1964 was optimistic. On Africa Freedom Day, 15 April 1964, a Chinese commentator assigned Africa a role which was clearly derived from Lenin's *Imperialism*:

> The progress and victory of the African national-democratic revolution is of major importance to the development of the world national-liberation movement. Africa has always been directly under the con-

---

the Chinese, were departing; most were expected to leave during September 1970. *NYT*, 23 September 1970. On Kan Mai, see *NYT*, 9 March 1965.

114. *PR*, 6 November 1964, p. 10; *NYT*, 12 February 1965. Houari Boumédienne, Ben Bella's successor, disbanded the militia.

115. China sought to import, as well as to export, scientific and technological information. In August 1964 China and the United Arab Republic agreed to promote mutual scientific and technical cooperation. *NYT*, 25 August 1964. One agreement was signed in late December. *PR*, 25 December 1964, p. 4. On 13 January 1965, Wu Heng, vice-chairman of the Scientific and Technological Commission, signed an agreement in Cairo calling for the exchange of scientists and students and the formation of a joint scientific board that would meet annually to coordinate the exchange of research between the two countries. *JMJP*, 15 January 1965, p. 4; *NYT*, 14 January 1965. Chou En-lai paid a visit to Cairo on 1–2 April 1965, probably to discuss the Asian-African conference. On 6 April a foreign affairs adviser to Nasser, Hussein Zulfacar Sabry, arrived in Peking. *JMJP*, 8 April 1965, p. 1. Among those present at a gathering for Sabry was Hsiao Hsiang-jung, director of the general office of the Ministry of National Defense. A few days later the Cairo newspaper *Al Ahram* reported that a group of Egyptian atomic scientists would fly to Peking soon to "acquaint themselves with various aspects of progress in the field of atomic researches achieved by Chinese scientists." The visit had been discussed by Chou and Nasser when they met in Cairo the previous week. *NYT*, 10 April 1965.

> trol of the imperialists and colonialists. It is here that they maintain the last bastions of the colonialist system. Africa is an important economic base for the very existence of West European and North American imperialist and colonialist countries, which rob the continent of its rich natural resources and exploit its vast manpower. Because of its geographical position and its many strategic minerals and raw materials, Africa holds a vital place in the war and aggression plans of the imperialist camp, headed by the United States. The African national-liberation movement's victories have dealt a heavy blow to the imperialists and colonialists; they constitute a powerful support for similar movements in Asia and Latin America and are a great contribution to the defence of world peace. No wonder the US imperialists are saying: "The future of Africa will seriously affect, for better or worse, the future of the United States."[116]

What was China's relationship to this contest to be? In December 1964 Chou En-lai spoke to the National People's Congress, giving a sweeping review of government work. He paid special attention to African cases in which armed struggle had played an important part, and he examined the lessons of Algeria and the Congo (L) in particular. Despite the blow recently suffered by Congolese antigovernment forces, of which Chou was keenly aware, he interpreted the African scene in a now-familiar language of exhortative optimism.[117] Chou was most revealing when he turned to the subject of Chinese aid. "With the development of its socialist construction," China had given increasing aid to other countries. Not only were "fraternal socialist countries" and newly independent countries to be supported, but China would support "countries which are not yet independent in winning their independence." Saying that Chinese assistance was given gratis or in the form of low-interest or interest-free loans, Chou insisted that China had "always done everything possible to help others."[118]

The implication was clear. As China's economic situation improved, she could afford to commit greater resources to the national liberation

116. *JMJP* editorial, 15 April 1964, from slightly abridged translation in *PR*, 17 April 1964, p. 9.

117. "The victory of the Algerian people in their national-liberation war has set a brilliant example for the national-liberation movement in Africa." The Portuguese colonies and Southern African territories were areas in which "the people [would] unquestionably win final victory in their fight for independence and freedom." And the people of the Congo would certainly defeat the United States "by strengthening their national unity and persisting in their long struggle." *PR*, 1 January 1965, pp. 6–20.

118. *Ibid.*, p. 19.

movement and to states seeking to "consolidate their independence." Listeners at home were alerted that larger foreign policy entries would have to be accommodated in future budgets. Chou may have had Vietnam in mind, although U.S. troops in South Vietnam then numbered only 25,000; probably he did not foresee that Vietnam would come to have an even more insistent claim on Chinese aid.

Within two months the situation in Vietnam changed dramatically. On 7 February 1965 the United States commenced systematic bombing raids on North Vietnam. United States forces in South Vietnam reached 265,000 by July 1966. Chinese policy makers were forced to consider two new demands: What support would North Vietnam seek in order to withstand the aerial assault? What resources would have to be readied for the contingency that Chinese troops might be drawn actively into the Vietnam War or that China herself might be attacked?

China undertook no abrupt changes in Africa. Instead she continued to prepare for the Asian-African Conference, at which the Vietnam War would doubtless be a topic—if China had her way, the chief topic. On the other hand, the momentum of Chinese activities declined. An observer could see that China's diplomatic network in Africa had ceased to grow, that few new economic ties were being agreed upon, and that guerrilla movements which China might support were not making headway. African leaders, especially those most unwilling to cooperate with China, were increasingly vociferous about Peking's interference. By early 1965 the context in which China sought to work was very different from that which favored her at the close of 1963.

China's glamor, the attraction of the novel and forbidden, had dimmed. Nor had every contact with China enhanced Peking's standing among African leaders. During the Congolese warfare of 1964, Peking showed that she could provide arms and training to revolutionaries in sub-Saharan Africa, a showing which cut both ways. She could perform a complex political and logistic task—but it could be directed against an existing government. China's nuclear program also altered her standing during this period. Some Africans approved, but most did not.

Impact of China's Nuclear Program

China exploded her first nuclear device on 16 October 1964. She declared that her aim in doing so was "to break the nuclear monopoly of the nuclear powers and eliminate weapons." She vowed never to be the first to use nuclear weapons, and she formally proposed a summit conference of all countries of the world to discuss "the complete prohibition and thorough destruction of nuclear weapons."[119] Responses from Africa fell into four categories. Some agreed that nuclear weapons in Chinese hands were good for both China and Africa and concurred with China's call for talks about the prohibition and destruction of nuclear arms. Others noted the technical accomplishment implied by the test but carefully held back approval of the test itself and agreed that a conference to discuss abolition of atomic weapons should be called. A third group was silent on the Chinese proposal, but politely acknowledged the accomplishment of the test. Others were silent or voiced disapproval.

The most outspoken support by an African government was given by Mali. In Hanoi, Modibo Keita signed a communiqué which was consistent with Mali's earlier refusal to sign the test ban treaty.

> In face of the stubborn refusal of imperialism to disarm and its determination, in defiance of the unanimous opinion of the peoples, to pursue the foolish policy of all-out armament, the strengthening of the self-defence capability of the Asian, African and Latin American countries becomes an urgent necessity.[120]

Moreover, the test was "a great encouragement to the Asian, African, and Latin American peoples who are struggling for national liberation and the consolidation of their independence." Keita voiced "vigorous support" for the call to a summit conference.

African national liberation movements, which could not sign the test ban treaty, were not under the pressures felt by governments to support the treaty. They were freer to accept the Chinese analysis and many did. According to a spokesman of the Zimbabwe African People's Union:

> It is a matter of necessity that People's China should have all means of self-defence to protect her integrity. Our brother, the People's Republic of China, is threatened by war bases around it, and nuclear weapons pointing at its heart. China is improving her defence capabilities, not to attack anybody but to ward off imperialist intrusion.[121]

The president of the Swaziland Progressive party, O. M. Mabuza, welcomed the proposal for a summit conference and said he regarded China's success "as an encouragement to the people fighting for national inde-

119. *PR*, 16 October 1964, pp. ii–iv.
120. *PR*, 30 October 1964, p. 8.
121. George Silundika, publicity and information secretary of the Zimbabwe African People's Union. *Ibid.*, p. 11.

pendence."[122] A representative of the Basutoland Congress party stated the test was a fitting victory for China and for revolutionary peoples throughout the world; it would strengthen the liberation movements in Asia and Africa and contribute to world peace.[123]

The majority of African comment was less enthusiastic. The Kenyan ambassador to China simply acknowledged a "great achievement in the field of atomic physics." Ketema Yifru, the acting foreign minister of Ethiopia, said only that "every country has the right to defend itself, and China is no exception."[124] Other African countries, agreeing that talks and disarmament were better than a perilous armed truce, cautiously approved the plan for a summit conference.[125] A similar range of comments was exhibited after later Chinese tests.[126]

Proliferation of atomic weapons is an unpopular policy. On the whole, African governments preferred a stalemate to a world of more nuclear powers. China's nuclear program likened her to the other nuclear states. She was sensitive to this vulnerability, and she has sought to negate criticism since the time of the test ban treaty, but with only limited success.

The idea that Chinese nuclear power somehow is at the service of the Afro-Asian people assumes agreement on a number of specifics: Who is the enemy? When and how should nuclear weapons be readied? And for defensive or offensive purposes? Who should decide what threats to make and whether nuclear arms are actually to be used? There were no such questions in 1955, and the Bandung conference avoided central disagreements. In retrospect, it appears that the second Bandung conference failed to materialize because the participants believed that their differences — particularly on Vietnam, the Soviet Union, and nuclear proliferation — were too deep to be avoided. Although Ho Chi Minh's effort to unify Vietnam under Communist leadership had an appealing anticolonial tone, China's criticism of the Soviet Union and her claim to need nuclear weapons were distasteful positions for most Africans.

122. *Ibid.*

123. *PR*, 23 October 1964, p. 12, quoting the Basutoland Congress party representative in Cairo, Ramaqele Tsinyane.

124. *Ibid.*

125. For example, Morocco expressed support for all proposals which aimed to secure peace and promote understanding among nations. The Moroccan statement, dated 21 January 1965, was not published until three months later; this delay suggests no special enthusiasm on China's part. *JMJP*, 13 April 1965, p. 5.

126. Second test, 14 May 1965: *PR*, 21 May 1965, pp. 6–8; *PR*, 28 May 1965, pp. 11–12. Third test, 9 May 1966: *PR*, 20 May 1966, pp. 30–33; *PR*, 27 May 1966, p. 38.

Second Asian-African Conference

A preparatory meeting for the Second Asian-African Conference was held in Djakarta from 10–15 April 1964. Chou En-lai had extracted a number of commitments to support the conference during his tour of ten African countries, and, in part as a result, the preparatory committee was broadly based. The committee decided that all African countries which were members of the Organization of African Unity (OAU) were to be invited, as well as the Governo Revolucionário de Angola no Exílio (GRAE), the Angolan revolutionary group which the OAU recognized at that time. Moreover, the delegates specified, "Representatives of all national movements from non-self-governing territories recognized by the OAU in Africa and from Asia, which have not yet attained independence, may attend the conference with the right to be heard."[127] This guaranteed the governmental character of the conference.

Chou En-lai traveled to Africa twice in the three months before the planned conference, indicating the importance he placed on it.[128] En route to the conference itself, the Chinese delegation of thirty-five stopped in Cairo. But on that day Colonel Houari Boumédienne deposed Algerian president Ben Bella, and when the delegation continued on to Algiers the plane was not given permission to land.

127. "Final Communique of Second Afro-Asian Conference Preparatory Meeting," in *PR*, 24 April 1964, pp. 6–8. On controversies during the preconference period, also see *ibid.*, pp. 5–6, and *PR*, 18 June 1965, pp. 16–18.

In July 1964 the OAU chose Algeria as the site; Algeria, just a month before the conference was to open, pleaded for a delay until 29 June 1965 because of material difficulties. At a seventh and final meeting of the preparatory committee in Algiers (8 June) a preliminary meeting of foreign ministers was scheduled to begin on 24 June and the conference itself on 29 June. The question of Soviet participation, which the Soviets themselves appeared to lay aside in August 1964, was revived after a reported five-month canvass of prospects by Moscow. The Soviet Union repeated her claim of being an Asian country in her note of 14 August 1964 to all Asian-African countries, but she insisted that she would "not allow the question of [her] invitation to be embarrassing to other African-Asian countries." *NYT*, 15 August 1964. On 2 June 1965 Moscow published an analysis, which said in part: "Forces have emerged within the Afro-Asian movement that are trying to split and, chiefly, isolate it from the socialist countries and the international workers' movement. And one can understand the countries which, at such a time, want to see the Soviet Union sharing in the deliberations at Algiers. . . . The presence of Soviet representatives at the forthcoming conference is bound to be beneficial." [180], 2 June 1965, pp. 7–8; *NYT*, 5 June 1965.

128. At the end of March he paid a thirty-six hour visit to Algiers after visiting Romania, and then he went to Cairo for a day. *PR*, 9 April 1965, pp. 10–11. Chou stopped briefly in Cairo and Khartoum on 4 June while en route to a four-day visit in Tanzania; he stopped again in Cairo on his return.

The first flight permitted from Algiers to Cairo carried two members of the Chinese embassy staff, who immediately met with Chou En-lai.[129] And, on the same day, Chinese Ambassador Tseng T'ao sought and received an interview with Boumédienne; he conveyed China's support for the new Algerian administration and urged that the conference be convened as scheduled.[130]

The growing pressure for postponement was uppermost in the minds of all major participants. On 21 June, thirteen African and Asian countries of the British Commonwealth requested a postponement; on 22 June they were joined by Uganda and Nigeria. (Lobbying among Commonwealth heads of government then gathered in London, the Chinese chargé, Hsiung Hsiang-hui, met at least three times with Nkrumah, once with Joseph Murumbi of Kenya, and twice with Ayub Khan.)[131] On 22 June, too, Ch'en I reached Algiers and voiced confidence in success of the conference.[132] He saw Boumédienne on 23 June. The same day Algeria's foreign minister, Bouteflika, returned to Algiers from Cairo, where he had talked with Nasser and Chou En-lai. Thus, China appeared to be at the center of efforts to salvage the conference. But it could not be saved.[133]

China's version of this debacle was that the delegates' safety and Afro-Asian unity were threatened by imperialist intrigue, and therefore China, with other states, took the initiative to effect postponement. In particular, China stressed the continuing validity of decisions made at Djakarta in April 1964, for she wished to preserve the Algerian site and the invitation list omitting Malaysia and the Soviet Union.[134] But there was little prospect that China's plans would meet with success. Chou En-lai and Ch'en I

129. The military attaché and a second secretary. *NYT*, 21 June 1965.

130. *PR*, 25 June 1965, p. 4.

131. *NYT*, 24 June 1965.

132. *NYT*, 23 June 1965.

133. On 24 June, Bouteflika's ministry announced a one-day postponement of the meeting of the foreign ministers. But the following evening, as final preparations were under way, an explosion shook the conference hall, and Algeria ordered another postponement of the meeting. Only thirty-six of the sixty-four expected delegations were present, and during the evening of 26 June the conference was formally postponed to 5 November 1965. According to reports, China and Algeria insisted until the last moment that the conference should be held; Algeria's arrest of Egyptian workmen who were in the hall when the bomb exploded further marred relations between Boumédienne and Nasser, who had been pressing for the safety of Ben Bella; the concatenation of doubts and divisions simply overcame Algeria and China. *NYT*, 27 June 1965; [183], 27 June 1965. A contrary speculation, that China sensed an adverse majority and may have been just as happy to see the cancellation of the June meeting, is advanced in [183], 20 June 1965, p. 1.

134. *PR*, 2 July 1965, pp. 4–7.

devoted weeks to bringing about the conference, but they were unsuccessful. Commentators speculated in confident tones that postponement of the conference until November would kill it once and for all.

In the uncertain weeks that followed, China sounded out Asian and African opinion. Her ultimate decision to abandon the conference was presaged on 8 September when Chou En-lai attacked Soviet "sabotaging activities" and said that it was a "question of principle" that the Soviet Union not take part in the conference.[135] He spoke during Ch'en I's visit to three of Africa's more radical states: Algeria, Guinea, and Mali.[136] Ch'en I may have set out to explain an already-firm Chinese decision to stay away from the conference, based upon the conclusion that the Soviet Union could not be excluded; on the other hand, his trip may have been a last-minute effort to obtain commitments against Soviet participation. In any case, two of the states he visited, Mali and Guinea, were among those which later supported China's call for postponement of the conference.[137]

In a *Jen-min Jih-pao* editorial on 23 October, China cited four reasons for postponement:[138] "differences exist as to whether or not the African-Asian Conference should oppose US imperialism," which presumably meant that China feared she could not muster a strong condemnation of U.S. actions in Vietnam; "the so-called invitation extended to United Nations Secretary General U Thant has not yet been cancelled"; the question of Soviet participation had again been raised; and new tensions and conflicts that have recently developed "among certain Asian and African countries," specifically the India-Pakistan clash. These say in sum that China no longer expected that the conference would serve her purpose. On 26 October China announced she would boycott the meeting.[139]

Nonetheless, Algeria apparently hoped for a conference with both Soviet and Chinese participation. The Algerian information minister said he saw no obstacles in the way of a decision by the foreign ministers to

135. *PR*, 17 September 1965, p. 9.

136. *PR*, 24 September 1965, pp. 4 and 7. Ch'en I also visited Syria, Pakistan, and Afghanistan.

137. *PR*, 5 November 1965, p. 9. The other two were Tanzania and Congo (B). Dick Wilson, in a persuasive account of this episode, says that Ch'en I "found that the chances of a round condemnation of America at Algiers were slight, and this was the major reason for Peking's sudden turnabout." [166], 18 November 1965, p. 327.

138. When the standing committee met on 14–15 October, for its first session since 26 June, China proposed postponement of the conference, and at the next meeting (19–20 October) China and Cambodia tabled a joint resolution for postponement *sine die*. On 22 October Chou En-lai sent a letter to the Afro-Asian countries explaining China's stand, which was spelled out even more graphically in a *JMJP* editorial. *PR*, 29 October 1965, pp. 5–12.

139. *NYT*, 29 October 1965.

invite the Soviet Union, and at the same time Boumédienne was endeavoring to persuade China to attend. He was unsuccessful. Despite her boycott, China remained intensely interested, as indicated by the presence of six Chinese newsmen at the 28 October meeting of foreign ministers. But at this point China's decision appears to have been firm. On 31 October NCNA denied reports that China would agree to attend if the conference were postponed three months and the Soviets excluded, insisting that "at no time will the Chinese Government trade in principles."[140] The conference was formally postponed on 1 November. Although the foreign ministers' resolution spoke of a conference at some future time in Algiers,[141] there was no prospect that it would be resurrected.

New and Old Means of Afro-Asian Cooperation

In 1963 and thereafter Peking encouraged and initiated several new instruments of Afro-Asian cooperation. She had not planned to rely entirely on a second Bandung, the conventional fronts, or the Afro-Asian People's Solidarity Organization.

The Asian and African Journalists Association (AAJA) claimed forty-eight member nations — surely an exaggeration — but Africans did participate in its activities.[142] After the military gained control in Indonesia in 1965, the AAJA secretariat in Djakarta was subjected to "ever-increasing difficulties" and interference, and it moved to Peking.[143]

China also made an effort in athletics. Sukarno organized the first Games of the New Emerging Forces (GANEFO) in Djakarta 10–22 November 1963 with Chinese support. An Asian Committee of GANEFO was set up in Peking in September 1965.[144]

China sought to wrestle control of the Afro-Asian Writers' Bureau from a Moscow-encouraged segment of the group.[145] The Chinese-sup-

140. Cited in [175], vol. 7, no. 9, October 1965, p. 27; also *PR*, 5 November 1965, p. 13.

141. Formal resolution in *PR*, 5 November 1965, p. 9.

142. *PR*, 10 May 1963, pp. 22–23. In 1965 China conducted an Afro-Asian journalists' course attended by Africans from five countries: South Africa, Southwest Africa, Basutoland, Bechuanaland, and the Congo (B). *SCMP*, no. 3507, p. 27. Africans from nine countries attended the Fourth Plenary Meeting (enlarged) of the AAJA Secretariat in Peking, 20–24 April 1966. *PR*, 29 April 1966, pp. 12–15 and p. 24.

143. *PR*, 21 January 1966, p. 27; *PR*, 14 January 1966, p. 24; *PR*, 4 February 1966, pp. 3–4.

144. *PR*, 22 November 1963, pp. 16–18; *PR*, 8 October 1965, p. 6.

145. A permanent bureau of the Afro-Asian Writers' Conference had been established in Ceylon. In mid-1966 Sino-Soviet differences in the organization came to a head. The Soviets encouraged a meeting of the Afro-Asian Writers' Conference in Baku. A few days later, the Chinese-sponsored group met in Peking and denounced

ported section met in Peking in June and July 1966 and decided that the Third Afro-Asian Writers' Conference would be held in China, although the Soviet-sponsored group had just decided the meeting should be in the Soviet Union. Much of the 15 July 1966 issue of *Peking Review* is devoted to the results of the mid-1966 meeting.[146]

In the Afro-Asian Organization for Economic Cooperation, China pressed to politicize the fifth conference in May 1966 and bar Soviet participation.[147]

The Peking Center of the World Federation of Scientific Workers was host in 1964 to a symposium, attended, in part, by representatives of eighteen African countries. Ch'en I urged all the scientists to present a "broad united front," and many participants signed a protest against U.S. imperialist aggression in Vietnam. Another symposium was going to be organized in Peking in 1968 and a liaison office was created in Peking for that purpose, but the cultural revolution intervened.[148]

The most daring Chinese move — though it came to naught — was her threat to create a "revolutionary United Nations." As long as most countries were members of the United Nations, China could criticize the organization's structure and activities but she was scarcely in a position to build a competing body. After Indonesia's withdrawal on 7 January 1965, however, China could argue that another important and populous state had found the United Nations wanting. On the other hand, as China did not wish to be committed to creating an alternative, she sought the best footing from which to diminish the value of the United Nations. Chou En-lai stated:

> The Chinese Government and people firmly support Indonesia's withdrawal from the United Nations. This is a revolutionary action which has greatly advanced [the struggle to demand that the United

---

the Soviet initiative as "splittist." *PR*, 17 June 1966, pp. 35–39; *PR*, 8 July 1966, pp. 33–39; *PR*, 15 July 1966, pp. 6–14 and pp. 38–55.

146. At the Peking meeting it was also decided to set up an executive secretariat in Peking to assist the bureau in Colombo in preparing the third conference. This ensured Chinese control.

147. Beni Mallal and Casablanca, Morocco, 16–19 May 1966. *PR*, 27 May 1966, pp. 34–37. The refused applicant was the Uzbek Chamber of Commerce. The issue had also arisen at the fourth conference. *NYT*, 9 December 1963.

148. In September 1963 a group of foreign scientists met in Peking to mark the center's founding and to begin work on the symposium. *PR*, 11 October 1963, p. 3. [127], pp. 203–213 gives an interesting account of this. A number of African participants did not sign the statement of protest against the Vietnam War circulated at the symposium itself in 1964. *PR*, 4 September 1964, pp. 11–18. It should be noted that the World Federation of Scientific Workers is a Soviet-sponsored organization.

> Nations correct its mistakes and undergo thorough reorganization]. At present the struggle is spreading ever widely both from within and outside the United Nations. If the United Nations does not correct its mistakes and make a thorough reorganization, then, to set up a revolutionary United Nations will be the general course of development. Our call for the consideration of setting up a revolutionary United Nations also helps to strengthen the right of Asian and African countries to have their say in the United Nations, helps their struggle for exposing the United Nations and demanding the correction of its mistakes and its thorough reorganization.[149]

Whatever momentum this initiative may have had was ended by Indonesia's decision to rejoin the United Nations.

China's commitments to new revolutionary Afro-Asian and global organizations did not immediately imply abandonment of the AAPSO, which had, after all, helped to bring her into contact with Africans in the past. At the fourth solidarity conference, which met in Winneba, Ghana, 9–16 May 1965, the Chinese delegation's leader, Liao Ch'eng-chih, emphasized the question of Vietnam; in discussing Africa, he dwelt on the case of the Congo (L).[150] On the pivotal issue of armed struggle the conference affirmed the "legitimate right" of Asian, African, and Latin American peoples "to answer the imperialist violence by revolutionary violence"—a phrase which constantly recurs in Chinese analyses and exhortations.[151] Sino-Soviet differences were overt, in the form of clashes between hostile factions from Ceylon and Cameroon.[152] However, in a step which promised China her greatest advantage from AAPSO participation since the Conakry conference of 1960, the Winneba conference confirmed an earlier AAPSO council decision that the fifth conference would be held in Peking in 1967.[153] It was also agreed to convene the Conference of Afro-Asian-Latin American Peoples in Havana in January 1966, and an eighteen-member preparatory committee, including China and the Soviet Union, was named to plan the event.[154]

When the tricontinental conference did meet in Havana, it threatened

149. *PR*, 9 April 1965, p. 9.
150. *PR*, 21 May 1965, pp. 14–17.
151. [10], p. 8.
152. *PR*, 28 May 1965, p. 14. On the conference's method of settlement, see [10], p. 72.
153. [10], p. 74. *PR*, 21 May 1965, p. 17, notes that the Sixth AAPSO Council, Algiers, March 1964, had unanimously recommended Peking as the site of the fifth conference.
154. [10], p. 73.

to snatch away China's opportunity to host the next AAPSO conference. "Throughout the conference," *Jen-min Jih-pao* explained, "the Soviet delegates tried in every way to form a new tricontinental organization to replace the AAPSO which has a history of eight years of struggle against imperialism."[155] Although a tricontinental solidarity organization was established, the conference did not decide whether it should supplement, replace, or stand apart from AAPSO. It did create a permanent committee on organization to draft a charter for the next such meeting, tentatively set for Cairo in 1968, and it created an aid committee.[156] A number of African liberation movements were represented, and the decisions of the conference were more militant in spirit than Chinese charges of Soviet peace-mongering would suggest. This may have been partly due to the deliberate Soviet choice of militant language, intended to undercut China's appeal to national liberation movements.

Nevertheless, China subsequently concluded that remaining within AAPSO would no longer serve her purposes. After proceeding as if to hold her own version of the Fifth Afro-Asian People's Solidarity Conference, in the face of Soviet moves to cancel the Peking venue, China decided to withdraw from AAPSO altogether. Soviet and Egyptian influence — doubtless coupled with the moderate concerns of other AAPSO members — eliminated Chinese opportunities within that structure.

Embassies

China continued to seek diplomatic representation in Africa. The Central African Republic recognized Peking as the "sole legal government representing all the Chinese people," and broke relations with Taiwan.[157] This arrangement did not endure, and relations with Peking were terminated just over a year later. During the brief period of diplomatic recognition there were encounters which demonstrated the reserve of the Central African Republic. In March 1965 President David Dacko told a visiting Chinese parliamentary delegation that it would be as impossible to transplant Centrafrican ideology to China as it would be to apply Chinese politics in the Central African Republic.[158] While visiting the Central African Republic in June 1965, Deputy Foreign Minister Chi P'eng-fei tried

155. *PR*, 21 January 1966, p. 18; *JMJP* editorial, 18 January 1966.

156. [115]; [197], vol. 20, no. 3–4 (1966), March–April 1966, pp. 5–9. The new aid group was the Committee for Assistance and Aid to the National Liberation Movements and to the Struggle against Colonialism and Neo-Colonialism. A separate group was set up to support Vietnam.

157. *NYT*, 3 October 1964.

158. [147], May 1965, p. 30.

to persuade her to oppose Soviet, Malaysian, and Congo (L) participation in the planned second Bandung conference, but his plea was rejected.[159] When relations were broken in January 1966, the Chinese colony in Bangui numbered about thirty.[160]

Events in Dahomey fit a similar pattern. Diplomatic relations were established; then, following a change in government, the Chinese mission and NCNA representatives were ordered to leave. As in the case of the Central African Republic, relations were established in 1964, before China's large-scale support to the Congolese antigovernment forces had been widely commented upon.

Soon after relations were established with the Central African Republic and Dahomey, Chinese policy in Africa suffered its first public reverse. The Mwami of Burundi, who was embroiled in a complex internal political struggle and was also aware of China's use of Burundi to contact revolutionaries in the Congo, ordered the Chinese to leave his country, and he suspended diplomatic relations. China's losses included her contacts with Rwandan exiles, who had been training in Burundi under Chinese experts in the hope that they might be able to return to Rwanda and seize power.

China established diplomatic relations with Zambia in October 1964 and with Mauritania in July 1965. Relations with Zambia followed shortly after her independence. However, China delayed recognizing Mauritania for fear of antagonizing Morocco, which had laid claim to large portions of Mauritanian territory.[161] Traditionalist Mauritania recognized China, among other reasons, to maintain her credentials with Africa's radical states.[162] As in the cases of the Central African Republic and Dahomey, Mauritania ousted a mission from Taiwan to make way for the one from Peking.

From 1966 to 1969 China was prominent in Africa in three ways: she continued economic aid programs and began some others, including the Tanzania-Zambia railway project; diplomatically, she became involved in unfriendly encounters with some African governments, while she remained friendly to others; she continued to support selected national liberation movements. Economic aid is considered in Chapter 4, govern-

159. [147], August 1965, p. 24.

160. [149], no. 962, 13–19 January 1966, p. 6.

161. Tung Chi-p'ing claims to have seen cables, routed between Peking and the Chinese embassy in Morocco, indicating that Mauritania wished recognition but that Peking had demurred for the reason stated. Interview, Cambridge, Massachusetts, 7–8 June 1965.

162. [93], pp. 419–420.

mental relations in Chapters 6 and 8, and relations with liberation movements in Chapter 8. After the Great Proletarian Cultural Revolution began in earnest in 1966, it took first place among Chinese political concerns. Much of China's normally active diplomacy was suspended. The period from 1966 to 1969 was, in most respects, one in which China's policy makers marked time in African affairs.

By mid-1969 Chinese diplomats in Africa were ready to resume an assertive foreign policy after a three-year hiatus. Ambassadors were dispatched to some African capitals, although in others the chargés in whose hands embassies were placed during the cultural revolution remained as chiefs of mission. In October and November 1970 China undertook diplomatic relations with two African states, Equatorial Guinea and Ethiopia, bringing to fifteen the number of African states with which she maintained relations, as follows:[163]

Northern Africa	*West Africa*	*Central Africa*	*East Africa*
Algeria	Equatorial Guinea	Congo (B)	Ethiopia
Morocco	Guinea	Zambia	Kenya
Sudan	Mali		Somalia
United Arab Republic	Mauritania		Tanzania (including a consulate in Zanzibar)
			Uganda

163. Diplomatic relations with Tunisia and Ghana had been broken. See Table 1 and the discussion in Chapter 6.

4 Economic Relations

Trade with Africa has been only a modest part of China's imports and exports. The full figures are set out in Table 2, but the following abstract shows the significance of this trade to China.

	1956	*1963*	*1966*	*1967*
Percentage of Chinese exports shipped to Africa (excluding South Africa)	1.9%	3.0%	5.9%	6.0%
Percentage of Chinese imports originating in Africa (excluding South Africa)	1.7%	4.4%	3.6%	2.9%

Africa's total trade is three to four times as large as China's, and, accordingly, trade between the two regions is not as important to Africa as it is to China. Despite this fact, each year China takes an important share of the exports of a few African countries. For example, more than 8.5 percent of Uganda's 1961 exports were bought by China,[1] and she purchased more than 7 percent of Egyptian exports in 1965.[2] These high figures reflect China's cotton purchases, and they show it is possible for China to be a major factor — but not the dominant one — in some African markets.

Economic advantage apart, trade has expanded as one facet of the development of Sino-African political relations. China's first office in Africa was the trade mission established in Cairo in 1956. China's intentions had been announced the year before:

> China, which has a population of 600,000,000, is devoting itself to peaceful construction. It has a big and growing market. It needs . . . cotton produced by Egypt. . . . China's silk piece goods, paper, tea,

1. [130], 1963.
2. [161], 1966. In the 1966–1967 season, from its beginning to 22 February 1967, China bought 10.5% of the Egyptian cotton crop. [163], 19 April 1967.

> cotton and woolen textiles have traditional markets in Asia and Africa, because the people there like them.[3]

China's first large purchase from Egypt was made in July 1955. In August, an Egyptian delegation to China negotiated a three-year trade agreement, putting economic relations on a continuing basis, and Cairo agreed to buy 60,000 tons of rolled steel within the year. At this juncture establishment of the trade offices was agreed upon, and large-scale trade began. Prior to 1955 only limited trade between China and African countries had taken place.[4]

These economic developments had a unique political significance. The fact that China—and the Soviet Union—took large quantities of Egyptian cotton at a time when world cotton prices were falling served to bolster the cotton-based Egyptian economy at a critical moment. Thus, when Cairo and Peking established diplomatic relations, an aura of goodwill, of anticipation that cooperation would grow, was much in evidence.[5] Sino-Egyptian cooperation set a pattern for Chinese relations with other states of the Middle East.

Sino-African trade from 1955 to 1967 is reviewed in Table 2. Exports increased sharply in 1955 and 1956 as Chinese trade with Egypt grew. Thereafter exports at least maintained their level through 1966, and usually they rose from year to year. China's severe economic difficulties forced Chinese sales down to $41 million in 1960 from $45 million in 1959; thereafter the trend was upward, even before economic recovery was general. By the mid-1960s a sharp increase in exports was recorded.

The volume of imported goods increased in 1955 and again in 1957 due to China's purchase of Egyptian cotton. Until 1961, in fact, the value of these purchases was well in excess of Egyptian purchases from China. In 1961 China sharply curtailed imports, and, from the $74 million high of 1960, the net value of imports fell to $39 million in 1961. This drop coincides with China's diversion of foreign exchange to the higher priority requirement of importing foodstuffs. African states were not in a position to supply the bulk food grains which China required, and imports from Africa fell more precipitately than China's imports as a whole.

By 1963 Chinese imports had recovered to $62 million. From 1957 to 1964 imports exceeded exports by $43 million; in 1965 alone China bought $37 million more from Africa than she sold. In 1966, however, this pat-

3. Summarized in NCNA, 25 April 1955.
4. [200], December 1955, p. 12; *ibid.*, April 1955, p. 13.
5. In 1954 and 1955 China also sought trade in Syria, Lebanon, and Saudi Arabia. [200], April 1956, pp. 5–8; [200], July 1956, p. 10.

Table 2
CHINESE TRADE WITH DEVELOPING AFRICA*
(f.o.b. in U.S. $ millions)

	Chinese Exports			Chinese Imports		
	Total Chinese Exports	*Chinese Exports to Africa*	*World Exports to Africa*	*World Exports to China*	*Chinese Imports from Africa*	*Total African Exports*
1955	1,420	22	5,090	1,490	26	4,430
1956	1,710	33	5,460	1,610	28	4,640
1957	1,710	43	6,040	1,500	47	4,620
1958	1,970	42	5,980	1,980	44	4,650
1959	2,230	45	6,000	2,190	49	4,820
1960	2,060	41	6,470	2,090	74	5,300
1961	1,600	46	6,540	1,600	39	5,430
1962	1,680	49	6,280	1,350	38	5,540
1963	1,720	52	6,760	1,420	62	6,240
1964	1,870	58	7,390	1,640	66	7,250
1965	2,020	78	8,170	2,120	115	7,650
1966	2,290	135	8,180	2,290	80	8,220
1967	2,070	125	8.330	2,350	67	8,330

* *Yearbook of International Trade Statistics* (New York: United Nations, 1969), 1967 volume. The figures are for trade between the "China Mainland" and "Developing Africa." The original note for "China Mainland" states: "Estimates based partly on import data of trading partners. Where exports to China (Taiwan) could not be distinguished from exports to China (mainland) they are shown as exports to China (mainland). Exports to Mongolia, Korea North, and Viet-Nam North are included under this heading. The intertrade of these countries and their trade with China (mainland) are excluded."

Figures in this table are for developing Africa. Developing Africa includes all countries of the continent except South Africa; the United Arab Republic is included in figures for developing Africa.

For the sake of convenient reference to the source, all trade is reported f.o.b. To obtain the actual cost to China of her imports, however, one must adjust the figures to incorporate freight costs. For a discussion of one such estimate, see *Current Scene*, vol. 7, no. 13, 1 July 1969; the editor estimates 10% as a rough figure for freight costs from Africa proper, and 13.5% for Mediterranean countries.

It should be noted that some very different figures appear in the *Direction of Trade Annual* (1963–1967), vol. 5. It gives the following for Chinese exports and imports in the African trade (figures obtained by summing the reported figures for Africa and the U.A.R.):

	Exports f.o.b.	Imports c.i.f.
1964	63.8	65.6
1965	114.5	130.9
1966	140.3	81.4
1967	119.0	59.6

The significant discrepancy is in Chinese exports to Africa in 1965 and 1966. If the *Direction of Trade* figures are more accurate than those of the United Nations report, China's trade in 1965 and 1966 has been considerably greater than reported in the main table.

tern was reversed, and exports to Africa sharply exceeded imports. China's 1967 exports to Africa were almost twice the value of her imports, and they represented about 5 percent of China's foreign trade.

Strategic Materials

A recurring theme in Chinese comment is that the United States and other industrial countries maintain their interests in Africa because of its mineral wealth. According to a *Hung-ch'i* article of 1961:

> Africa possesses very rich mineral deposits and agricultural resources, especially diamonds, petroleum, gold, cobalt, uranium, lithium, and other rare metals of great strategic importance.[6]

"If not for Katanga's uranium," says a Belgian character in a Chinese play as he addresses an American general advising the United Nations mission in the Congo, "you'd never have made your first atomic bomb." The general replies, "If not for our atomic bomb, Katanga's uranium would be worthless as stones."[7]

Cobalt, which may be used to harden steel or in a nuclear program, has been sold to China by Morocco, according to journalist John Cooley. He claims that two shipments aggregating 3,985 tons were made in 1960. United States officials reportedly cautioned Morocco against trade in cobalt, but "Western intelligence in Hong Kong" discovered a further 4,000 tons had been shipped furtively in 1963.[8]

Other items in Sino-African trade excite less interest. China has imported cotton from Egypt, Sudan, and Uganda, copper from Zambia, phosphates from Morocco, cloves from Zanzibar, incense from Somalia, trucks from Morocco and Algeria, maize from South Africa and Rhodesia, and other goods. She has shipped in return a variety of consumer goods, equipment for development projects, and arms.[9] What else might interest China? Uranium deposits may have been an early attraction, but China has discovered large domestic deposits of this ore in Sinkiang.[10] Although Chinese petroleum experts have visited Africa, they may have been more

6. [209], 1 April 1961, translated in Joint Publications Research Service, no. 8759, p. 48.

7. [208], p. 36.

8. [22], pp. 170 ff. Cooley also asserts that a March 1964 Sino-Moroccan trade agreement stated China would buy 5,000 tons of "non-ferrous metals," which may mean cobalt.

9. Arms shipments to Tanzania were said to have reached 11,000 tons. *NYT*, 17 March 1966.

10. [44], p. 74.

interested in tips to aid China's own drive toward self-sufficiency than in the prospect of trade.[11] China's building of the Tanzania-Zambia railway may have been intended, in part, to improve Chinese access to Zambian copper.

For the most part strategic materials do not figure prominently in China's quest for economic relations with Africa. Alexander Eckstein has said that the most conservative estimates sustain the judgment that China's own mineral and energy resources are "adequate to support a high level of industrialization in China."[12]

Aid

Chinese credits and grants are shown in Table 3. Whether grants were actually transmitted to the grantee and whether credits were actually used are questions to which the available data cannot supply a complete answer. This limitation should be borne in mind.

Chinese foreign credits are usually made available in annual increments over a term of years. A typical agreement provided ten equal allotments over a decade. Although announced credits exceeded $350 million by mid-1966, the amount which China had actually become obligated to make available was much smaller. And some available credits have gone unused. The principal recipients to mid-1966 were Algeria ($50 million), Congo (B) ($25 million), Ghana ($42 million), Guinea ($10 million), Kenya ($15 million), Mali (almost $20 million), Somalia ($20 million), Tanzania ($16 million), and the United Arab Republic ($85 million). Few of the credits to Ghana were used, and Kenya's allotment, according to one report, was not drawn upon at all.[13]

Early in 1966 a series of reports implied that China lacked the capacity to offer goods useful to African development and claimed that Chinese credits to some African countries were not being used. The *New York Times* reported, after Nkrumah's ouster and the subsequent end of Chinese aid to Ghana, that "most of the Chinese projects have yet to get off the ground."[14] Another correspondent reported that in Cairo "one does not hear any more of the much-trumpeted promise by Peking to provide

11. [22], p. 72. Chinese petroleum experts visited oil-producing Algeria in early 1964.

12. [29], p. 310, note citing [140], p. 113.

13. [174], 14 July 1967, p. 16. Earlier the same paper reported that credits had begun to reach Kenya "in the form of goods whose poor quality made them unsalable, or else goods which Kenya is already producing in ample quantity." [174], 29 April 1966.

14. *NYT*, 2 March 1966.

Table 3
CHINESE AID TO AFRICA: COMMITMENTS TO MID-1966

Date	*$ Million Grant*	*$ Million Credit*	*Recipient*	*Comment*
1956		5.00	Egypt	Since repaid
APR 58	.17		Algeria	
1959	10.00		Algeria	Reported arms aid
12 SEP 60	2.80		Congo	Stanleyville
13 SEP 60		10.00	Guinea	
1959–1960	In kind		Guinea	15,000 tons rice
18 AUG 61		19.60	Ghana	
22 SEP 61		19.60	Mali	
19 OCT 61	.06		Tunisia	
13 DEC 61	.13		Somalia	Medical supplies included
21 AUG 62	In kind		Algeria	9,000 tons wheat; 3,000 tons rolled steel; 21 tons medical supplies
15 JAN 63	.10		Morocco	
9 AUG 63	3.00	20.00	Somalia	
11 OCT 63		50.00	Algeria	
24 DEC 63	.02		Algeria	
27 JAN 64	.10		Algeria	
FEB 64		22.40	Ghana	
20 FEB 64	.50		Zanzibar	
10 MAY 64	2.80	15.00	Kenya	
16 MAY 64	.01		Tanganyika	
8 JUN 64		14.00	Zanzibar	
17 JUN 64	2.80	42.00	Tanzania	
1964		5.00	Congo (B)	
3 AUG 64	.02		Algeria	
30 AUG 64	See *Comment*		Congo (B)	5,300,000 CFA francs for refugees expelled from Congo (L)
1964		4.00	Central African Republic	
1964		20.00	Congo (B)	
DEC 64		80.00	U.A.R.	
21 APR 65	2.99	12.04	Uganda	
JUN 66	2.80	5.60	Tanzania	
JUL 66		4.00	Mali	In foreign currency
8 JUL 66		2.10	Tanzania	For joint shipping line

$50 million in industrial credit for the five-year development plan."[15] He also noted that Algeria had drawn only $3 million of the $50 million available to her. Worldwide, China pledged $330 million in aid in 1964 but only $50 million in 1965.[16] China even failed to use her initial survey of the Tan-Zam railway route to demonstrate technical skill: it was reported that the Chinese survey team was composed of railwaymen, not surveyors, and that their list of requisitioned equipment did not contain surveying tools.[17]

It is possible that China was uncertain how best to counter what she perceived to be Soviet and American threats to her in the latter part of 1965. With the passing months American air strikes remained confined to Vietnam, reinforcing reported American assurances that China would not be attacked if Chinese troops in North Vietnam were limited to logistic and railway tasks. Mao Tse-tung felt sufficiently sure of himself to launch the Great Proletarian Cultural Revolution, tentatively in November 1965 and irreversibly in April 1966. In the much less important sphere of African aid operations there was also evidence that, by mid-1966, China was ready to proceed in the usual way. It was announced that the major part of the £16 million China had pledged to Tanzanian development had already been "committed" and China advanced an additional £3 million, of which £1 million was a grant.[18] At the same time, Uganda's minister of finance announced that negotiations were under way to use China's credit. Shortly thereafter China lent Mali $4 million in foreign currency; part of this was to repay debts and to provide transit facilities at Dakar.[19] In July, China and Tanzania announced their plan to create a joint shipping line.[20] During the next four months development projects were begun or completed in Mali, the Congo (B), and Guinea.[22] In April 1967, Algeria was granted a loan of $2 million in hard currency,

15. *NYT*, 13 February 1966.

16. *NYT*, 16 February 1966. Of the U.A.R., he added: "Apart from a $5 million foreign exchange loan that has been repaid, the U.A.R. has not touched the promised $80 million Chinese credit."

17. [174], 29 April 1966.

18. The £5 million promised Zanzibar before its union with Tanganyika was committed to projects, as was more than £4 million of the credit extended Tanzania. China's first £1 million grant to Tanzania had been duly received. [162], 17 June 1966.

19. [194], 14 and 16 June 1966; [177], 6 July 1966.

20. China put up £1.5 million as initial capitalization. Half the sum is a loan to Tanzania for her share. The loan is to be repaid to China out of profits over a ten-year period beginning in 1977. The initial plan called for two ships. *NYT*, 8 July 1966; [190], 8 July 1966.

21. *NYT*, 26 September 1966.

22. [195], 8 October 1966 and 25 February 1967.

presumably implementing earlier credits;[23] in the wake of Egypt's disaster at the hands of Israel, China promptly announced another hard currency loan of $10 million and 150,000 tons of wheat.[24]

In addition to credits, China made cash grants and emergency contributions. Budgetary or plan subsidies of about $3 million or £1 million have been reported offered to Kenya, Somalia, Tanganyika (twice), and Uganda. It is reported that budgetary aid to Somalia was half in cash and half in consumer goods.[25] Several small emergency contributions have been made; for example, Somalia received Y150,000 in flood relief in 1961–1962 and medicines of equal value.

Since 1966 China has not stated the worth of grants and credits. Many references to assistance do not distinguish projects which are using prior credits from those being newly financed. Extension of Table 3 beyond 1966 would therefore be misleading. Another way to portray China's development aid in Africa is to list projects which have been mentioned in press accounts, sometimes with journalists' estimates of their value. Table 4 surveys reports of selected projects in Tanzania and Guinea from 1966 to 1970 and lists the credits from which they were presumably funded.

These examples illustrate the variety of Chinese aid projects and their pertinence for development. Light industry, agriculture, medicine, and transport are emphasized. China also sponsors occasional show projects.

Tanzania-Zambia Railway

There have been numerous Chinese technical assistance programs, and many Chinese technicians have come to Africa to implement them.[26] All prior projects are dwarfed by the Tanzania-Zambia railway: it will run from the Zambia copper belt to the Tanzanian port of Dar es Salaam. Zambia will be freed from dependence on Beira, the Portuguese-controlled

23. One milliard old francs, roughly $2 million. Radio Algiers, 21 April 1967.

24. Radio Cairo, 11 June 1967; *NYT*, 26 June 1967.

25. *NYT*, 25 January 1965.

26. No comprehensive summary of Chinese technicians and advisers in Africa is available. The following scattered reports, however, give a good picture of the numbers involved. *Tanzania.* The Chinese ambassador put their number at 200 in July 1966 and said more would arrive in August. [147], October 1966 p. 30. An Associated Press dispatch in January 1968 estimated there were 400 Chinese military instructors, technicians, and agricultural experts in Tanzania. About 150 railroad surveyors arrived three months later. [190], 13 April 1968. In September 1970 Chinese in Zanzibar alone were estimated to be between 400 and 500. *NYT*, 23 September 1970. *Congo (B).* A 1967 agreement called for twenty Chinese medical and public health personnel. *NYT*, 9 February 1967. *Ghana.* Chinese technicians who left Ghana after Nkrumah was overthrown numbered 207. *NYT*, 12 March 1966.

Table 4
EXAMPLES OF CHINESE CREDITS AND AID PROJECTS:
TANZANIA AND GUINEA

TANZANIA

Value in $ million	*Recipient and Type of Aid*	*Date of Credit or Grant*
.5	Zanzibar. Grant.	FEB 64
14.0	Zanzibar. Credit.	8 JUN 64
2.8	Tanzania. Grant.	17 JUN 64
42.0	Tanzania. Credit.	17 JUN 64
2.8	Tanzania. Grant.	JUN 66
5.6	Tanzania. Credit.	JUN 66
2.1	Tanzania. Credit for joint shipping line.	8 JUL 66
14.0	Tanzania-Zambia. Estimated value of Chinese survey for Tan-Zam Railway.	1967
336.0	Tanzania-Zambia. Estimated value of loan for Tan-Zam Railway construction (May include preceding item.)	JUL 70

Projects Undertaken 1966–1969	*Description*	*Source of Data*
Joint shipping line	Sino-Tanzanian line. Two 10,000 ton vessels. China lent Tanzania's initial capital of £750,000. Opened in mid-1968.	[190], 8 July 1966 and 12 January 1967; [179], 6 July 1968.
Textile mill	Foundation stone of Friendship Textile Mill laid 29 July 1966. Part of the £16,000,000 Chinese commitment to development. 3,000 workers to be supervised by 150 Chinese.	[190], 30 July 1966.
Tan-Zam Railway (preliminary survey)	Nyerere given preliminary report prepared by small Chinese team.	[162], 14 October 1966.
Dam building	Experts for construction of a £5,000,000 dam at Kibunda.	[179], 9 December 1966.
Tan-Zam Railway (1967 agreement)	China agrees to finance and construct the Tan-Zam Railway. Commits to survey and design at cost of $14,000,000.	[190], 11 September 1967.
Farm implements factory	Value £174,000. Financed from long-term Chinese loan.	*Daily Nation* (Nairobi), 12 February 1968; *SCMP*, no. 4119, p. 29, 11 February 1968.
Shoe factory	Opened at Mtoni, near Zanzibar Town. Value £100,000.	[190], 16 February 1968; *SCMP*, no. 4122, p. 27.
Agricultural development	China to assist in massive agricultural plan.	[190], 13 July 1968; [179], 25 July 1968.

Table 4 (Continued)

Projects Undertaken 1966–1969	*Description*	*Source of Data*
Pharmaceutical plant	A Chinese-built gift.	[190], 26 August 1968.
Tan-Zam Railway (extension)	China agrees railway will run from Kapiri Mposhi in Zambia to Dar es Salaam, avoiding need to shift goods.	Radio Lusaka, 13 February 1969.
Tan-Zam Railway (construction)	Survey completed in 1969; Zambia, Tanzania, and China begin construction in 1970.	See pp. 96–103.

Note: A more extensive list of Chinese projects, including some very minor ones, can be found in George T. Yu, *China and Tanzania: A Study in Cooperative Interaction* (Berkeley: University of California Center for Chinese Studies, 1970), pp. 51–61.

GUINEA

Value in \$ million	*Type of Aid*	*Date of Credit*
10.0	Credit.	13 SEP 60

Projects Undertaken 1966–1969	*Description*	*Source of Data*
Hydroelectric plant	Dam and hydroelectric plant at Pita opened in January 1967.	[195], 25 February 1967.
Dam	At Tinkisso.	*Ibid.*
Sugar refinery	At Madinaoula.	*Ibid.*
Steel plant	Annual output of 60,000 tons.	*Ibid.*
Railway to Mali	Chinese agreement with Guinea and Mali to build connecting railway.	Radio Bamako, 28 May 1968.
Groundnut oil factory	Foundation stone laid in Dabola.	Radio Conakry, 10 December 1968.
Railroad repair	China agrees to repair the Conakry-Kankan line.	Radio Conakry, 31 October 1969.
Agricultural development	China promises to assist Guinean agricultural development.	*Ibid.*
Cement works	China agrees to aid construction of a cement factory.	*Ibid.*

Note: On 21 January 1966 Guinea's minister of economic development lauded Chinese aid projects, citing a match and cigarette factory opened in Conakry in 1964, a tobacco plantation at Beyla, a tea plantation and factory at Macenta, and a dam at Pita. See [147], March 1966, p. 34. China has not stated the value of recent projects. One estimate is that her total aid commitments to Guinea reached \$70 million by 1970. [147], December 1970, p. 8.

Mozambican port. China will provide a loan for construction costs and rolling stock; moreover, Chinese engineers, who have completed a survey of the route, will supervise the construction. At this writing details of the sum lent and credit terms have not been published, but reports at the signing of the three-nation agreement in July 1970 speculated that the loan would be $336 million, interest free, to be repaid over thirty years.[27] Construction began in 1970, and it is expected to be completed in 1975. China's annual outlay will therefore be roughly $70 million. By comparison, China's flood relief to Romania in 1970 was estimated to be $23 million,[28] and her 1970 aid to North Vietnam was estimated to be $200 million.[29]

Five years of negotiation, survey, and design had passed by the time China, Tanzania, and Zambia signed the loan agreement. Peking first made the aid offer in 1965. In August 1965 a small Chinese team began preliminary survey work in Tanzania. In September 1967 China signed an agreement to finance the entire railroad, although Tanzania and Zambia reserved their assent pending completion of a thorough engineering survey. It is especially noteworthy that China committed herself to the Tan-Zam railway project at the very height of the Great Proletarian Cultural Revolution. Disorganization in the Ministry of Foreign Affairs was severe, but the cultural revolution did not prevent China from undertaking successive steps of this project in a fairly orderly manner.

At the end of 1969 a negotiating team led by a vice-minister of railroads, Kuo Lu, traveled to Lusaka for further talks. Kuo lingered in Zambia and Tanzania for almost a month beyond the announced successful end of talks,[30] prompting speculation that the parties had failed to agree on financial terms. Nevertheless, survey work was soon completed, and quantities of construction equipment, rails, cement, and other goods were unloaded in Dar es Salaam during the winter. The final signing certified the three parties' prior decision in principle to construct the railroad.

Why did Tanzania and Zambia accept Chinese aid for a project of such scale? Both very much wanted the railroad, and they could obtain funds from no one else. Tanzanian President Nyerere stated succinctly: "It was not as if we had alternate proposals to choose from. We should, indeed, have welcomed Western offers, but the only firm offer we had was

27. Baltimore *Sun*, 13 July 1970.
28. *NYT*, 16 July 1970.
29. [166], 4 June 1970, p. 4.
30. *SCMP*, no. 4533, p. 23 (1 November 1969); *SCMP*, no. 4537, p. 37 (8 November 1969); *SCMP*, no. 4543, pp. 21–22 (16 November 1969); SCMP, no. 4549, p. 29 (24 November 1969); *SCMP*, no. 4559, pp. 26–27 (9 December 1969).

from China." Even as late as 1967 there were reports that Zambia still hoped to evoke a competitive offer, but none was forthcoming.

How do Nyerere and Zambian President Kenneth Kaunda view China? Ideological companionship between China's leadership and the African statesmen is tenuous at best. Nyerere's commitments in the Arusha declaration and Kaunda's proclamation of "humanism" are certainly inconsistent with Chinese ideological preferences. At the final signing, Li Hsien-nien spoke of the "revolutionary struggle against US imperialism and its running dogs," but the Tanzanian and Zambian spokesmen offered no more than a wish for a "just and peaceful world order in which imperialism, fascism, and colonialism will have been banished forever."[31] In another context, Nyerere has said that Chinese aid is encumbered by fewer strings than aid from any other country.[32] The two African states appear ready to accept development funds from any donor who can do the job and who is willing to refrain from unacceptable political interference in local affairs.

Would China perform? Were Tanzanian and Zambian authorities troubled by the uncertainties of the cultural revolution? The influential *East African Standard* in neighboring Kenya put it this way:

> There is . . . a question-mark over whether China, torn to the point of instability by its internal convulsions, is in a position to carry out its commitments. If it can meet its economic pledges to Zambia and Tanzania without seeking political rewards and favours, its services will be welcomed, and its present unhappy image in the rest of Africa greatly improved.[33]

The step-by-step ordering of the project enabled Tanzania and Zambia to observe Peking's performance of each task before they committed themselves further. China experienced great pressure to keep her end of the bargain: if she failed to meet major commitments, future projects would be difficult to develop and African states would be less certain of the value of political ties with Peking. Pressures of this type persist.

If Zambian and Tanzanian willingness to join with China to build the railroad is straightforward, China's willingness to commit herself so heavily requires a more elaborate explanation. Political gains will certainly accrue. The failure of Western nations to make firm counteroffers was interpreted by many Africans as a decision to refuse help. China's presence

31. *PR*, 17 July 1970, pp. 16–17.
32. *NYT*, 25 May 1967.
33. [162], 7 September 1967.

in the two states is assured while construction continues — and probably thereafter. Third world nationalists see in China's aid the promise of future largesse; this response may be most pronounced among national liberation movements inclined to join China in common cause for other reasons. China implies the African political stance she desires by saying of the two cooperating governments:

> In international affairs [they] have always upheld justice, opposed the imperialist policies of aggression and war and supported the national-liberation movements in Asia and Africa, thus making positive contributions to the cause of the Afro-Asian people's unity against imperialism and winning the praise and admiration of the Afro-Asian countries and peoples.[34]

Successful completion of the railroad will testify to Chinese skill, energy, and economic strength. Finally, since Zambia will no longer be dependent upon railroads in Mozambique and Angola, Zambia will be protected from retaliation which Portugal might invoke if she is angered by Zambian plans and policies toward Africa's southern tier and its liberation movements.

Portugal has had leverage because Zambia must transport her copper to the sea for shipment. Anticipated economic gains, including access to Zambian copper, may figure in China's calculus. But her primary economic interest could just as well be the desire to export. Some speculations predict that repayment of the loan will be accomplished, in part, by Tanzanian and Zambian purchases of Chinese commodities. In effect, this would mean that part of the loan would be in Chinese consumer goods. Even if this does not occur the railroad guarantees China entrée for her exports to both countries.

Thus we note that China may achieve both evolutionary and revolutionary objectives through the railroad. Of course, it is not known whether these arguments decided Peking's commitment. A search for causes or prerequisites should also emphasize Tanzanian and Zambian initiative: the two countries created an attractive opportunity that was unlike any other which China had been invited to support. Peking had only to satisfy herself that she could perform successfully and that diversion of resources from domestic construction was a wise allocation. If Chinese experience in railroad construction was insufficient to convince Peking that she could complete the project, the matter must have been settled by an analysis of the preliminary survey. Peking's readiness from the outset to discuss the

34. *PR*, 17 July 1970, p. 16.

full project as Tanzania and Zambia conceived it suggests confidence based on a priori grounds of domestic experience and ideological conviction. The allocation problem was not pressing at the beginning: small sums in 1965–1967 and perhaps $7 million a year for the survey and design in 1968–1969. Less than $70 million a year is budgeted for 1970–1974. If one argues that costs would be partially offset by expanded exports, the anticipated cost would be even less. Long-term evolutionist aims may be advanced at a relatively modest cost to short-term evolutionist aims, the postponement of the extension of some domestic Chinese railroads.

Revolutionist goals that the railroad may advance should be clearly distinguished from the crude notion of "Chinese penetration." "Red Guard Line Chugging into Africa" was the headline in the *Wall Street Journal*: "The prospect of hundreds and perhaps thousands of Red Guards descending upon an already troubled Africa is a chilling one for the West."[35] The revolutionist political thrust of the railroad is much more subtle and much less direct. Encouragement of national liberation movements, greater Zambian self-reliance, and validation of Chinese anti-American and revolutionary symbols are the principal revolutionist components of the railway project. If these have an effect, it will be through the actions of indigenous African political groups. Direct political activities of Chinese railroad personnel in Tanzania and Zambia are likely to be severely limited for linguistic reasons. However, Peking will be able to acquire a knowledge of rural conditions and social structure in regions served by the railroad if politically-adept bilingual personnel accompany the construction teams.

The characteristics of highway and railroad construction suit Chinese capabilities and objectives. Chinese engineers know the required technology. Roads and railroads are highly visible, permanent landmarks which serve many people and are prerequisites to modern economic activity. Construction gives Chinese personnel access to otherwise unknown regions. If the route is difficult, construction affords China a chance to display her prowess in engineering and construction. The work is arduous, sometimes dangerous, and entails a demonstrable sacrifice by individual Chinese in behalf of the local populace.[36]

In this light, China's choice of road and rail projects for other important commitments is a significant complement to projects in light industry, medical care, and agriculture. In Zambia, Peking has undertaken to

35. 29 September 1967.

36. Three Chinese killed during work on the Lusaka-Mankoya road were declared martyrs serving the people. *JMJP*, 3 December 1969, p. 3.

construct and improve two highways, from Lusaka to Mankoya and to Kaoma.[37] Before Modibo Keita was deposed in the Mali coup of November 1968, Peking agreed to build the Guinea-Mali railway, at an estimated cost of $20 million.[38] Speaking of the agreement, Mali's foreign minister said such aid was effective, of high quality, and that it was "not in any way detrimental to sovereignty or mutual respect."[39]

These examples show that China can cooperate with African governments on major projects. The cultural revolution did not preclude an active aid policy. Peking is able to plan commitments as long as ten years in advance, the time from her first proposal on the Tan-Zam railway to its anticipated completion. She has funded diverse projects, and many of her largest undertakings were plans conceived initially by the recipient states. Although political aims are sometimes evident, for example in outright grants and in the construction of transmitter facilities, they are more commonly attained indirectly through performance of a conventional economic task.

China's Official Position

During Chou En-lai's tour of Africa in 1963–1964, he laid down eight principles governing Chinese aid policy. The rules, he said, were strictly observed by the Chinese government. They were the most important public commitment made by Chou during the trip. They merit close consideration, both as an appeal to Africans and as an assault on Soviet activities.

> First, the Chinese Government always bases itself on the principle of equality and mutual benefit in providing aid to other countries. It never regards such aid as a kind of unilateral alms but as something mutual. Through such aid the friendly new emerging countries gradually develop their own national economy, free themselves from colonial control and strengthen the anti-imperialist forces in the world. This is in itself a tremendous support to China.

China has urged "equality and mutual benefit" in Asian-African relations since the Bandung conference. When imperialism is weakened, Chou argues, China gains strength. This idea echoes guidance once given by Moscow to Communists everywhere when the Soviets urged action to protect the "socialist base."

37. Agreements signed 14 February 1969 and 30 January 1970. *SCMP*, no. 4593, p. 26.

38. [166], 15 August 1968, p. 302.

39. *PR*, 31 May 1968, p. 8.

> Second, in providing aid to other countries, the Chinese Government strictly respects the sovereignty of the recipient countries, and never asks for any privileges or attaches any conditions.

By raising the second issue, China calls attention to conditions which sometimes accompany aid from other donors. For example, the United States insists that states which have nationalized the property of United States citizens without suitable compensation are ineligible to receive aid. This point masks the question of allocation: Why does one African state receive a large Chinese grant or credit, another only a small one? China employs aid as a reward and as a promise. Past actions are rewarded; there is a promise that, if certain implied conditions are met, aid will be forthcoming.

> Third, the Chinese Government provides economic aid in the form of interest-free or low-interest loans and extends the limit for the repayment so as to lighten the burden of the recipient countries as far as possible.

The third point distinguishes China from states which, rather than subsidizing aid, see loans and their repayment as business propositions.[40] It also calls attention to China's repayment of Soviet development loans, despite severe economic trials.

> Fourth, in providing aid to other countries, the purpose of the Chinese Government is not to make the recipient countries dependent on China but to help them embark on the road of self-reliance step by step.

The burden of development is mainly on the developing countries. This is another way of reminding African states that China requires her own resources for domestic development, and it also anticipates her inability to sustain massive aid operations. The point is consistent with the view widely held by economists that most investment for development must be generated within the developing country.

> Fifth, the Chinese Government tries its best to help the recipient countries build projects which require less investment while yielding

40. China has reportedly extended the repayment period for three projects in Tanzania: the textile mill, radio station, and agricultural tool factory. [148], fourth quarter, 1969, p. 26.

quicker results, so that the recipient governments may increase their income and accumulate capital.

Quick results are always an enticement. But China may also have used this argument to shift African attention to projects that could be financed by indigenous resources, or with modest Chinese support. If the African states set their sights on ambitious schemes, they would almost surely need to seek Soviet and Western aid. It is hardly to China's advantage to try to match the aid given to Africa by prosperous industrialized states; nor does China wish to export equipment in demand within the country — except for usable foreign exchange. One Tan-Zam railway can be built. Several could not be undertaken simultaneously.

> Sixth, the Chinese Government provides the best-quality equipment and material of its own manufacture at international market prices. If the equipment and material provided by the Chinese Government are not up to the agreed specifications and quality, the Chinese Government undertakes to replace them.

This is an attractive warranty, but whether it will be effective depends on China's pride in a good reputation and on the strength of her desire to keep customers.

> Seventh, in giving any particular technical assistance, the Chinese Government will see to it that the personnel of the recipient country fully master such technique.

This implies that other donors do not wish to teach, but seek instead to monopolize technique and to exploit their advantage for economic and political gains.[41] Technical assistance accompanied by training has a longer-lasting economic effect than technical assistance alone. The trainees

41. A representative of the Peking-based Afro-Asian Writers' Bureau commented: "A casual comparison will show that there is a world of difference between Chinese aid to us African people and the so-called aid which the Soviet revisionists publicize. Here is an example of a Soviet expert. Before he leaves home, he insists that his many requests be satisfied: He demands a villa with air conditioning in each room, a fine car, and local servants. This is not all. Even more shameful is the fact that the Soviet experts would not allow any worker of the recipient country to stay around while they were doing designing work and drawings. They were afraid that the local workers would learn their 'professional secrets'." *PR*, 17 March 1967, p. 27. He describes Chinese experts as "brothers" who "painstakingly explained the proposed designs." His comments prove only that China wished to make the contrast in these terms.

would be grateful to China for an opportunity they would otherwise not have had.

> Eighth, the experts dispatched by the Chinese Government to help in construction in the recipient countries will have the same standard of living as the experts of the recipient country. The Chinese experts are not allowed to make any special demands or enjoy any special amenities.[42]

Again, China distinguishes her experts from those of the Soviet Union, Europe, and America. Moreover, she appeals to a sense of community binding Chinese experts and their African counterparts.

The eight points urge African self-reliance, distrust of other donors, and recognition of a community of interest with China. At the same time, China commits herself to nothing beyond her means. The eight points are also an apologia for the small scale of Chinese aid. Much as anti-United States and anti-Soviet appeals helped create an ideological substitute for true defensive capability, these points are a substitute for a more generous aid program.

Motive and Evaluation

In large measure China's economic aims appear to be simply those of normal commerce. Cotton and cobalt might have been bought elsewhere, but it was convenient to buy them from Africans.[43] If China purchased maize from South Africa, as is widely believed, it was done for economic reasons; the political cost was high.[44] There are other reports that China has struck some very hard commercial bargains and interpreted clauses in trade agreements so severely that economic relationships have been endangered.

Some activities are partly political in character. Chinese displays at trade fairs and a vast number of exhibits promote the Chinese presence.

42. [198], pp. 149–150.

43. Allocation of cotton purchases among the U.A.R., Sudan, and Uganda have been quite uneven and do not display a readily discernible political pattern. China may simply have sought the best price.

44. Despite repeated Chinese denials, reports of this trade have been insistent. A Kenyan cabinet minister was convinced that trade continued at least until 1964, and he asserts that the African National Congress was also convinced. [162], 28 October 1965, p. 4. See also [56] and *NYT*, 22 January 1965. It is a curious fact that South Africa's economics minister, queried in parliament on the value of South African exports to China, replied that he "did not consider it to be in the national interest to disclose these figures" and declined to explain why. [154], 8 February 1964, p. 5.

The purchase of Somali incense seems to be a political courtesy. Outright grants are certainly political gestures.

The more militant states and those more openly anti-Western have received the bulk of Chinese aid. The Central African Republic received a small credit, probably a reward for diplomatic recognition. The largest loans have gone to a handful of countries and just three — Algeria, Tanzania, and the United Arab Republic — have received most of the credits. Which states maintain diplomatic relations with China but received neither grants nor credits (other than, say, small sums in disaster relief)? There are, first of all, the northern African states of Morocco and Tunisia, and — until a loan was made in 1970 — Sudan. Tunisia spoke out against some Chinese political positions, and relations were broken in 1967. Burundi and Dahomey had short-lived relations with China and did not receive aid. Equatorial Guinea established relations in late 1970. All others have received some Chinese assistance.

In summary, Chinese aid is given to nonaligned governments whose leaders believe that Chinese aid is desirable. They must also judge the political intrusions which could accompany it — implicit political demands and the improper activities of technicians — to be tolerable or subject to control.

Peking seeks several objectives through economic action. She wants expanded markets and economic advantage. Moreover, aid projects form part of China's political presence and are an opportunity for Chinese personnel to learn more about African societies. Although the relationship between aid and political deference to a donor is rarely made obvious, Chinese leaders know that states which anticipate Chinese aid are more likely to take public stands friendly to China than if they believed aid impossible.

Kenya and Somalia have voiced complaints about Chinese aid. But others have welcomed it and have gone out of their way to stress that China exacted no political quid pro quo. President Alphonse Massamba-Debat of the Congo (B) said in April 1967 that Chinese assistance was "free from any ties" and that cooperation with China was proceeding well.[45] When Nyerere said Chinese aid had fewer strings than that of

45. [179], 10 April 1967. As late as September 1970 China felt obliged to attempt to still reports of Sino-South African trade. "Recently, the press of U.S. imperialism and its accomplices has incessantly manufactured and spread rumours, slanderously accusing the People's Republic of China of trading with the white colonialist authorities in South Africa and Rhodesia," said a spokesman of the Ministry of Foreign Trade; he went on to say that all economic and trade relations had been "long severed." *PR*, 4 September 1970, p. 31.

any other donor, he also asserted that Tanzania was not even obliged to buy Chinese goods in order to receive credits.[46]

It remains to be seen whether Chinese trade with Africa will maintain its present level or increase, and whether promised credits will actually be used. It does appear that China, uncertain how best to proceed, hesitated in early 1965, and then resumed aid activity in 1966. From mid-1965 Peking pressed for a role in the Tan-Zam railway. The maintenance of China's new resolve through a period of diplomatic turmoil and economic dislocation is all the more remarkable. It is evidence of a decision — doubtless made at the highest level of China's leadership — to uphold the initiative in Africa despite the cultural revolution. And it suggests that the diverse groups within China — however varied their reasons, and however severe their differences on other issues — agreed that these commitments were useful to make.

46. *NYT*, 25 May 1967. But it was not claimed that China's aid to Tanzania took the form of convertible currency. On the other hand, China has made selected hard-currency loans and grants to meet particular needs of recipients.

5 The Enemy and Persistent Struggle

The events related so far are episodes of foreign policy. At the outset that policy was based on broad principles, with little precise definition. With time it has coalesced and become more detailed. Today China's African policy includes both broad lines and specific policies guiding Chinese action toward each of many governments and movements. Chapter 8 surveys Chinese policies toward the nation-states of Africa and nationalist movements. Chapter 9 focuses on broad lines of policy and their implications.

To link events to policy — and to prepare to assess that policy — it is useful to get some preliminaries clearly in mind. The assertion that China has a revolutionary intention requires extension and completion: What does it mean, and by what mechanisms is such a revolution to be achieved? The assertion that China must be taken seriously requires consideration of the view that China has failed, or suffered severe setbacks. Do events expose an ill-designed policy, or is the African context inherently so hostile that Chinese policy is tried in vain? What is distinctive about Chinese policy? Has it a dynamic which merits special attention? Why is it insufficient to view Chinese moves as power plays when she is on the initiative, or as coping when she is on the defensive — in the simplistic style typically considered adequate to analyze the foreign policy of other states?

The record of China's supposed setbacks and failures is given in Chapter 6, and China's revolutionary model is presented in Chapter 7. The distinctiveness of Chinese policy is the subject of this chapter.

The argument of these three chapters is that Chinese policy turns on an irrefutable view of the world, perpetuated by concepts of will and action which form a distinctive circular reinforcing system; that setbacks are rationalized by invoking this circular mechanism; and that the institutional structures of the Chinese revolutionary model, when employed in accordance with a further set of strategic requirements that are also sensitive to reinforcement processes, form an action system with unique power.

This brief introduction to themes in Chinese policy does not attempt a thorough statement of the relationship between ideology and foreign policy, or of organizational doctrine and action abroad. A few key features are isolated and identified. Their relation to ideology and internal organization is rich and profound, but beyond the scope of this study.

Identifying the Enemy

Mao Tse-tung holds that "there are many contradictions in the process of development of a complex thing, and one of them is necessarily the principal contradiction whose existence and development determine or influence the existence and development of the other contradictions."[1]

This must be as true of the international situation as it is of the domestic situation or the instance of imperialist oppression of semi-colonies which Mao cites. Mao further insists that one or another side of the contradiction may be stronger at any given time: it may form the "principal aspect of a contradiction." Imperialism was stronger than the Chinese people in 1937, but the Chinese people would become the principal aspect of the contradiction, and imperialism would be overthrown.[2]

> The study of the various states of unevenness in contradictions, of the principal and non-principal contradictions and of the principal and the non-principal aspects of a contradiction constitutes an essential method by which a revolutionary political party correctly determines its strategic and tactical policies both in political and in military affairs. All Communists must give it attention.[3]

This is the method which, some believe, guides CCP decision making, but China's public statements do not contain explicit justifications for judging that a contradiction exists, that one among several is the principal contradiction, or that one aspect of a contradiction dominates the other.

No complex decipherment is required to discern whom China considers to be her enemies. As amply illustrated, Chinese statements label enemies repeatedly, and they sometimes identify an enemy as the "main enemy." But if two forces stand in contradiction, there must be struggle

1. [224], vol. 1, p. 331.
2. *Ibid.*, p. 334.
3. *Ibid.*, p. 337.

between them; the form of struggle must be open to identification. Specifying an enemy requires the identification of an antagonistic relationship. Once such a relationship is noted, the claim will be politically effective only if events are seen to demonstrate its existence. The CCP's first problem is to find the chief contradiction; its second is to persuade potential political effectives that the contradiction—however it is described—exists and is decisive.

The task consists of three parts. The contradiction must be shown to exist. Second, it is alleged to be central: the contradiction (in Situation A) is related to other contradictions (in Situations B, C, and so on) in source and in consequences; its origins are akin to the origins of all that is oppressive and unjust; and a favorable outcome will have desirable repercussions elsewhere. Third, seeming counterevidence and contrary interpretations must be blunted—at least to a degree. That degree is determined by the extent to which doubts in the minds of potential political effectives can be accepted without too severe a risk to the sought-for outcome.

How does China approach these tasks in didactic statements, in the Chinese material directed to an African audience? An excellent example—one which illustrates the themes which China put forth in the late 1950s and early 1960s, and which remains the standard coin in 1970—is Li Hsien-nien's speech to visitors from Congo (B):

> At present, the African people's struggle against US-led imperialism, colonialism and neo-colonialism is developing in depth and the flames of armed struggle keep on spreading. From their practice in struggle, the broad masses of the African people have come ever more clearly to see through the US imperialist ambitious design of trying to replace old colonialism and realize that US imperialism is the most dangerous enemy of the African people. Dauntless in the face of US imperialism, the African people are liquidating its military bases and smashing its subversive activities, winning a series of brilliant victories. We believe that the African peoples, further strengthening their unity and persevering in protracted struggle, will certainly drive US imperialism and colonialism and neocolonialism out of the African continent and the African peoples will surely win complete victory in national liberation![4]

The "most dangerous enemy" is U.S. imperialism. How is the United States in confrontation with the people of Africa? Through relationships

4. *PR*, 24 July 1970, p. 6.

that are categorized as imperialism, colonialism, and neocolonialism. In a sense, colonialism and neocolonialism are forms of imperialism. Since most Africans acquired political independence between 1956 and 1963, the charges of U.S. imperialism on that continent must rest heavily on the concept of neocolonialism. Peking must demonstrate the focal position of neocolonialism; she must also have a way to answer those who are unpersuaded, who object to the neocolonialism doctrine on whatever grounds.

The doctrine of neocolonialism is not merely one of several which China proclaims; it is an essential assertion, without which China's hopes and the acceptance given to Chinese views cannot be properly understood.

The doctrine of neocolonialism holds that anything less than full economic autonomy implies subordination to the illegitimate power of foreign economic interests. It has enjoyed wide acceptance, as the following resolution of the Second Conference of Independent African States, Addis Ababa, 15–24 June 1960, testifies:

> ERADICATION OF COLONIAL RULE FROM AFRICA: MEANS TO PREVENT NEW FORMS OF COLONIALISM IN AFRICA
>
> New forms of colonialism could be introduced into [the emerging nations of Africa] under the guise of economic, financial and technical assistance. . . . The Independent African States [should] be wary of colonial penetration through economic means and . . . institute effective control over the working machineries of foreign companies operating in their territories.[5]

The issue is to distinguish proper from improper consequences for the domestic economy. Are prices fair? Are investments mutually beneficial, and are the benefits fairly shared? Is the weaker partner under duress? If the country's resources are being sold, are the terms fair to the future? And are political strings attached? The neocolonial doctrine is important and relevant because almost all normal economic relations between strong and weak partners can be viewed as relations forced upon the weaker on terms not freely chosen. Doubtless some economic relations *are* exploitative in this sense. Though corporations are free to compete, exploit, and expand, their struggle for profit is considered to be an aim of national policy. Herein lies the key to the power of this doctrine: *in some instances* it is clearly and unmistakably correct.

Chinese sensitivity to what now is called neocolonialism was evident

5. [76], pp. 154–155.

as early as 1953, when Chou En-lai charged that "under the pretence of 'aid' [the United States government] is actually trying to control and seize all the British and French colonies in Asia and Africa."[6] By the end of 1955 Chinese commentators had asserted frequently that the United States sought to replace onetime colonial rulers.[7] The phrase "neocolonialism" itself may have been coined by Nikita Khrushchev late in 1955, when he cautioned new nations to be wary of efforts by imperialist states to gain and exercise influence.[8] China employed the term soon thereafter.

As first analyzed by Peking, neocolonialism would spare the new colonial powers from frequent resort to armed force. Using economic aid programs and alliances, such as SEATO, the new colonialists would act with more delicacy and subtlety than their forerunners. But this would be to no avail, the Chinese commentator insisted. As Khrushchev said, "the capitalists will not do anything for nothing; without profit capital does not exist." Therefore the shift from old to new colonialism, which would still be obliged to extract profits, would not slow the movement against colonialism.[9] The contest was cast in the language of a titanic struggle:

> The colonial powers are not resigned to their defeat. They are making desperate efforts to maintain what remains of their colonies. They are also trying to reimpose their dark rule on the countries which have taken the road of independent progress. . . .
>
> But the desperate efforts of the colonial powers cannot avert [the end] of the colonial system which is on the verge of collapse. The use of violence, suppression and other old forms of colonial enslavement has failed to intimidate the people in the oppressed nations who are awakened and struggling for independence. Instead, it has aroused greater indignation in the people of those nations who are rising more resolutely and bravely to fight for their national independence and freedom.
>
> The resort to the new form of colonialism of giving "aid" to backward countries is also doomed to failure.[10]

A second strength of the doctrine is its seeming explanatory power. Highly convincing cases of exploitation aside, many others can persua-

6. NCNA, 5 February 1953.

7. NCNA, 11 April 1955. This dispatch details U.S. involvement in Africa, mentioning military bases, economic agreements, and capital investment.

8. Khrushchev's speech of 29 December 1955 noted U.S. Senator Estes Kefauver's disparagement of "old colonialism" and asked if Kefauver meant to praise *new* colonialism. He was met by "stormy, prolonged applause." [159], vol. 7, no. 52, p. 16.

9. [228], 20 January 1956.

10. *SCMP*, no. 1235, p. 27 (*JMJP*, 21 February 1956).

sively be labeled "neocolonialist." United States opposition to the Anglo-French-Israeli attack on Egypt was portrayed by China as proof that the United States intended to replace the older colonialists in the Middle East. Africans were warned that the ouster of Lumumba and creation of a "puppet" regime demonstrated neocolonialism at work. *JMJP* editorialized that "if, today, US imperialism uses this dirty and foul tactic against the lawful government of the independent Congo, tomorrow it may also use it against other independent countries of Africa."[11]

Repeatedly Peking warned that neocolonialism would be a live force. When Ghana won independence, China cautioned that "the struggle of the Ghana people was not yet ended" because British influence persisted and the United States was actively expanding its influence in Africa.[12] Celebrating anticolonialism day in 1958, Peking stressed with special emphasis America's intention to replace the old colonialists.[13] At the founding of the China-Africa People's Friendship Association in 1960 Kuo Mo-jo charged that "US imperialism—the new colonialism—is actively making inroads upon the African continent."[14] Similar warnings were voiced throughout the 1960s. Blanket warning increased the availability of neocolonialism as a doctrine, as an explanation to which those seeking some understanding of the web of economic relations might turn. China was not alone in maintaining the doctrine: the governing Communist parties declared in November 1957 that "the imperialist circles of the United States," as part of an effort to bring most of the world under their sway, were "trying to enmesh the liberated peoples in new forms of colonialism."[15] More recent discussions by pro-Moscow groups continue to mention neocolonialism, in substance and by name, though not with the insistent and repetitious rhythm which characterizes Chinese statements.[16]

Li Hsien-nien's references to American military bases and subversive activities were intended to persuade his audience that Washington harbored imperialist or neocolonialist designs. The Libyan revolutionary government, only a few months before Li Hsien-nien spoke to the guests from Congo (B) in 1970, endorsed the view that a United States air base was undesirable and forced Washington to abandon it. As Li spoke, a treason trial was under way in Tanzania; the state's star witness had implicated

11. *SCMP*, no. 2413, p. 22 (*JMJP*, 3 January 1961).
12. *SCMP*, no. 1486, p. 17 (*JMJP*, 6 March 1957).
13. *SCMP*, no. 1760, p. 46 (*JMJP* editorial, 24 April 1958).
14. *SCMP*, no. 2247, p. 28 (NCNA, 18 April 1960).
15. "The 1957 Moscow Declaration," in [55], pp. 46–56.
16. For example, [148], no. 39, fourth quarter, 1969, pp. 7, 10.

a United States government official in a plot to bring about the overthrow of Nyerere.[17] Existence of military bases, the alleged subversion, and other demonstrable fragments contribute to the conviction that neocolonialism is being practiced.

Li's assertion that United States imperialism is the "most dangerous enemy" is a claim on every African's attention. Following the quoted passage Li states, "Your struggle in Africa is not isolated," and then he quotes from Mao Tse-tung, "A new upsurge in the struggle against US imperialism is now emerging throughout the world."[18] Struggles in Palestine, Indochina, and Africa are described as one common effort. China and the Congo (B) are also engaged in a "common struggle."

To meet objections, to preserve the convincing character of her argument, Peking must consider apparent counterevidence. She dismisses United States troop withdrawals from Vietnam as "camouflage."

> To put it bluntly, the so-called "political solution" in the Middle East and the so-called "peaceful settlement" in Indo-China put forward by US imperialism and its accomplice are refurbished versions of the Munich policy of the thirties, a plot aimed at stamping out the flames of the armed struggles of the Palestinian and other Arab peoples and the three Indo-Chinese peoples against US imperialism and at realizing the division of the world by the "super" powers at the expense of small nations. . . .
>
> No matter what tricks US imperialism and its accomplice may resort to, they cannot deceive the daily awakening peoples of the world, nor can they save themselves from their doomed defeat in the Middle East, Indo-China and other parts of the world.[19]

Thus, America should not be judged by her claims of peaceful intention. The United States is still striving for neocolonialist control.

In this single speech Li Hsien-nien uses three arguments which establish the enemy as neocolonialist: citation of facts, the claim that opposition to the enemy in Africa is part of a worldwide struggle, and the refutation of incompatible reports. Li even implies, by referring to the superpowers as he does, that Moscow and Washington are in collusion. The struggle against neocolonialism and revisionism is a single struggle.

17. Potlako Leballo, head of the Pan-Africanist Congress, a Chinese-supported group, said the supposed leader of the plot had been in repeated contact with a U.S. Information Service officer in London. *NYT*, 19 July 1970.

18. *PR*, 24 July 1970, p. 6.

19. *Ibid.*

As long as the United States strives to maintain or improve her freedom of choice in the world, China will be able to cite her actions as proof that Washington seeks neocolonial control. Facts that seem to be to the contrary can be brushed aside as trickery, camouflage, and fraud. This is the sense in which China's identification of the enemy — United States imperialism, plus a collusive Soviet partner and numerous puppet players — is irrefutable.

Alone, this concept of an enemy against whom struggle must be waged would be strong political doctrine. But China goes further, and she calls for struggle of a certain *quality*, struggle in conformance with selected principles of action. Several of the most important of these are introduced in the following sections.

Preconditions for Ultimate Victory

The African people "will surely win complete victory," Li Hsien-nien declared.[20] The theme has been stated again and again. Liu Shao-ch'i told a Moscow audience in 1952:

> Where the teachings of Marx, Engels, Lenin and Stalin are correctly applied on the basis of concrete conditions in the given country, where the experience acquired by the Communist Party of the Soviet Union in revolution and construction is correctly drawn upon, victory is always ensured.[21]

After 1958 Peking's spokesmen said repeatedly that right analysis, right action, confidence, and will would guarantee Africa's victory against imperialism. "We can eliminate all the misfortune caused by colonialism," one declared, "provided we have no unrealistic ideas about imperialism and constantly strengthen our solidarity and support for each other."[22] A further step to guarantee success, according to an assessment of national liberation in *Hung-ch'i* [Red Flag], is to build an internal united front to struggle alongside all forces opposing imperialism.[23]

A companion article developed the two central themes of handling disappointments and making correct analyses. A weak force may suffer setbacks, but revolutionary dialectics assure ultimate victory.

20. *Ibid.* Sometimes the "victory" to which Chinese commentators refer is an explicit victory in anticolonial revolution, but at other times the comment omits any distinction between anticolonial national revolution and internal social revolution.

21. NCNA, no. 1137, 11 October 1952.

22. *SCMP*, no. 1760, p. 50 (24 April 1958).

23. *SCMP*, no. 1827, pp. 1 ff. ([209], 1 August 1958). The problem of the united front is considered more fully in Chapter 7.

> Some decades ago there existed in Russia and China only a few Marxist groups formed by a few dozen people. They weathered temporary failures and waged fresh struggles; finally they defeated all the outwardly strong reactionaries and became the parties in power in these two great countries. This is revolutionary dialectics.[24]

Only a few men are required to form the nucleus of a revolutionary group. If they comprehend that failure is temporary, they will take heart and struggle again. By overcoming the *subjective* obstacles to persistence, a determined revolutionary force can be built. Ultimately it will succeed.

However, the revolutionary force is also obliged to assess the objective situation correctly. A correct assessment, the commentator said, will show that final victory is within reach:

> Ten years ago, Comrade Mao Tse-tung pointed out: "To underestimate the significance of the victory of the Second World War will be a great mistake." He also said: "To overestimate the strength of our enemies and underestimate the revolutionary forces will be a great mistake." This equally applies to the appraisal of forces at this new historical turning-point today. The situation in which the East Wind prevails over the West Wind has paved the way for the final victory of the struggle of the people the world over. No force can turn back the fast-moving wheel of history. The new-born forces will certainly defeat the forces of decay. The speed of advance of the forces of peace, democracy and socialism will certainly surpass the people's expectations.[25]

His optimism mirrors its time: the weeks after the commune movement was launched, the height of the Taiwan Straits crisis of 1958. If this was a way of saying to Moscow that Soviet support could achieve a decisive victory for China and the Soviet Union together, it was also the assumption behind Peking's later charges that Moscow had turned down ready opportunities. Moscow failed to discern the principal aspect of the contradiction between imperialism and socialism. Soviet unreadiness to act with the vigor China believed desirable revealed revisionism at work. Peking believed victory was attainable with the right analysis, and she also believed that the CCP knew which analysis was correct.

Avoiding "unrealistic views of imperialism" and acknowledging that the world balance of power favors victory, strengthening international solidarity, uniting the people, and waging persistent struggle: together,

24. *SCMP*, no. 1837, p. 42, ([209], 16 August 1958).
25. *Ibid.*

these steps would assure victory. This guarantee is a ritual component of Chinese exhortations in Africa.[26]

The requirement to wage persistent struggle implies further components of the formula for victory: will, struggle itself, continuing recruitment, and a sense of strategic time.

Will

Belief in victory is a doctrine of will. It is the insistence that, in the long run, the just cause will triumph. If the revolutionary purpose is to be sustained against hardships, setbacks, and discouragement, the revolutionaries must sustain their own morale. The belief that one's sacrifices will not be made in vain contributes importantly to morale. The task of political officers is to help the guerrilla army maintain its integrity as a fighting force, not merely the achievement of ideological goals.

A second doctrine of will is the "man over weapons" doctrine. Mao Tse-tung holds that man, rather than technology, is decisive in a struggle. Guerrillas operating against the Portuguese in Mozambique, for example, cannot hope to match the airpower or firepower available to Portuguese troops. If they accept this doctrine, they could confront the Portuguese with less awe of their superiority.

The power and credibility of this doctrine are rooted in reality, and it is a correct observation about military action. If a government's men

26. A few examples will illustrate the emphasis given these themes: *SCMP*, no. 1295, p. 45 (on Africa Freedom Day in 1959): "As long as the people of all African countries strengthen their unity and persist in their struggle, no amount of difficulties can block the African people's road to victory." *SCMP*, no. 2405, p. 26 (*JMJP*, 20 December 1960): "The Chinese people firmly believe that in the international situation in which the East Wind prevails over the West Wind, it is certain that colonialism will be finally and completely abolished by relying on the national liberation struggle of the peoples now going on in Asia, Africa, and Latin America and by relying on the great unity of the peoples of the socialist countries, the revolutionary masses of the people of the capitalist countries and all oppressed nations. The complete collapse of colonialism is inevitable." *SCMP*, no. 2452, p. 22 (3 March 1961): Liu Shao-ch'i cabled Gizenga's Stanleyville government that the Congolese people "united as one and persisting in struggle, will eventually defeat the plot of imperialism." *SCMP*, no. 2480, p. 26 (*JMJP*, 15 April 1961, on Africa Freedom Day): "The African people . . . still have to wage a persistent and indomitable fight. . . . A broad united front is a reliable guarantee for the African people to win victory in their struggle against new and old colonialism." *SCMP*, no. 2722, p. 28 (14 April 1962): The African people would win "if they united closely and persisted in the struggle with high vigilance." *PR*, 24 August 1962, quotes Ch'en I at a Peking reception: "Experience has shown," he said, commenting on restored unity among independent Algeria's new leaders, "that a people united are invincible in their anti-imperialist struggle."

are unreliable and the government cannot count on help from those whom it governs, technological advantage may not spare it from military and political defeat. In actual cases, government troops and bureaucrats often perform adequately and some members of the populace do render aid. In Portuguese Guinea the guerrillas' extensive control appears to have reached a limit; some members of the population in areas the guerrillas do not control alert the authorities to attempted incursions, which are efficiently countered. But in China the revolutionaries were able to overcome the government advantage in guns and equipment.

A third doctrine of will anticipates and softens failure. Defeat would challenge the CCP's claim to correct analysis, if defeats were not anticipated as a normal and inevitable contingency of struggle. Mao Tse-tung wrote in 1947:

> We know with a sober mind that there will still be various obstacles and difficulties in our path of progress and we should be prepared to cope with maximum resistance and struggle by all enemies at home and abroad.

His warning was repeated in a review of the international situation in 1960.[27]

China's unhappy experience in the Congo in 1961 not only brought about renewed charges of neocolonialism, but it also forced Peking to make additional explanations and rationalizations of failure. The "situation" — a reminder of objective circumstance which the actor is given and cannot control — was "difficult and complicated."[28] But even failure can be put to good advantage — as a source of understanding:

> It is of course impossible for the national liberation movement in Africa to be all plain sailing. The Congolese national liberation movement has suffered a setback as a result of US imperialist intervention under the UN flag. . . . But the flames of the Congolese revolution can in no way be put out; the Congolese nationalists have learnt bitter lessons from the setback at the cost of bloodshed and are rallying their forces to wage a new struggle.[29]

If anything, failure requires an added measure of will. In an unfavorable situation the object is "to continue struggling" and turn "the un-

27. *SCMP*, no. 2171, p. 3 ([209], 11 January 1960), quoting "The Present Situation and Our Tasks."
28. *SCMP*, no. 2663, p. 23 (16 January 1962).
29. *SCMP*, no. 2873, p. 21 (*JMJP*, 1 December 1962).

favorable into the favorable"; it is even more important to adhere to the "general strategic policy for defeating the enemy."[30] That policy, in turn, rests on respecting the enemy tactically but despising him strategically.

> If we do not scorn the enemy strategically, we will not only lose our revolutionary determination under unfavorable conditions, but will not be able to seize victory under favorable conditions due to the loss of our revolutionary determination, thus damaging the revolutionary cause.

How is the breakdown of will to be withstood? Not by reckless and haphazard battle, which could also damage the revolution, but by three political steps. The people's "revolutionary confidence and determination" is to be heightened (although the precise methods are not specified); rightist influence on the people is to be eliminated; and the people are to be guided toward an understanding of the essence of imperialism and reaction.[31]

In summary, in the Maoist view, what a man believes he can do has a decisive effect on what he actually achieves. If he believes that he will win, that he will win despite technological disadvantage, and that he will win despite today's losses, then his chances of winning are improved. These are doctrines of will: in helping to maintain struggle once begun, they reinforce struggle itself.

Struggle

Two forms of struggle are implied in China's calls to wage "protracted struggle." One form is political struggle to expose imperialist and neocolonialist designs and block them by persuasion and the use of institutional power. The second form is armed struggle, the conduct of revolutionary guerrilla war. Both forms can be enlisted in the assault against neocolonialism. Conventional politics can be practiced by governing nationalists with whom China cooperates. Armed struggle can be waged against colonial authorities and against governing nationalists with whom China does not cooperate. In the first instance, Chinese calls for protracted struggle are in the nature of slogans for political action, interesting but not commanding special power. Armed struggle, however, marks a

30. *PR*, 11 January 1963, pp. 10–15 ([209], 5 January 1963). In addition to the rather familiar theme that "the road of revolution is not without its twists and turns and is sometimes beset with difficulties and setbacks when certain detours and temporary retreats are necessary," the author makes the even stronger assertion that "victory is impossible without paying a considerable price."

31. *Ibid.*

dividing line; the radical political party which takes "the road of armed struggle" draws special Chinese praise. That act means for China, as no other act or words mean, that the party is a serious revolutionary group.

It is in the context of armed guerrilla warfare, therefore, that struggle most clearly complements the Maoist emphasis on will. Struggle toughens revolutionaries; it is a source of political lessons and fighting skills. Chinese comment even suggests that a proper revolution is impossible without struggle.

Consider one theme in Mao Tse-tung's military writings: the successful commander, Mao writes, adapts prior experience to the new concrete circumstances he must meet.[32] He does not imagine that local commanders will always succeed — elsewhere Mao said that he would be pleased to be correct 70 percent of the time and wrong but 30 percent — but he insists that failures be studied for the lessons they yield. He sketches the career of a hypothetical local commander who rises from simple soldier to a high post by successively adapting the lessons of past Communist struggles and his personal experience to increasingly complex arenas of battle. The implication is clear: without the experience of armed struggle, he could not have mastered the arts needed by a commander. Repeated many times, this process leads by Darwinian selection to the creation of a tough and able leadership at all levels of command.

The CCP also believes that struggle forces imperialism to expose itself. Crude violence and repression undertaken in the name of the international status quo actually legitimize revolution, for armed struggle rips away the cloak of gentility. Those people who had earlier been unwilling to take hazardous action decide that revolution is the only road, that one must "oppose counterrevolutionary violence with revolutionary violence."

Neither of these Maoist propositions (that struggle teaches fighting skills and sharpens political consciousness) can be disproved. The first is intuitively convincing, and the second is too complex for intuitive analysis. Prolonged struggle could, just as easily, demonstrate its own futility. For those who remain within a movement committed to armed struggle, however, these two propositions contribute to the momentum of revolutionary war. Certainly revolution provokes suppression, which drives guerrillas outside normal society, bans them, and forces them to sustain their armed challenge. Maoist requirements militate against a gradual abandonment of struggle, which might enable individual guerrillas to return to their homes. Struggle guarantees the solidarity of the guerrilla band.

32. For example, [223], p. 78, or [224], vol. 1, p. 182.

Recruitment

To sustain itself against hardship and defeat, a guerrilla organization must maintain its strength and win new recruits. Maoist canon implies that there is a place for any sincere recruit. An a priori ideological test is not demanded, since the most unlikely recruit may, through conversion, reject his past and adhere to the united front of the moment.[33]

Within a guerrilla group, the object is to retain those who are already committed. Ideological ignorance and error, even with a strict Maoist political organization, can be dealt with by steps short of expulsion: Mao uses the analogy of a doctor treating a patient.[34] The injunction to learn from failure assumes that men who fail are to be given another chance. Incompetence will not be tolerated forever, but the pragmatic, inventive, reflective, and decisive leader — precisely the kind of man on whom a guerrilla effort must depend — is retained even though he commits some errors due to inexperience or miscalculation.

Guerrilla tactics must conserve manpower. The enemy is engaged, but the safety of the main force is paramount. Men are committed to action only in clearly favorable circumstances. The guerrilla force does not gamble on one grand victory; it guards itself to fight another day. Guerrilla war assumes that, if the present encounter is unfavorable, there will be better opportunities in days ahead. The issue is not only whether the revolutionaries can outwit their foe, it is also whether they can outwait him.

Time

In China and abroad, the CCP assumes that revolution is a long affair. Quick success is not promised. Explaining the Chinese revolution, Peking often mentions that twenty-eight years passed from the CCP's formation in 1921 to seizure of state power in 1949. Except for some flashes of optimism in 1958, the CCP has always referred to many decades — at the least — being required to build a true Communist society. The need for patience and persistence is central to the Maoist revolutionary plan.

The future is almost sure to bring forth an objective reality more conducive to revolution than the present. If the revolutionaries can keep their sense of goals, if they can maintain their organizational integrity and will to act, they will be prepared to seize the opportunity. Time is on their side. The revolutionaries expand their own force and strike at the enemy

33. Witness the early life of Chu Teh, as told by Edgar Snow in [118], pp. 379–391.
34. See Mao Tse-tung, "Correcting Unorthodox Tendencies in Learning, the Party, and Literature and Art," in [18], p. 392.

when they can, but governmental erosion sets the stage for the seizure of state power. The capacity of the existing state may be undercut from within (economic breakdown, political ineffectiveness, social disarray), from abroad (invasion), or by some combination of these elements aggravated by the obligation to suppress the armed revolutionaries. Chinese guerrilla war embodies this sense of time.

In 1938 Mao defined "strategic protractedness" as the interim goal for China's anti-Japanese forces. That meant "gaining time to increase our capacity to resist while hastening or awaiting changes in the international situation and the internal collapse of the enemy."[35] Mao proposed to pursue this goal by "many campaigns and battles of quick decision," a series of encounters, each of which was a swift strike followed by rapid relocation and preparation for another fast and mobile assault. Simultaneously, the army pursued political action among the people; this could be put to good military use in the future. Ultimately Japanese power in China ended because of the American onslaught against the home islands. The consequent changes in China created a new, decisive, but not uncomplicated, opportunity for the CCP.

Reinforcement of Will and Action

In the Maoist view, the party is an organizational device to sustain purpose over time. Struggle is normal and universal. Struggle is a long-term preoccupation and the essence of politics. Persistent struggle guarantees victory; although the enemy will never give up willingly, the process of struggle itself will force him to more desperate acts, which in turn will win men and women to the revolution. In the end the enemy will be overcome.

The Chinese characterization of the neocolonialist enemy, according to the discussion above, is irrefutable. Armed struggle, once undertaken, provokes the local government and outside powers to take practical measures in response. Those measures are ambiguous; they usually have unwanted consequences; typically some can be interpreted to show that an outside power, be it the United States, France, or Britain, hopes to maintain some measure of permanent control.

Once a group of men begin an armed struggle, it is difficult to draw back. The enemy, perceived to be hostile, plays its part. If it is effective, the guerrillas will suffer defeats. Peking blames these setbacks on enemy machinations and on the immaturity of the political situation, but she insists that both can be overcome. The spectacle of the struggle under way,

35. [223], p. 156.

the CCP claims, will shift the balance of forces, draw the people away from the existing government into active support of the revolution. Having anticipated defeat, and being firmly persuaded that victory will be theirs, the guerrillas will struggle on and adapt universal notions of guerrilla warfare to the conditions of the region in which they are fighting. They will inflict many small defeats on the enemy. Because their cause is that of the people, even the use of guerrilla techniques by the antiguerrilla forces cannot defeat them. Man will triumph over weapons. When circumstances combine to shift the principal aspect of the contradiction between the revolutionaries and the suppressing forces, the revolution will be victorious.

In practice, of course, revolutionaries do not always succeed. Will may lessen, guerrillas may come to doubt the revolutionary purpose, villagers may perceive the guerrillas as thugs or bandits, the government may be discriminating and effective in its use of force: as a result the armed enterprise could dwindle and disappear. Nonetheless, the CCP formula for revolution, a complex of ideological, organizational, psychological, and strategic doctrine, *if fully implemented* is a coherent and practical body of belief likely to serve an armed band far better than slogans and mere enthusiasm. Because it touches on most of the important strengths and weaknesses of a guerrilla initiative, it is well-suited to its purpose. Not every facet of the formula has been considered here. The role of army, party, and united front is discussed in Chapter 7; other considerations, especially those of military strategy, development of civil-military base areas, and the broader context of ideology, are beyond the scope of this study. The doctrines described here are central notions sufficient to show that maintenance of revolutionary momentum can be rationalized despite a hostile reality, small numbers, and repeated defeats.

Maintaining revolutionary momentum is the key to the Maoist system of reinforcing will and action. A convincing enemy, who will not go away, is the first and essential requirement. The catalyst is the inauguration of armed struggle. Once warfare has begun, belief in ultimate victory emboldens the revolutionaries to strike again and again. The lessons of armed struggle reassure them that victory will and must be theirs, that nothing less is tolerable. The Chinese revolution itself clinches the argument for those who would doubt.

6 Disappointments and Setbacks

No simple judgment is possible of the adequacy or inadequacy, the success or failure, of Chinese policy. Too many incomparables must be weighed. Moreover, the short term cannot be calculated against the long term. Confronted by the twin problems of scope and time, which bedevil all systematic study of political action, commentators employ makeshift devices to pass from the descriptive to the judgmental mode. Their devices, in turn, structure the language of future political commentary and analysis.

The consequences for understanding Chinese policy are especially acute, because the issues which move China to political action (not to mention Peking's political style) are often outside the personal experience of the audience. Typically, the observer has no personal or independent resources with which to challenge the designation of policies as successful or unsuccessful. He may, however, insist that judgments rest on some explicit evidence and argument, and that they not exceed the limits of acknowledged assumptions concerning scope and time.

Among all the stories that are told, those which best summarize impressions of the observer (using an irrefutable event to convey his judgment of a complex or contradictory situation) are cited and recited. The need for a clear point of reference, a salient act, is very strong. Such an act, revealing and consequential, summarizes the past and promises to affect the future. In searching for keys to social intricacy, students and statesmen grasp what they consider concise, meaningful, strategically decisive, and convincing. The episodes considered in this chapter are cited to show Chinese inadequacy and failure. The problem is to determine in what sense, and to what extent, that showing is justified.

In several of these cases, suspension or rupture of diplomatic relations is the key act. In some instances, China's foothold was so tenuous that local political changes destroyed it overnight. But the cases belie the argument that those severing relations did so as a last resort because of grievous interference, or to attain goals in foreign relations. Rather, the African governments broke relations to meet domestic requirements unique in each situation, and for which China had only peripheral relevance. It is hard to imagine that Chinese diplomats would have acted differently than they did, even if they had known they could avoid expulsion by doing so, except in the cases of Tunisia and Ghana, which Peking appears to have deliberately provoked.

Diplomatic relations, present or absent, are a clear index in the eyes of most commentators. To sever existing relations is a highly-charged and symbolic act. Since most states do not effect a diplomatic rupture without intending to show profound disapproval of the other country, the breaks between China and African countries seem to imply that China committed grave and improper deeds, forcing African retaliation. A close examination of the cases, however, shows that the implication is not always well founded.

Expulsion of individual diplomats and correspondents is also an extreme act. The likelihood that improper conduct occurred is high, but the problem is to compare the expulsion, on the one hand, with the continuance of diplomatic relations despite the impropriety, on the other.

Peking's inability to achieve what she wanted in the second Asian-African Conference and in the Afro-Asian People's Solidarity Organization can be documented. The outcome was unfavorable to the policies Peking favored, and the organizational maneuvers she had undertaken. It is important to weigh the gravity and extent of Peking's disappointment.

Commentators tend to consider involvement of greater numbers of personnel (diplomats, technicians), access to regions (diplomatic relations, joint shipping lines), commercial interdependence (trade), identity or commonality of views (Mali's refusal to sign the 1963 nuclear test ban treaty), the capacity to conceive and consummate announced plans (conferences, technical aid projects), and the entry of friends and clients to posts of authority (Abdul Rahman Mohammed Babu) as indices of success. Indices of failure take the opposite: reduced personnel, severed relations, falling trade, disagreement, inability to accomplish significant plans, and a dearth of friends and clients in authoritative positions. In a typical situation, however, one index may suggest success (the Tan-Zam railway) while another may indicate failure (rupture of diplomatic relations). There can be demonstrable agreement and demonstrable disagreement. No useful purpose is served, in this author's judgment, by venturing that Chinese influence in Africa is greater at one time than another. On the other hand, it can be useful to record that China's opportunity to act has increased or decreased at a particular place and time, to endeavor to understand why this is so, to consider the likelihood that similar changes will occur elsewhere at other times, and to speculate whether the change will have secondary effects on China's *future opportunity* to act (in creating further opportunities or damping opportunities which already exist).

Political commentary on China's African policy during the late 1960s assumed that a simple "failure" of policy was possible.[1] Attuned to the evident dissimilarities between Chinese views and those of African governments and movements, their impressions confirmed by the decline of China's diplomatic relations, some commentators judged events against Peking's maximum hope and pronounced a failure. The episodes considered in this chapter contain much evidence that China faced obstacles and did not overcome them. Deep reservoirs of suspicion on the part of some African governments are revealed. Nonetheless, some episodes frequently cited to illustrate failure seem, on close examination, to yield no clear lesson, but rather to be ambiguous.

Burundi

Diplomatic relations, established on 23 December 1963, were "temporarily suspended" on 29 January 1965 by Mwami (King) Mwambutsa.[2] No specific public charges were made against China at the time. However, the move was made two weeks after the assassination of Premier Pierre Ngendandumwe, which precipitated a crisis in relations among the Mwami, Tutsi "extremists," and moderate Hutu politicians. Speculation that China might have been involved in the killing of Ngendandumwe, who was counted among the Hutu moderates, was quashed by the acting premier named in his stead.[3] Nonetheless, those jailed in the wake of the assassination included a former premier, Albin Nyamoya, who was associated with Tutsi elements which had developed contacts with China.[4]

In August 1965 a Taiwanese official visited Burundi, and the Mwami was later said to have agreed to establish closer relations.[5] But the Mwami's

1. One scholarly essay was frankly titled "China's Failure in Africa." [143]. The theme was recurrent in the American press.

2. *PR*, 5 February 1965, p. 10. For another overview of internal Burundian politics, see [147], November 1970, pp. 18–20.

3. The acting premier, Pie Masumbuko, blamed "Watusi extremists" for the killing. "Some people are saying Ngendandumwe was killed by the Americans," Masumbuko said, "some say he was killed by the Chinese. I say both are false." *NYT*, 22 January 1965.

4. *NYT*, 26 March 1965. Nyamoya's government had been turned out by the Mwami, who invited Ngendandumwe to form a new government, shortly before the assassination. [183], 6 February 1966.

5. [147], October 1965, p. 40.

position became less tenable. On 19 October 1965 a group of Hutu officers in the gendarmerie attacked the royal palace; although the Mwami escaped, his premier was badly wounded.[6] The attempted coup gave an excuse for a Tutsi group to seize and execute virtually all of the Bahutu political leaders in Burundi.[7] However, this action did not propel the Tutsis into unqualified power. The premier retained his post while recuperating in exile, and an uneasy calm enveloped Burundi political life. The United States ambassador was expelled on suspicion of being in contact with conspirators, but even this was not a signal of "extremist" control. The foreign minister, Marc Manirakiza, wished to incorporate the Hutus into a viable political framework under the Mwami's authority.[8] When asked whether the United States ambassador's forced departure might have significance for a resumption of relations with China, Manirakiza replied only that the matter was not one to be decided at present.[9]

In July 1966 the Mwami's son, Prince Charles Ndinzeye, deposed his father and Tutsis came to power. On 30 August the foreign minister[10] announced in Kinshasa that Burundi would resume diplomatic relations with Peking. Burundi appears to have been on the verge of reversing the Mwami's decision to suspend relations, but resumption did not occur. On 28 November 1966 Premier Michel Micombero seized power and formed a national revolutionary council drawn from the military. The Mwami's reign and the unstable tripartite politics mentioned above ended. The governing Tutsis no longer needed power to bargain against the Mwami. Burundi's new government sought to settle major differences with the Congo (K) and Rwanda, whose leaders viewed the return of Chinese embassy personnel with alarm.[11] Diplomatic relations had not been resumed as of August 1970.

It was important to China that she support Rwandan refugees and Congolese revolutionaries from Burundi; moreover, before Nyamoya's

6. [183], 6 February 1966.

7. *NYT*, 10 March 1966. Those executed numbered at least eighty-six, including the presidents and vice-presidents of both houses of parliament. In a sense, this was reprisal for Hutu success in the relatively free elections conducted earlier in 1965.

8. [183], 6 February 1966.

9. [149], no. 963, 20–26 January 1966, p. 7.

10. Pie Masambuko, who made the announcement after concluding a mutual security agreement with the Congo (L) and Rwanda. *NYT*, 1 September 1966.

11. President Micombero urged restraint on Rwandan refugees in Burundi, some of whom had received Chinese-supported training in guerrilla tactics before the break in relations with China. "Their behavior must not harm our foreign relations. They must abstain from any gesture or action likely to be interpreted as a commitment on our part to any subversive enterprise." 5 December 1966, cited in [147], February 1967, p. 26.

ouster in January 1965, China had developed close rapport with the governing Tutsis. The risks involved in supporting "extremists" installed in the government must have seemed worthwhile. The Mwami's uncharacteristic intervention was a sign of his political weakness; within two years the "extremists" were in power. As late as August 1966 there were men in the highest echelons of Burundi politics who favored resuming diplomatic relations with China. In May 1967, despite the absence of diplomatic relations, a Burundi cabinet member visited Peking to talk with Chinese officials.[12]

China did not blunder, and her diplomats were not expelled because of hostility to revolutionary politics. The setback, which was real enough, was wrought largely from within Burundi and was a consequence of the country's complex factionalism. Though Peking lost contacts, the Mwami's flirtation with Taipei was unsuccessful too. Interest in the resumption of diplomatic relations remained lively. It is incorrect to cite Peking's expulsion from Burundi as proof of a failure of Chinese policy.

Central African Republic

On 1 January 1966 Colonel Jean Bedel Bokassa seized power from his cousin, David Dacko, and five days later he ended diplomatic relations with China.[13] Bokassa told the press that relations were broken because arms and documents ascribed to a purported Armée Populaire Centrafricaine, which was controlled by "Chinese or pro-Chinese Centrafricans," had been uncovered. Dacko had known of the plotters, said Bokassa; in seizing power he had saved Dacko's life, for sooner or later Dacko would have been rejected by the "pro-Chinese extremists."[14] That is what the public was told; its essentials seem unconvincing. Elsewhere Bokassa asserted that his reasons for undertaking the coup were purely domestic;[15] that is the view of Victor T. Le Vine, the leading American analyst of Centrafrican affairs.[16]

12. *JMJP*, 5 May 1967, p. 6.

13. *PR*, 14 January 1966, pp. 4 and 24. China asserts that a day before the expulsion order was issued, 5 January, the new foreign minister told the Chinese chargé that the government of Centrafrica wished to continue diplomatic relations. See also *NYT*, 2 January 1966; [183], 2 January 1966.

14. [149], no. 962, 13–19 January 1966, p. 6.

15. [187], 23 January 1966, pp. 1 and 3.

16. [147], April 1966, p. 8. Arguing that the cold war and the presence of foreigners were largely irrelevant to the spate of military takeovers which had just occurred in four African countries, Le Vine considered the counterevidence of the Centrafrican case. "Colonel Bokassa . . . claimed that some 'Young Turks' in government and the military . . . had been involved in an attempt to set up a so-called 'People's

Le Vine's opinion — that Centrafrica established relations with China in order to obtain the $4,000,000 loan negotiated at the same time — is also held by André Givisiez, a correspondent of *Afrique Nouvelle* (Dakar).[17] If the loan was the only tie, China's mission would appear to have rested simply upon opportunism. However, even before the coup, Le Vine identified a group of Young Turks within the administration and the army who had acclaimed Dacko's recognition of China and had watched the revolutionary developments in the Congo (B) with interest.[18] Bokassa's charges concerning the Armée Populaire Centrafricaine were directed against this group. Some were imprisoned, and others fled.

Again, there does not seem to be a useful lesson for China's policy makers. The embassy was a listening post; it also provided access to Centrafricans interested in China. Even if one acknowledges the existence of plans for a people's army and accepts other evidence supposedly proving misconduct,[19] Chinese activities were not large scale or brazen. Expulsion must be counted as a loss, but an acceptable one and one not likely to have been avoided by any alternative Chinese policy.

Dahomey

Diplomatic relations were established on 12 November 1964 and severed on 2 January 1966,[20] following the third takeover of the government in two years by the Dahomean army led by General Christophe Soglo. Neither the original decision to establish relations nor the subsequent break is readily explained. And although the Chinese embassy opened in December 1964, Taiwanese representatives remained in Dahomey until April 1965; some were even invited to official receptions. Soon after

---

Army' with Chinese help. It is possible, but it must be remembered that the Chinese were considered troublemakers in the CAR long before the coup, and that they only set up their embassy in Bangui as part of the price for a $4,000,000 loan. The alleged plot of the 'Young Turks' was, in my opinion, one of the pretexts for the coup, not its cause. The general political and economic malaise of the country . . . is more likely the real cause."

17. [149], no. 963, 20–26 January 1966, p. 16.

18. He defined them as a "small group of young (average age about twenty-five), well-educated, highly placed men" who appeared content to work within the framework of the governing party although little represented in its Comité Directeur. "As they increase with students returning from abroad (10–15 per year) they may be more difficult to handle." [147], November 1965, p. 19.

19. In January 1966 the government announced discovery of a cache of arms in the headquarters of the Bureau de la Sécurité Intérieure de l'Etat and displayed leaflets on guerrilla war found in the former residence of Chinese diplomats, hardly a revelatory discovery; Bokassa said that the government had found Chinese checks totaling about $2,800 made out to Centrafrican citizens. [147], March 1966, p. 23.

20. [149], no. 961, 6–12 January 1966, p. 5; [152], 9 January 1966.

Soglo's second intervention (November 1965), Taiwan's ambassador to Togo made two visits to Dahomey. Whatever prompted the Dahomean government to establish relations with Peking, it appears that Soglo was never convinced of the desirability of maintaining them. No reason was given for breaking relations. Dahomey reestablished relations with Taiwan on 21 April 1966.[21]

The ties between Dahomey and China were even more tenuous than in the case of Centrafrica, which had at least hoped to profit from an aid agreement. There was one group which publicly favored Chinese-Dahomean relations: the Union Générale des Etudiantes et Elèves Dahoméens urged diplomatic ties.[22] Some persons among Dahomey's youth, now politically ineffective, do believe ties with China would be desirable.[23]

Since mutual interests were few and relations had been expected to end for some time, there was probably little China could have done to preserve them. China's operations were not large; the activities in Dahomey were undertaken by a small Chinese contingent of about ten. In short, the loss of the embassy was a setback, but it was neither a turning point nor a major defeat.

Ghana

China's troubles in Ghana were precipitated by the overthrow of Kwame Nkrumah on 24 February 1966. Yet the Chinese diplomats did not close their embassy and leave until 5 November. Unlike the cases of Burundi, Centrafrica, and Dahomey, China's loss in Ghana was substantial. There is no evidence of compensating political gain. Appeal to radicals may have been fostered by China's continuing attachment to Nkrumah. But for Ghana herself, the measure of Nkrumah's following is the complete collapse of his Convention People's party. There are Ghanaians who would prefer a radical alternative to the post-Nkrumah government, but there is no evidence of strong pressure or capable men working for Nkrumah's return.

Did China provoke the rupture, or was the "unilateral suspension" (as China termed it)[24] wholly a Ghanaian affair? The final step was taken by Ghana, but only after a series of charges and countercharges that continued for eight months. The immediate provocation for the break was a strongly-worded, unfriendly Chinese note accusing Ghanaian "authori-

21. [147], June 1966, p. 41.
22. [176], 26 August 1964, p. 4.
23. For example, a Dahomean was among the youth celebrating May Day in Peking, May 1967. *JMJP*, 2 May 1967, p. 6.
24. *PR*, 4 November 1966, p. 5.

ties" of "yet another grave step . . . in pursuing their anti-Chinese policy." They were "playing the role of a flunkey of imperialism." Circumstances indicate that China hoped to have her embassy expelled. Four days before China delivered the note in Accra, Ghana had broken relations with Cuba; there was no Chinese technical assistance left to lose.[25] Moreover, Accra was involved in a campaign to save money by closing diplomatic missions abroad,[26] and by December the number of Ghanaian missions had been reduced from sixty-two to forty-three.[27] It is reasonable to conclude that Chinese diplomats in Accra thought Ghana would use the note of 1 October as a basis for breaking relations.

Why might Peking have wanted to end relations? As long as China maintained diplomatic ties, she was in an uncomfortable position vis-à-vis Nkrumah. Nkrumah had come to Peking on the day he was deposed, en route to Hanoi. He then made his way to Conakry via Moscow. Sékou Touré insisted that "the attitude of each nation towards the rebellion of the military traitors of Ghana will be our criterion for judging the honesty of each of these States and their relations with Africa."[28] Ghana's former foreign minister, Alex Quaison-Sackey, upon his return to Ghana from China, told a news conference that Nkrumah had asked for Soviet and Chinese aid in resuming power; Quaison-Sackey did not expect the request to be granted.[29] The new Ghanaian government professed to believe that China was giving aid to Nkrumah. It charged that "the Government of the People's Republic of China had begun shipment of substantial quantities of arms and other war materials to the Republic of Guinea with a view to assisting Kwame Nkrumah to return to Ghana to stage a counter-revolution." China retorted that the charge was sheer fabrication and a vicious slander but carefully persisted in calling the new Ghanaian leadership the "Ghanaian authorities," a phrase which reserved the question of its legitimacy.[30]

Rumors of possible Chinese support for Nkrumah continued. One report circulating when relations were broken — attributed to intelligence sources in Conakry — was that China had given Nkrumah more than

25. [168], 28 September 1966. Chinese technicians were expelled immediately after the coup, and the embassy staff was limited by Ghana to eighteen. Ghanaian note of 28 February 1966, paraphrased in *PR*, 11 March 1966, p. 7.

26. [168], 16 July 1966. The Peking embassy was not among those Accra reportedly planned to close. Several Asian missions were to be closed and a new one opened, in Australia, to serve Ghanaian interests in the Far East.

27. [195], 24 December 1966.

28. Radio Conakry, 2 March 1966.

29. *NYT*, 3 March 1966.

30. *PR*, 25 March 1966, pp. 8–9.

$1,000,000 to aid his efforts to retake power.[31] Whether such reports were true or not, China felt some obligation, even as she continued relations with Accra, to keep her distance from those who overthrew Nkrumah. Perhaps she calculated that the risk of offending Guinea, Mali, and Congo (B), which had each offered hospitality to Nkrumah, might prove more costly than an outright affront to the new rulers of Ghana. Or China may have resolved to embarrass the Soviet Union, which waited only a few weeks to acknowledge the Ankrah government. The conclusion is that China did not want to give up her embassy in Accra, but she was caught in ideological and symbolic loyalties which could not be reconciled. Once a break was decided upon, the affair would be exploited to expose Moscow's essential conservatism. It is quite possible that China's action was not undertaken with any expectation that Nkrumah could return to power; rather, Peking's move guaranteed other African radicals that Chinese support would endure despite any setbacks they might encounter. Only a few months previous to this, China had embraced Boumédienne with unseemly haste, winning a bad reputation among Ben Bella's supporters in Africa. Peking may have sought to restore her standing among members of Africa's left.

It remains to calculate China's loss. By November 1966, the embassy, like others she had lost, was little more than a listening post. The damage had already been done. The guerrilla training camp to which China had dispatched instructors, a camp not only for Africans from dependent territories but also for those from independent countries including Nigeria, Gabon, Upper Volta, Niger, Cameroon, Rwanda, Zambia, Malawi, and Tanzania, had been shut down months before.[32] China's aid operation had also ceased, though only a small part of the promised $42,000,000 was used, with the expulsion of all 207 Chinese technical assistance personnel.[33] China's motives for creating her presence in that particular way are not known, but the coup disrupted plans for an extended stay in Ghana. However, the sharp curtailment of Chinese activities was a by-product of the coup, not a sign that China had been unwise to pursue those activities while they had been sanctioned by Nkrumah. The diplomatic break came only after China's principal assets had disappeared.

31. *NYT*, 26 October 1966.

32. *NYT*, 10 June 1966. Seventeen Chinese military personnel, including three colonels, engaged in training at various times from late 1964 until the coup. [38], p. 60. The same source includes photographs of Chinese instructors conducting training sessions.

33. *NYT*, 12 March 1966. According to [38], 430 Chinese left Ghana in the wake of the coup.

Tunisia

China's relations with Tunisia were never warm. As noted in Chapter 3, they were agreed upon only after long delay, and thereafter China bore blunt criticism from the president and leading nationalist figure, Habib Bourguiba. In 1965 Bourguiba referred to China's policies in Asia and Africa as "colonialism camouflaged as ideology."[34] He said, in response to an interviewer's question as to whether there was a real danger of Chinese penetration in Africa:

> Yes, as long as one observes [China's] desire to infiltrate herself a little bit everywhere, to provoke difficulties, to aggravate existing contradictions, to arm and train guerrillas against the established regimes. Chou En-lai doesn't deny it and tells anyone who listens that Africa is ripe for revolution.
>
> But as far as I'm concerned I have the impression that China will have a great deal to do before casting our continent into anarchy and subversion. Many Africans are distrustful, or are frankly allergic. I don't foresee Chou En-lai's winning in the near future.[35]

China countered Bourguiba's remarks, and lodged a verbal protest against Tunisia's advocacy of a "two Chinas" solution to the United Nations deadlock on Chinese representation.[36] Relations were so strained that Bourguiba's son, the secretary of state for foreign affairs, stated that they would be broken if Peking continued to "provoke Tunisia or to slander the Tunisian Chief of State."[37]

On 15 September 1967 China protested to Tunisia formally. Acts protested included the detention of a Chinese table tennis coach and a staff member of the embassy, but the harsh language of the Chinese note was its key feature:

> Standing on the side of US imperialism, the Tunisian Government has been trying to split and disintegrate the Arab people's anti-imperialist front. This has greatly enraged the Tunisian and other Arab people and encountered their firm opposition. The Tunisian Government is finding itself in an increasingly bad fix. In trying to use its opposition to China to divert the attention of its people and cover up its own crime of entering further into the service of US

34. [147], October 1965, p. 56.
35. [185], November 1965, p. 57.
36. *JMJP*, 20 November 1965; *PR*, 26 November 1965, p. 25.
37. [147], February 1966, p. 30.

> imperialism and Soviet revisionism and selling out the interests of the Tunisian and other Arab people, the Tunisian Government will certainly come to no good end.[38]

Tunisia demanded an apology, and she said that all Chinese embassy personnel would be declared persona non grata if the apology were not delivered by a certain date. She then declared that no new Chinese diplomats could be sent to Tunisia until her terms were met. China branded this an insult and said that it had become "totally impossible for the Chinese Embassy to continue its work in Tunisia."[39] On 27 September, China's embassy staff left Tunisia.[40]

Peking need not have used the language that she did in her 15 September note. Either she sought to end relations or the authors of the note were unskilled in diplomacy. In any case, the note probably reflected the turmoil which beset the ministry of foreign affairs at that time and in the weeks immediately preceding, consequent upon the Great Proletarian Cultural Revolution. If its authors intended to provoke a break in relations, they may have calculated that it was advantageous to identify with radical Arab states, then attempting to explain to themselves Israel's swift victory in the third Arab-Israeli war.

Bourguiba's stubborn unwillingness to refrain from public criticism of China and his insistence that foreigners in Tunisia conform to the government's judgment of proper conduct set the stage for the suspension of relations. Peking was unyielding, perhaps because of the cultural revolution. She apparently judged that an embassy in Tunis was not worthwhile unless Chinese spokesmen could speak as they pleased. Bourguiba, however, was unwilling to tolerate propaganda and political interference. From China's point of view, there was more to lose by silence than by a break in relations. There is no reason to believe that relations will be reestablished in the near future.[41]

Kenya

On 29 June 1967 the Chinese chargé d'affaires, Li Chieh, was declared persona non grata. Li was the fourth Chinese official to be forced

38. *PR*, 22 September 1967, p. 29.
39. *PR*, 13 October 1967, p. 39.
40. Radio Peking, 28 September 1967.
41. In August 1968, the Tunisian leadership sought to link dissidence at the University of Tunis with a group which, it alleged, had ties to the Chinese embassy before it closed. [103], pp. 24–25.

to leave Kenya in two years.[42] Although precise charges were not publicly disclosed in the first three cases, all were surrounded by accusations that China paid Kenyans opposing the Kenya African National Union (KANU). Incidents in March 1966 coincided with the break between Kenyatta and Oginga Odinga, who lost his post as deputy president of KANU on 13 March, and the subsequent trial of strength in which Kenyatta proved his decisive superiority.

On 10 March the defense minister revealed that Kenya had lodged protests (with China, the USSR, and three other countries) that Kenyans were being given military training without the consent of the government. Four hundred Kenyans were said to be involved.[43] Colin Legum reported that there was some evidence that approximately £100,000 had been made available to Kenyatta's opponents to help them capture the KANU conference at which Odinga was deposed.[44] And on 24 March the minister of home affairs stated that between June 1964 and December 1965 some £400,000 had been spent in attempts to undermine the Kenyan government.[45] No record of donors and recipients was made public. But it was clear in context that China had taken a major role—and that the expulsions of an embassy clerk and the third secretary were countermoves.

The stage was set for further attacks on China. Kenyan newspapers, which had published many reports of disruption and disorganization in China's cultural revolution, were quick to publish portions of an inflammatory pamphlet issued in Hong Kong under the name of the New China News Agency. Even in the likely possibility that the pamphlet is a forgery, as one Chinese embassy asserted,[46] its publication is an intriguing incident in cold war politics.

The pamphlet is titled "New Diplomats Will Bring the Great Proletarian Cultural Revolution to Africa." Diplomats who returned to China for the cultural revolution will "return to Chinese embassies in Africa . . . with new officials who will be assigned to Chinese embassy staffs in various countries. . . . [They] consider themselves primarily as revolutionary

42. Wang Te-ming, NCNA correspondent, was asked to leave on 22 July 1965. He was linked to an effort to seize the governing party's headquarters. [162], 26 July 1965. On 10 March 1966, a clerk, Chang, of the Chinese embassy in Nairobi was ordered out. A few days later Yao Ch'un, third secretary, was forced to leave. March 1966 cases also involved Soviet, Czech, and Hungarian diplomats and newsmen.

43. *NYT*, 11 March 1966.

44. [183], 20 March 1966.

45. [162], 25 March 1966.

46. [162], 17 March 1967, reports that a Chinese embassy spokesman in Kampala, Uganda, described the document as a forgery.

workers." Chou En-lai purportedly instructed the "new revolutionary diplomats" to "form militant local Red Guard units to purify the revolutions in Africa as the Chinese Red Guards have purified and perpetuated the glorious Great Proletarian Cultural Revolution." The Kenya People's Union — Odinga's new party — was said to be "dedicated to the just demands of all the people of Kenya."[47] This language was sure to inflame highly-placed Kenyan readers. The governing party, KANU, issued a statement expressing no surprise that a Chinese publication would praise the Kenya People's Union. It then warned:

> Events in Africa during 1966 and continuing instability in some parts of the continent make it easy, and in fact inviting, for some countries to feel that they can meddle in the affairs of African states. Forces are anxious to sow the seeds of suspicion among neighboring states.
>
> Confusion and instability in Africa benefits such forces. It is important that the African countries be on their guard against the intrigue and manipulations of these forces whose only purpose must be to destroy that which we are trying to build. . . .
>
> Any party in Kenya which relies on the inspiration and support of outsiders cannot be regarded as a genuine nationalist organization and must be looked upon with suspicion by the people of this country.[48]

Use of the pamphlet by KANU to impugn Odinga's group did not preclude doubts about its authenticity, which was the subject of a formal inquiry.

Three months after Li Chieh was asked to leave Kenya, Peking attacked the late Tom Mboya, the minister for economic planning and development. In a letter to the *East African Standard*, the embassy took issue with a speech by Mboya:

> Mboya has come out to help US imperialism out of its difficulties. He even venomously places US imperialism that is aggressive in nature on a par with the People's Republic of China that has been persistently opposing imperialism and uttered the nonsense that not only the Americans of the CIA had to be watched, but also the Chinese.
>
> Mr. Mboya's intention is very obvious, that is, to divert the atten-

47. [162], 14 March 1967, p. 4.
48. [162], 16 March 1967.

tion of the Kenya people from their anti-US struggle and to sow discord in and sabotage thc friendship between the Kenya peoples. . . .

Mr. Mboya's fabrications and slanders can only result in dropping on his own feet the rock he has lifted.[49]

Mboya replied by quoting from the KANU manifesto and from a speech delivered by Kenyatta in mid-1965. The president of Kenya had said:

> It is naive to think that there is no danger of imperialism from the East. In world power politics the East has as much design on us as the West and would like us to serve their own interests. This is why we reject Communism. It is in fact the reason why we have chosen for ourselves the path of non-alignment and African socialism. To us Communism is as bad as imperialism. What we want is Kenya nationalism which helped us to win the struggle against imperialism.[50]

It is accurate to say that China took risks in her clandestine support of political factions, her support was exposed, and China has been obliged to watch the faction to which she gave greatest support suffer a disastrous fall in political fortune. Kenyatta's remarks were made two months before the first Chinese was expelled. Knowing Kenyatta's attitude and his decisive role in KANU, might China have acted otherwise? Rather than be passive, China undertook certain ventures. Their exposure is in part a consequence of good Kenyan police work, enhanced by the government's wish to suppress and scatter Odingist opposition. China suffered a serious decline in respectability and her assets are further from the center of power than they were in 1965. Moreover, she is now suspect.[51]

Results of the election of 1966, in which dissidents who broke away from KANU were forced to contest their seats, suggest that the KANU mainstream occupied a secure position. Conscious of that, the government has declined to sever relations with China despite incidents which would surely have led to a break in other countries. Chinese hopes of 1965 have

49. [162], 27 June 1967.

50. *Ibid.*

51. On the other hand, although the sample was small, China's embassy in Nairobi could have reported with pleasure the results of an opinion poll showing that Chou En-lai and Mao Tse-tung stood high in the estimate of KPU members even in May 1967. A total sample of 500 were asked, "Which non-African Political Leader do you most admire?" Choices included Wilson, Johnson, Chou En-lai/Mao Tse-tung, and Kosygin/Russian. The KPU members ranked Chou/Mao (13%), Gandhi (11%), Kosygin/Russian (9%). Among the full 500, results were Johnson (19%), Wilson (11%), Chou/Mao (6%). [89], pp. 79 and 90.

proven to be empty. Revolutionary slogans have failed to be effective. Maintaining the nominal Chinese presence and watching it closely, Kenyatta avoids an appearance of inflexibility. China has been disappointed, but above all she has been constrained by a firm and efficient host government.

United Arab Republic

Relations between China and the United Arab Republic are mutually respectful, each party recognizing the intentions of the other and approaching the other with a certain wariness. Leadership in the United Arab Republic, like that in Kenya, has had confidence in its ability to host an important Chinese presence; several joint ventures have even been undertaken. At times relations have been strained. The narrow question to be considered here is whether China's revolutionary enthusiasm led her to a setback in Egypt in 1965 when members of a small pro-Chinese faction were arrested and tried.

In August and September 1965 twenty-five members of a pro-Chinese group, led by an attorney, Mustafa Agha, were arrested.[52] Eleven were brought to trial, identified as members of the Arab Communist party, and charged with plotting to overthrow Nasser and to establish a People's Republic of Egypt.[53] China was not mentioned during the brief public portion of the trial, but one journalist, doubting that China intended to foment a coup, did write that those on trial were reliably reported to have been in close touch with the Chinese embassy.[54]

According to the report, one NCNA employee was asked to leave and a military attaché was transferred because of involvement in the case. Moreover — and more significant — China's long-time ambassador in Cairo, Ch'en Chia-k'ang, left Cairo in December 1965. Although he became a deputy foreign minister soon after returning to China, Ch'en may have left earlier than planned as a result of the trial.[55]

The striking aspect of this episode is the restraint with which it was handled. Public denunciations were avoided, and the trial was largely private.[56] The importance of a small group of self-proclaimed revolutionaries was not allowed to outweigh mutually useful relations between China and Egypt. China's interest in the Agha group — if there was such an interest — may have been related to her opposition to Soviet dominance

52. *NYT*, 17 October 1965, attributing the numbers to "informed sources."
53. *NYT*, 31 January 1966.
54. *NYT*, 16 February 1966 and 31 January 1966.
55. *JMJP*, 9 February 1966, p. 3; *NYT*, 31 January 1966.
56. Two concurrent security trials, one involving large numbers of Moslem Brotherhood members, were held in open court.

of the Egyptian Communist party. China and Egypt have disagreed on many important issues, but the Agha trial did not appear to signal a Chinese setback.

The Afro-Asian Idea

As the Sino-Soviet dispute worsened, Chinese ceased to attend meetings of the Moscow-sponsored organizations which had formerly given them their first contacts with Africans. Peking's differences with Moscow extended to the proposed Second Asian-African Conference and to the activities of the Afro-Asian People's Solidarity Organization.

China's hope to recapture the magic of Bandung in 1965 was not fulfilled. The sources of her disappointment, described in Chapter 3, stemmed from a political universe unfriendly to issues, positions, and concerns China considered to be paramount. Peking probably could not have mustered the majority needed to exclude the Soviet Union from Algiers; the prospects were not bright that a round condemnation of United States actions in Vietnam, which China considered a central aim of the conference, would be achieved. Others foresaw a tortured confrontation between Moscow and Peking, accompanied by pressures to take sides on uncomfortable issues; with no clear benefit in view, many governments preferred to avoid the proposed conference altogether. When Peking calculated that the outcome would be unwanted and decided not to attend the Second Asian-African Conference, she assured its indefinite postponement.

China could not achieve a conference on terms desirable to her. Its abandonment was a sign that African and Asian states, for the most part, preferred to utilize existing bodies — regional groups, the Commonwealth, the United Nations — and direct bilateral contacts to attain their political and economic goals. A public forum beset by uncompromising ideological struggles offered little. It is correct to cite this instance as evidence that China's foreign policy was uncongenial to many governments, some unwilling to be put on record against the United States in words not precisely of their own choosing, others refusing to become enmeshed in Sino-Soviet quarrels. The risk of alienating Washington and Moscow was real, and probably weighed. If Peking believed that the Vietnam War, especially America's bombing of North Vietnam and rapid introduction of combat troops into South Vietnam, would prove a rallying ground for governments otherwise prone to give domestic construction and traditional political ties first importance, she was wrong. In November 1965 China was not demonstrably less free to act than she had been a year earlier, but a major initiative, to which she had closely tied her prestige, and through which she may have hoped to legitimize some components of her stand against imperialism and revisionism, had slipped from her hands. This was an undoubted disappointment.

China's alternative was to organize events herself. As noted in Chapter 3, she did initiate some small conferences. She made a home for the Afro-Asian Journalists Association, a secretariat of the Afro-Asian Writers Bureau, and the Peking Center of the World Federation of Scientific Workers. These steps were useful because they provided a means to invite non-Chinese to Peking. The very existence of such centers challenged their counterparts, in which the Soviet Union had substantial influence. The fact that Peking was forced into narrow initiatives revealed her weakness; the broad united front was neither broad nor united.

The hope that a Chinese physical setting would assure political advantage lay behind Peking's efforts to bring the Fifth Afro-Asian People's Solidarity Conference to Peking. The fourth conference (Winneba, Ghana) had decided that Peking should be the site of the fifth, but Soviet distaste for that plan led to a drive to shift the site to Algiers. China insisted that Peking remain the site. Moscow was formally successful, but no fifth conference, under any auspices, has been held up to December 1970.[57] Following the AAPSO council meeting at which it was decided not to hold the fifth conference in Peking, China definitively turned her back on the AAPSO secretariat in Cairo:

> It must be pointed out that the present Permanent Secretariat of the Afro-Asian People's Solidarity Organization in Cairo is already in the control of the Soviet revisionists. Correct propositions put forth by the secretaries of the different countries who defend the revolutionary line of solidarity against imperialism and stand for what is just have long been arbitrarily suppressed. As a matter of fact, the Permanent Secretariat has already degenerated into a tool of the Soviet revisionists for implementing their counter-revolutionary line. We therefore declare that we shall henceforth have nothing to do with this organ.[58]

By withdrawing from the secretariat China distinguished herself from the Soviet Union, among those most prone to a radical analysis, and avoided the indignity of possible defeat at AAPSO meetings. The cost, lost avenues of contact with Africans, was less than it would have been before

57. The Eighth Session of the Council of the AAPSO, Nicosia, Cyprus, ended on 16 February 1967. China charged the meeting was illegal and did not attend. The council decided that the fifth conference would not be in Peking, but in Algiers. *PR*, 24 February 1967, pp. 24–27.

58. Text of statement issued by the Chinese Committee for Afro-Asian Solidarity, 17 March 1967. *PR*, 24 March 1967, pp. 21 and 31.

China had embassies on the African continent. By 1967 Peking had alternative means to contact Africans who might be attracted to her world view. Nonetheless, withdrawal from AAPSO signifies political defeat. China certainly was set back in her drive to lead the Asian-African states, although claims that China has become isolated are exaggerated.

Other Disappointments and Losses

The record of disappointments and setbacks would be incomplete without mention of other episodes, less important than those described above, in which events failed to conform to China's hopes.

About 1960 China began to receive African students in Chinese institutions, as she had earlier received students from Eastern Europe and Asia. The one lengthy account of living conditions among the African students, Emmanuel John Hevi's *An African Student in China*, is polemical in style but it has not been refuted. Hevi tells of inadequate teaching, the beating of a Zanzibari student who sought to buy a package of cigarettes, and Chinese efforts to manipulate the African Students' Union (of which Hevi was secretary general). He cites six causes of student dissatisfaction: undesirable political indoctrination, language difficulty, poor educational standards, inadequate social life, outright hostility, and racial discrimination. Although China resisted efforts by some of the students to claim their return tickets, by April 1962 most had left China. Hevi offers the following figures:[59]

Roll of African Student Nationalities in China, 1961–1962
(April 1962)

Country	*Came to China*	*Left China for Home*	*Still in China*	*Threatening to go home*
Chad	1	Nil	1	Nil
Congo (Gizenga government)	3	3	Nil	Nil
Ghana	4	3	1	Nil
Cameroon (UPC)	36	34	2	Nil
Kenya	2	2	Nil	Nil
Somalia	48	30	18	10
Southern Rhodesia	1	1	Nil	Nil
Sudan	1	1	Nil	Nil
Uganda	4	4	Nil	Nil
Zanzibar	18	18	Nil	Nil
United Arab Republic		Figures not known		
Totals	118	96	22	10

59. [49], pp. 116, 119–143. One review disputes Hevi's version of the Zanzibari's fight: Kojo Amoo-Gottfried in *Race*, April 1964, pp. 72–74.

If Hevi's account is accurate, China was unprepared to approximate the expectations of students who had come to Peking to obtain academic training. Attempts to obtain political advantage were transparent, and those responsible lost respect. The result was a dismal failure in cultural diplomacy, which received wide attention in Africa. China has not undertaken to provide academic training for African students again. Indeed, during the cultural revolution the universities and technical institutes have been closed to regular work. Africans have gone to China to obtain specialized training, presumably in guerrilla techniques, but no reliable summary of the numbers involved has been compiled, nor has there been any assessment of the quality of their experience in China.

In an analogous fashion, China has lost opportunities for political gain by failing to meet economic commitments or meeting them in a manner some Africans found unsatisfactory. Kenya's receipt of poor quality goods, and goods duplicating locally available commodities, was noted earlier.[60] The prime minister of Somalia, commenting in 1967 that Chinese aid had been greatly reduced, complained that China had delivered goods late and then demanded cash payment. How was it possible to repay the Chinese loan (and a loan from the United States), he asked, when there was not even enough money to pay the staff working on development projects?[61] These reflections did not mean that Somalia had decided to forego Chinese aid, for soon thereafter the prime minister disclosed plans to seek Chinese help for tobacco and rice cultivation,[62] but they suggest that Somali economists might approach future Chinese promises with caution. Reports circulated in 1968 that China was holding Zambia to the letter of a grain import contract, and that Zambian exporters suffered severe financial losses due to shrinkage of the grain during shipment. Such tough business practices could offset the diplomatic uses of the trade; nonetheless, Zambia has gone ahead and accepted Chinese financing of the Tan-Zam railway. Reports of disaffection with Chinese aid and trade practices are sufficiently numerous to justify the conclusion that Peking sometimes errs, or places economic gain above political gain.

From time to time Chinese representatives visit African states with which China does not maintain diplomatic relations. It is distinctly possible that it was harder for Chinese to make such visits by 1969 than it had been a few years earlier, but there is no way to be sure of this. In mid-1968, Senegal, which recognizes China but does not maintain diplomatic

60. Chapter 4, note 13.
61. Radio Mogadishu, 16 May 1967.
62. Radio Mogadishu, 8 August 1967.

relations, expelled two NCNA correspondents under circumstances which linked them to student demonstrations.[63]

Great Proletarian Cultural Revolution

Has the Great Proletarian Cultural Revolution, which began in 1966, adversely affected China's capacity to act in Africa? It is impossible to make a definitive judgment now, but five hypotheses appear valid:

(1) The efficiency and effectiveness of Chinese embassies in Africa suffered. Ambassadors and other staff members were called home for extended stays. The prior steady accumulation of contacts and opportunities suffered. In some instances, as in the case of Tunisia, the cultural revolution also may have intruded on policy processes.

(2) Supporting facilities in China, including the foreign ministry, were preoccupied with internal disputes. Interruption of schools and universities interfered with the training of specialists. Although there is evidence that they have always been made of papier-mâché, people's organizations and friendship societies appear even less important than they were in the past.

(3) Moderate economic recession may have increased competition for funds, making it harder for projects concerned with Africa to obtain support. However, this speculation must be weighed against China's agreement to finance the Tan-Zam railway.

(4) The cultural revolution shows there is no single "Chinese path to socialism." It reveals that even within China there are serious arguments about proper revolutionary and developmental strategies.

(5) Though the vastness and audacity of the cultural revolution may attract some African adherents and win them to commitment, it makes it more difficult for China to conduct a united front strategy. It will surely be more difficult for China to win the support of the moderates among those who are critical of existing African institutions.

If these statements are borne out, the cultural revolution has hindered China in Africa. This study argues that one component of China's African policy is preparation for future revolutionary opportunities. Chinese leaders believe that her sense of purpose is more durable than that of her opponents. The cultural revolution illustrates a conflict between short-term and long-term strategies. The CCP leadership has conducted the cultural revolution, at least in part, to maintain an attachment to revolution within China. Some important assets for her long-term revolutionary strategy in

63. [173], 23 June 1968, p. 27.

Africa are threatened in the process: informed embassy personnel who know local revolutionaries; a body of experience ready to be applied in Africa; a mystique surrounding the Chinese revolutionary style, helping it to attract adherents and frighten opponents; a sense that China's analyses are scientific and more perceptive than those of her opponents; and, finally, the very assurance that the CCP can speak decisively and with one voice. The immediate tactical requirements of a long-term revolutionary strategy at home have jeopardized the long-term revolutionary strategy abroad.

Given the possibility that China's revolutionary determination would otherwise fall below a crucial threshold and her entire revolutionary enterprise abroad be abandoned, the CCP leaders who orchestrated and led the cultural revolution may have been quite consistent to act as they did. That does not mean that they have accomplished their aims within China. Unanticipated costs may become visible, but it is evident even now that a toll has been exacted—a toll paid with Chinese prestige.

National Liberation

No African government owes its existence to Chinese support, nor does any governing African leadership today acknowledge Peking as the sole source of correct doctrine. Peking has overthrown no African government, nor has any African government been dangerously threatened by revolutionaries dependent on China for their doctrinal or material existence. If one were to say that Peking succeeds only by installing client regimes in the African countries, and otherwise fails, then failures would be recorded. Such a judgment would be internally consistent, but misleading.

China has supported some successful revolutionaries (Algeria, Zanzibar) and some who have failed (Cameroon, Congo). Of those China supports at the present time, some have a prospect of seizing power (Portuguese Guinea), while others appear to be far from making any serious attempt to seize power (Rhodesia, South Africa). African groups receiving Chinese support have risen and declined, been strong in one locale and weak in another; their fortunes reveal no single pattern of waxing or waning opportunities for China. Rather, there are always some groups or factions ready to deal with China, and there are always some African revolutionaries ready to be quoted in support of Chinese positions. Where liberation movements leaning to Moscow and to Peking compete, the Soviet-supported groups do appear better organized and more substantial, but no competing group can show a decisive advantage in attainments within the region to be liberated. National liberation movements are considered in Chapter 8. It is sufficient to note here that there is no Albania in Africa, nor a North Vietnam; but revolutionary movements which accept, in varying degrees, key Chinese views continue to keep their footing in a very unsettled political milieu in which revolution is possible. In the short term, there has been no signal expansion of Chinese freedom to act, through the vehicle of the client or closely allied government. For the long term, however, China's freedom to act remains real.

Conclusion

This chapter has shown that some of the incidents commonly cited to prove that China has suffered a general setback in Africa have been misread. The spectacular cases show that China has been the victim of bad luck, of untimely coups, and even of the uncontrollable aggressiveness of indigenous radicals. Many Africans were wary from the beginning of China's motives and intentions. In noting caution among African leaders in 1965 or 1967, observers may not have been demonstrating that Africans were newly persuaded that China's aims were in some ways incompatible with their own, but rather that the observers had become more alert to hear Africans speak in that vein.

On the other hand, China has met with impressive political defeats in the Afro-Asian arena. To cut her losses, she has been forced into narrowly autonomous initiatives. In particular, when faced by the full thrust of Soviet influence, China has repeatedly been forced to retreat.

Finally, the cultural revolution brought China a bad world press; accounts were often exaggerated, but damaging nonetheless. The Great Leap Forward of 1958 was not characterized by the anarchy, street fighting, and public power struggles which marked the picture of the cultural revolution circulated abroad. However unsuccessful the Great Leap Forward was economically, it was dedicated to propositions which many found appealing: rapid industrialization, the use of otherwise underemployed labor, and the call for physical labor by office workers. The appeal of the cultural revolution is narrower. Its attraction is stress on the solution of problems through action, the creation of an omnicompetent populace of worker-peasant-student-soldier, and the abolition of bureaucracy. These are more abstract and less tangible than backyard furnaces, irrigation projects, and the communes. Even the most romantic among Africa's revolutionary left may view the cultural revolution with considerable dismay.

Despite missteps and shortcomings, bad luck and true failures, most of China's capabilities remain intact. To go from the observation that China has suffered some setbacks to the judgment that China's political assets can be dismissed is unwarranted. Through a series of inopportune choices, such as a purge of those in the diplomatic service with African experience, China could depress her capability suddenly and with great effect. For her capability consists above all of intangibles: contacts, familiarity with the local scene, ability to speak a language, or some established sense of mutually advantageous dealings. Capabilities of this kind are largely embodied in individual men and women. China's second important asset, the string of diplomatic missions and NCNA offices, is almost wholly intact and even being expanded. In sum, although China's position could be wiped away by stupidity or a gross insensitivity to prevailing conditions, there is no reason to believe that this will happen.

7 The Chinese Revolutionary Model

Copyists, imitators, plagiarists, and avowed disciples would have looked to the Chinese revolution even without urging. State power is a prize, and men believe that special knowledge can win it for them in their own countries. It is not surprising that some men turn to China's experience, just as the post-1917 revolutionary generation sought lessons from the Bolshevik Revolution. To school non-Chinese in revolution, the CCP has put forth versions of its own experience as a model to be copied.[1]

The imitator must first grasp the Chinese model, choose those portions he judges worth copying, and then strive to reproduce parts of the model in an environment for which they were not intended. The leader of a foreign revolutionary movement can draw from an array of documents, studies, slogans, myths, exhortations, and interpretations, emanating from many sources, to form a view of China's revolution. If a revolutionary confined himself to Mao Tse-tung's *Selected Works* and a few other authorized statements, his task would be simplified, but he would still not be able to find a source picturing the "model" in a schematic form such as that adopted for this study. The Chinese revolutionary model discussed in this chapter is a framework drawn from accounts by the CCP, consisting of essential elements which presumably could be adapted to revolution elsewhere.

What criteria of selection would he use? Most of those who have self-consciously copied elements of the Chinese experience have been remarkably selective. They have chosen what they thought would be applicable to their own countries; they have not copied those lessons which appear peculiar to China. At that level of generality, Peking has no argument with selectivity; the CCP warns specifically against mechanical

1. See [216]. Tang Tsou and Morton Halperin consider the problem of Maoist strategy and foreign policy in [126], elaborating many features of the revolutionary model.

adoption of one country's experience by another. It does not say, however, how movements are to distinguish what is applicable from what is not, what is necessary from what is contingent upon local variations. State power is so elusive that leaders of movements fear they will forfeit success if they make a wrong choice of aim or method. Peking contends too that success stems from persistence and a clear and fixed purpose. The absolute requirement of certainty must somehow coexist with correct adaptation of the Chinese model to fit foreign conditions—and then, even so, conditions are subject to change with time. The revolutionary must be self-assured and resolute; he must also take cues from his own experience and be flexible.

In choosing aims, a movement's leadership could confine itself to antiforeign objectives, or it could attempt social revolution through class struggle. The cultural revolution has suggested yet a third option: adopting China's aim to transform men. The leaders' prior aims and perceptions of national circumstance will shape the questions they ask about China's experience. It is unlikely that more than a very few foreign revolutionaries would subscribe to the demand for cultural revolution in the form voiced by the Mao-Lin leadership in 1967. Those who did would find it hard to reconcile their demand with the institutional and structural emphasis of this model, much as cultural revolution proved incompatible with the CCP bureaucracy in 1966.

The cultural revolution has also revealed that China's leaders disagreed sharply among themselves. The CCP's claim to certitude is less credible than before. If Soviet insistence on one true vision of scientific socialism was shattered by the Yugoslav separation and Khrushchev's later denunciation of Stalin, Chinese claims to a well-ordered party were dashed by the denunciation of Liu Shao-ch'i.

In 1955, when China began relations with Africa, she did not insist that others adopt her revolutionary model. China had proposed her revolutionary model as a plan for action from 1949 until it proved unworkable in several Asian countries. Lack of success and a changing world context led Peking to approach Asian governments in peace; conciliatory diplomacy developed gradually from 1953, and it was unambiguous at the Bandung conference of 1955. Thus, when China began relations with Africa, she did not insist that her revolutionary model be adopted. After 1957 a reversal set in: prompted by a changing view of the balance of forces in the world, China once again urged others to take up revolution as the CCP had practiced it.[2] In early 1961, when published espousal of

2. A. M. Halpern notes that China redefined her relation to other regions after

the model was again temporarily muted in deference to the Moscow conference just completed, internal Chinese comment still strongly asserted the usefulness of her experience for the third world. The *Bulletin of Activities* of the People's Liberation Army (PLA) claimed:

> No country in this world has had more experience than we. We all understand that theory is derived from practice; because we have more combat experience, we should therefore have more superior military theories. . . . The summing-up of our military experience is not only for ourselves but also for the benefit of other countries and nations which are still not yet liberated. They are very much in need of the kind of experience which will enable them to crush imperialism and feudalism and to gain independence and democracy.[3]

Another *Bulletin* author insisted that China tell African leaders about her experience, including "the revolutionary experience of the Communists of this generation." He cautioned, in keeping with earlier comment, that "they must depend mainly upon their own personal experience, for foreign assistance can come only second." Adopting a device to make Africa's situation clear to his military readership, he drew comparisons to key stages in Chinese revolutionary history: the implication is that the unfolding African revolution will pass through similar stages.[4] A Chinese

---

sputnik, with a strong affirmation of the Chinese revolutionary model. Unmistakable signs appear in speeches at China's tenth anniversary celebrations on 1 October 1959. Liu Shao-ch'i said: "Revolution and construction in China have features peculiar to this country. But it is also possible that some of these important special features may reappear in some other countries. In this sense, Chinese experience is to a certain extent of international significance." Ch'en I observed that Chinese successes were a "tremendous encouragement to all the oppressed nations and peoples of the world fighting for their liberation. In the Chinese people they see their own tomorrow. They feel that everything the Chinese people accomplished they too should be able to accomplish. They draw unlimited confidence and courage from the victory of the Chinese people. The Chinese people see their yesterday in all the oppressed nations." [45], p. 8, citing [232].

3. [227], 10 March 1961, pp. 315–316; speech of Marshall Yeh Chien-ying.

4. "At present some parts of Africa are going through experiences similar to what we experienced in China sixty years ago in the Boxer uprising. Some of the events were like those which occurred during the Hsin-hai Revolution [1911], while others resembled what happened around the 'May 4th' [movement of 1919]. We had not yet begun the period of the Northern Expedition and that of the War of Resistance against Japan, and we were still far from the events of 1949 in China. Africa at present is mostly occupied with fighting imperialism and colonialism. Its fight against feudalism is not so important, and, moreover, its role in the Socialist revolution is in a dormant phase." [227], 25 April 1961, pp. 484–485. For another translation, with a slight difference of meaning, see [5], p. 178.

commentator in 1964 likened events in the Congo (L) to events of the Chinese revolution.[5]

Chinese publications widely distributed in Africa stress China's revolutionary experience. Didactic *Peking Review* articles on "The Struggle for Proletarian Leadership in the Period of the New-Democratic Revolution in China" and "The Chinese Revolution and Armed Struggle" contained detailed analyses of the development of China's revolutionary strategy and institutions.[6] Where their distribution is not proscribed, works by Mao Tse-tung are available individually and in collection, including a special volume of *Selected Military Writings*.[7] Other works available in some African bookstalls offer an instructive romanticization of the Chinese revolution.[8] These materials comprise a revolutionary source book.

Three elements were forged together to make the Chinese revolution: a revolutionary (Communist) party, an army, and the united front. Each element underwent continuous change, a process Liu Shao-ch'i implied when he referred to party-building, armed struggle, and the united front. His phrasing captures the active, purposeful effort implied by the three structures.[9] The object was to build a uniquely defined Marxist-Leninist party suited to Chinese conditions, a Maoist guerrilla army, and an increasingly broad (but controlled) united front. With hindsight this becomes a stylized picture of the three components, though it was hardly possible for the CCP leadership to foresee that form during the early stages of the revolution.

Each component performs an essential function. The party mobilizes

5. "Like the Chinese people the Congolese people have also been compelled to take up swords and embark on the road of armed struggle after suffering defeat in their revolution and after investigation and study." Moreover, "there is no doubt that US imperialism will also resort to the tactics of deceit and cajolery in the Congo," as the writer alleges it did in China. *SCMP*, no. 3248, pp. 22–24 (*JMJP* editorial, 24 June 1964); *PR*, 3 July 1964, pp. 15–17.

6. *PR*, nos. 8–12 (1962), 23 February 1962 and in weekly installments thereafter; *PR*, 10 August and 17 August 1962. French and English editions of *Peking Review* are distributed.

7. Published in an English edition in 1963 and a French edition in 1964.

8. The following were bought at an Accra bookstore in 1964: Miao Min, *Fang Chih-min, Revolutionary Fighter*; Ch'en Ch'ang-feng, *On the Long March with Chairman Mao*; Soong Ch'ing-ling, *The Struggle for New China*; Kuo Mo-jo and Chou Yang, compilers, *Songs of the Red Flag*; Liu Pai-yü, *Flames Ahead*; a collection on the period 1945–1949, *The Great Turning Point*. More general works included Rewi Alley, *Land and Folk in Kiangsi*; *Cultural Life of the Chinese Workers*; Lu Hsün, *The True Story of Ah Q*; and Liu Chao-lin, *A Girl and her Mynah*. Pamphlets of works by Mao Tse-tung were numerous and inexpensive; for example, *Report of an Investigation into the Peasant Movement in Hunan* was priced at sixpence.

9. [126], p. 82.

support, maintains an organization, preserves a clear vision of the future, sponsors decision makers, and endeavors to guarantee legitimacy for their decisions. The army is a party instrument to be used when force, or threat of force, is needed to preserve the party and accomplish CCP objectives.[10] As an institution the united front borders on fiction, although groups are set up to embody the united front and to enlist men and women for united front purposes. Those purposes are a diluted or tactical form of doctrinal orthodoxy chosen in part for their broad appeal. Finally, since the task of revolution is a struggle against hostile entrenched forces, the three institutions are harnessed together against those who would bar the party's way.

Spatial and temporal sensitivity characterize the model. The strategy of encircling cities from the countryside, for example, showed sound judgment about political and geographic realities. Protracted war uses time and human weariness to best advantage. Taken together, these yield the Maoist doctrine so often quoted: "Enemy advances, we retreat; enemy halts, we harass; enemy tires, we attack; enemy retreats, we pursue." The model is also sensitive to human wishes, weakness, and determination. One summary of psychological insights is the "man over weapons" doctrine. Spatial, temporal, and psychological sensitivities served the CCP only because they contributed to sound political and military judgments; it is hard to imagine that such sound judgments would have been made if the leadership had been less subtle in its idea of action.

Marxist-Leninist canons and CCP statements combine in a body of doctrine, an ideology. CCP leaders profess to analyze society, choose objectives, and select means to attain ends by thought and action which accords with ideology. Doctrine suggests what China's leaders expect other governments to do. It embodies a common mode of discourse through which the work of army, party, and united front can be concerted. It is the source of assurance that time will be to the revolutionary's advantage. It defines opponents. Organizations, beliefs, and the tactics of political action are specified in the revolutionary model. As Tang Tsou and Morton Halperin have pointed out, Maoist doctrines were devised to achieve ambitious goals in a hostile setting and with meagre means, by an apt combination of political and military struggle.[11]

The Party

The party creates the army and united front, selects strategies and tactics, and receives and interprets Marxist-Leninist doctrine in its own

10. *Ibid.*, pp. 84–87.

11. *Ibid.*

fashion. It is the core of the model and the source of command. The party dominates the army. "The Chinese Red Army," Mao remarked, "is an armed force for carrying out the political tasks of the revolution."[12] The party "wages war" against warlords, landlords, comprador bourgeoisie, and foreign aggressors, as the times demand.[13] Party judgments guide the army. "Having made a clear-headed appraisal of the international and domestic situation on the basis of the science of Marxism-Leninism," the party saw that all attacks by reactionaries could be and had to be defeated.[14] War serves the world-revolutionary political objectives of Marxism-Leninism.[15]

The party dominates the united front, as affirmed in a widely-distributed article published in 1961:

> The basic feature of the Chinese people's democratic united front is that this united front is led by the Chinese Communist Party. All its other special features are inseparably connected with this basic feature.[16]

It follows that the Chinese revolutionary model cannot be followed in a country in every respect unless a Communist party is created. Lenin noted, even before the CCP was formed, that the creation of Communist parties in every country was a crucial step.[17] However, China has not called publicly for creation of Communist parties in Africa. This is an omission of greatest importance: African Communist parties are few, small, and — from China's view — ideologically impure. No formally organized Communist party in continental Africa has taken the Chinese side in the Sino-Soviet dispute.[18] In country after country no organized party exists at all. Why has the CCP allowed this contradiction, urging use of its model in a region which has few appropriate groups to implement the model, and yet not urging that parties be created?

12. *Ibid.*, p. 86; see [224], vol. 1, p. 106.
13. [223], pp. 268–269.
14. *Ibid.*, p. 345.
15. Even in the muted language of the anti-Japanese united front, Mao Tse-tung foresaw achieving "perpetual peace" by revolutionary war: "Once man has eliminated capitalism, he will attain the era of perpetual peace, and there will be no more need for war. . . . The revolutionary wars which have already begun are part of the war for perpetual peace." [223], p. 223.
16. [215], p. 11.
17. [132], pp. 23–25. In 1970 China circulated Uruguayan comment that success in the democratic revolution is impossible without a Marxist-Leninist revolutionary party. *PR*, 11 September 1970, p. 22.
18. [196], 1968, and 1970. See [192], January 1965, pp. 190–196, which counts the UPC as a Communist party, and designates it pro-Chinese.

The CCP may have considered Africans unready to create Communist parties. In China's own case no Communist party existed until 1920 or 1921, although a republic had been founded ten years earlier. By likening "some parts of Africa" to pre-1921 China,[19] the CCP may have been suggesting that the absence of Communist parties was normal. On the other hand, indices of social and economic development show that many African states are advanced in comparison with China in 1921. The view that only the internally-generated creation of a party proves that conditions for its creation are ripe is temptingly plausible. Yet the CCP itself took form under Soviet tutelage, and the tradition that established parties should help fledgling parties has never been repudiated by the CCP. Neither parallels to China's past nor the failure of Africans to take initiative seem, therefore, to prove Africa is "unready." The answer must lie elsewhere.

China probably doubts that reliable parties can be established today. If China brought Communist parties into being without guarantees that they would shun the Soviet side of the Sino-Soviet dispute, the effort could prove self-defeating. It would certainly be hard to obtain such guarantees since many previously established African parties have taken the Soviet side. Some commentators doubt that covert Chinese grants to Africans have produced much ideological commitment.[20] Knowing that declared leaders of a Marxist-Leninist party would soon be confronted by Soviet blandishments and that they might defect, the CCP has simply chosen to sidestep that danger.

Helping to form parties would also anger local governments. At a time of strong nationalist feeling, Africans whom China would like to recruit to an anti-imperialist united front might recoil against Chinese tutelage. In states which have accepted a Chinese embassy such steps might jeopardize the embassy itself.

Finally, the CCP may have feared that bodies formed under Chinese auspices would alienate radicals already organized in their own circles. Or it may have feared the prospective leaders' well-demonstrated passion for forming self-centered circles, responsive only to their own demands—personalist rather than ideological movements. An alternative was open: win the allegiance, however incomplete or qualified, of indigenous radical bodies. By so doing the CCP would save itself from fathering bodies whose paternity could never wholly be denied; and whatever charges of outside interference Chinese support might spark could be countered by the unassailable local roots of the radical group itself.

19. [227], p. 484.

20. For example, [108].

The model clearly requires a Communist party, but China has been silent on the issue. She has not granted the Marxist-Leninist label to those radical groups which she has urged to revolutionary action; she has spared them public criticism. By an ideological test, it would be very difficult for Peking to judge that these revolutionary groups are truly Marxist-Leninist. On the other hand, they are more than nationalist groups. Each is a nationalist and revolutionary movement which is the *most radical* among all movements in the country seeming to have the *capacity to persist* and a *significant possibility of success*. If there is no opposition which is distinctly more radical than the existing government, or if none of the groups which profess to be radical appears sufficiently capable of becoming an effective political force, China will not support oppositionists. In one case, Egypt, the Communist party split, generating a faction which commentators have termed "pro-Chinese"; China's evident embarrassment at that turn of events illustrates her policy.

Perhaps China now considers any anti-imperialist action useful, regardless of its source. Again a comparison to the period before 1921 may be helpful. From the May Fourth Incident (1919) until the CCP was formed (1921), China's "new democratic revolution" was led, according to Mao Tse-tung, by the proletariat. Mao advises:

> No matter what classes, parties or individuals in the oppressed nations join the revolution, and no matter whether or not they are conscious of this fact and fully understand it, so long as they oppose imperialism, their revolution becomes part of the proletarian-socialist world revolution and they themselves become allies of this revolution.[21]

Chinese appeals to Africa have called on the people to wage a protracted struggle. The issue of proletarian hegemony during the new democratic revolution has not been pressed. China has insisted on uniting the people and waging unremitting struggle without mentioning proletarian hegemony.[22] The question is whether struggle — specifically, armed struggle — can serve CCP goals in the absence of an indigenous Communist party. CCP leaders have answered affirmatively. Perhaps they believe that armed struggle creates the preconditions for a Maoist party to come into existence.

21. [222], pp. 15 and 18.

22. The doctrine of proletarian hegemony has not been suppressed, but it does not appear to guide African policy and is not mentioned in discussions of Africa. [214], published early in 1962, reasserts the doctrine forcefully.

The Army

Armed struggle certainly requires military organization. The Chinese army performed political as well as military tasks,[23] but always under party leadership. If no party exists, consider Mao's warning:

> Without a political goal guerrilla warfare must fail, as it must if its political objectives do not coincide with the aspirations of the people—and their sympathy, cooperation and assistance cannot be gained.[24]

We can imagine a guerrilla army with political goals coinciding with popular aspirations that are not articulated by any Communist party. In fact, at a stage inappropriate for the formation of a party, there could be political goals of a primitive character to be sought by armed struggle. Armed struggle would, in turn, promote political consciousness. Later, when conditions were right, a party would be formed. In this hypothetical case, China's model is not applied in every respect, but is borrowed insofar as consciousness permits. As political consciousness grows, the model would be adopted in more detail.

China has advocated armed struggle in three types of African states. In self-acknowledged colonies and in white-supremacist states the enemy is evident. A general call for armed action in such states costs China little. If an indigenous group opts for armed struggle, Peking can support it with few reservations. China has also advocated armed struggle in some African states which are already independent and are not white-supremacist states. In such cases China treads very cautiously and appears to be a follower, not a leader.

Where opposition to an existing government does not serve China's purpose, where the government deals with China and appears to have the capacity to crush or contain opposition, China has withheld support from oppositionists. Before publicly encouraging struggle in a named country, Peking must envision a clear advantage. The record of her public commitments in Africa warrants the conclusion that she has supported armed struggle only if it promised to advance a radical purpose, and if the group to be overthrown was an inviting target. These cases have not required subtle political discrimination on China's part. Even more important,

23. [224], vol. 1, p. 106: "Besides fighting to destroy the enemy's military strength, [the Red Army] should shoulder such important tasks as doing propaganda among the masses, organizing the masses, arming them, helping them to establish revolutionary political power and setting up Party organizations."

24. Cited in [126], p. 86.

China publicly urges armed struggle only if it will probably be begun regardless of what China says or—better yet—if it is already under way.

If armed struggle is not suited to every case, why does China dwell upon armed struggle in her comment on Africa? China seeks to hasten the development of political opposition groups and guide them toward conceptions of action closely akin to her own. She must say what is distinctive about China's experience. If oppositionists are choosing among alternative patterns of action, China will lose by default if her pattern is not advertised. A revolutionary army conducting protracted struggle is the hallmark of the Chinese style; since it was not present in the Russian revolution, Peking can make some claim to originality for her revolutionary model. China must talk about armed struggle to advance her model. She seeks to avoid two dangers: unreasonable jeopardy to useful intergovernmental ties, and ill-chosen attachment to half-hearted oppositionists. She moves from the general to the specific only when her conditions are met. Her revolutionary posture is clear, but intergovernmental relations go on and she is sparing in her concrete support to oppositionists.

Armed struggle can be undertaken by anyone. China's indiscriminate general celebration of revolutionary war must influence some Africans to undertake violence even though Peking has no contacts with them and would not jeopardize other interests for their sake. China probably looks upon such violence with favor. China's prescription for revolution can succeed only if it is tried. Therefore, though Peking may stop short of linking her prestige to small-scale violence which has little chance of success, every organized radical opposition can potentially grow in scale and win public Chinese support. The CCP has repeatedly emphasized that revolution is the best school for training revolutionaries. Moreover, once armed struggle is underway, it is an example to others who may also profit by the instability it breeds in adjacent territories.

China's model, complete only in retrospect, is too elaborate for the actual conditions of social and political organization which prevail in many African countries. Rather than withdraw her model, China apparently has elected to guide African radicals across the transitional period until conscious Maoist struggle is possible. It is as if some Chinese foresee a process in two stages: first, draw scattered oppositionists into some form of organization and action (preferably armed action); second, transform a radical nationalist organization into a group borrowing heavily from the Chinese revolutionary model. At some time in the future an indigenous Maoist party will be required, but until then the CCP can provide strategic, doctrinal, and organizational guidance. Chinese guidance need not be detailed or direct. No special political or military sophistication is required to follow the cues found in Chinese publications. The Chinese can have occasional contacts with opposition leaders, who may meet with Chinese embassy and NCNA representatives or visit China. If the oppositionists undertake armed struggle, castigate imperialism, and support China on some key issues Peking might conclude that the situation was maturing. China's wariness toward unproven groups (whose actions could cost China important diplomatic and economic assets) would persist. Where China would like to see large-scale opposition to existing authority develop, Chinese leaders may believe that their guidance spells the difference between determination and discouragement among the revolutionaries.

China wants a "new democratic revolution" in Africa, but there are few Africans whose ideological purity she trusts. Their number will grow, CCP leaders probably believe, but in the meantime China will stand in their stead. The very special rendering of Marxism-Leninism to which China is now committed narrows the ranks of Africans who would meet Peking's ideological standards, with the result that there is no sign that China is passing an ideological baton to Africa. China could retire from the transitional role more quickly if she were ideologically less demanding. China remains guardian of orthodoxy herself, however, and opens the united front to all Africans equally. The relationship between the CCP and African radicals is clarified if one considers a worldwide united front of which China is the proletarian hegemon.

The United Front

Armed struggle and united front tactics are not considered incompatible by the CCP; on the contrary, they are pursued together. In 1938 Mao Tse-tung said:

> [The main task of the CCP is] to unite with as many allies as possible and, according to the circumstances, to organize armed struggle for national and social liberation against armed counter-revolution, whether internal or external. Without armed struggle there would be no place in China for the proletariat and the Communist Party, and it would be impossible to accomplish any revolutionary task.[25]

By the 1960s the arena of armed struggle was outside China. The Chinese united front was not isolated from events. In 1961 Li Wei-han wrote that upholding "the great unity of the people of the world" was one of the main features of the domestic Chinese united front. Moreover:

25. [223], p. 270.

> The united front of the Chinese people is an important component part of the united front of the people of the world. The Chinese Communist Party has always made the unity of patriotism and internationalism its starting point and joins the unity of the Chinese people to that of all the people of the world.[26]

Chou En-lai spoke of the "broadest united front" when he addressed the National People's Congress in December 1964; at its core were the "forces of Marxism-Leninism" uniting revolutionary people everywhere against imperialism, reaction, and modern revisionism.[27]

If China were to maintain hegemony in a worldwide united front, giving it form and exercising control over it, she would have to perform tasks like those performed by the CCP in the domestic united front during China's revolution. Even if the united front were largely a fiction of the Chinese imagination, it would require some structure and lines of communication, which the CCP would create. The CCP would also choose issues in which the influence of members of the united front could be useful, and it would control the ways in which influence was exerted. It would endeavor to maintain hegemony, refusing to share ultimate authority. The problem of assuring control might seem acute because the Maoist united front is extensive, not narrow. The CCP had to expand the united front within China even as it maintained control.[28]

Because of the nature of a united front, "control" has two meanings. Control of some structures which broadcast united front appeals is definite, but control of the united front — which lacks constitutional machinery to be seized or offices to be won — is nebulous. The united front is so vague that its membership rises and falls with successive ad hoc appeals. By insisting that it define the united front, the CCP precludes any competition for leadership. Since the CCP chooses the positions taken by the front, persons who take contrary positions (even those who have a record of taking the positions of the front) are simply outside the front. By this manipulation of words, "control" is maintained for contrary elements within the front are not allowed to speak for it.

It is not enough simply to maintain the united front; it must prosper and adapt. To succeed, the revolutionist must subject the front to continual

26. [215]; *PR*, 18 August 1961, p. 11; *PR*, 1 September 1961, p. 14.

27. *PR*, 1 January 1965, pp. 16–17.

28. [214], p. 5: "As the experience of the Chinese revolution has fully proved, the working class must, on the basis of the consolidation and expansion of the worker-peasant alliance, win over all the forces that can possibly be won over and unite with over 90% of the country's population; only so can it establish a strong, overall leadership for the revolution."

transformation. Imagine the CCP as the center of a number of concentric rings. The outermost ring includes those who are objectively contributing to the united front in the CCP view, however minor their contribution may be. A person in the outermost ring develops greater consciousness or becomes more active, and he then steps into a ring nearer the center. The CCP has consistently endeavored to move men and women toward the center of the united front. Simultaneously, it sought to strengthen the innermost ring of true Marxist-Leninists and to enlarge the number who occupied this position; that is, it has sought to enlist more party members and to improve the reliability of those already enrolled. The net effect in China was the molding of a Communist party largely out of peasant stock, but terming itself the vanguard of the proletariat, a proletariat now augmented by the inclusion of "rural proletarians." The CCP probably envisions a similar process in each African country, as well as throughout the world.

Chou En-lai's remarks to Algerian FLN cadres in December 1963 suggest that he believed the FLN could carry out such a transformation within itself. Chou apparently invited Ahmed Ben Bella to declare, at some suitable future date, that the FLN was a Marxist-Leninist party. Fidel Castro, already a successful revolutionary, had pronounced the Marxist-Leninist character of his movement before either Moscow or Peking had done so. Commenting on Chou's speech, Benjamin Schwartz has written that "the essence of the true proletarian class nature is now not only detached from the industrial proletariat, it is even detachable from constituted Communist parties."[29] Chinese judgment replaced any objective test of whether or not a person was Marxist-Leninist.

It is important to recall that the CCP was never a fixed homogeneous group of staunch Marxist-Leninists. It constantly sought new recruits. Only within the party was political education truly intensive. All recruits were considered politically deficient. By entering the party they declared their intention and willingness to undergo political education. The decisive criterion for recruitment was neither the past (class origin) nor the present (current belief), but a possible future (what the recruit might come to believe). Seen in this light, Chinese overtures to African militants are not ideologically bizarre. The CCP assumes that human material is plastic. It does not assume that men can always be molded precisely or without cost; it estimates that a certain political effort will produce changes of various degrees among the members of a group subjected to training. The CCP preference for struggle stems partly from the belief that struggle

29. [112], p. 106.

against a hostile environment guarantees *self-sustaining* political development. From China's point of view, the best result would be continuous low-cost transformation of a group in directions which parallel those preferred by the CCP leadership. In Chou's eyes the FLN, with its special history of successful guerrilla struggle, is a unique candidate to duplicate the Chinese experience in an African setting.

Algeria's revolution was similar to China's in some respects. The Front de Libération Nationale, a party of rather strict discipline, sought to enlist Algerians of many political persuasions in the common cause of revolutionary struggle. It created an army, the Armée de Libération Nationale (ALN), which bore the brunt of fighting the French. Over a period of eight years the FLN maintained its coherence; it even created a provisional government. Of all nationalist movements in Africa, the Algerian revolution most closely paralleled China's experience. In large measure, however, the similarities were coincidental. There is no reason to believe that the FLN and ALN were based upon the Chinese model. The difficulty of disentangling cause and coincidence is nonetheless a real one, for the FLN leaders knew of China's revolution and sought her support after they committed themselves to an armed struggle. China has sought to identify herself with the Algerian revolution and has repeatedly praised it. On the other hand, the FLN was not a Communist movement. Its ideology was nationalist in a profound sense. Only by looking at an unrepresentative handful of its postindependence programs might China conclude that the FLN could establish a Marxist and Maoist state, rather than merely discard the French colonizers; with another perspective, Peking might even have damned the FLN's adoption of neocolonialist ties to France.

Comparability

If African conditions were wholly unlike those of China in 1921–1949, the model would be inapplicable and irrelevant. In what ways are African conditions like those of China and in what ways are they different?

Africa is not free of misery and oppression. Yet famine, internecine war, and confining governmental traditionalism — all characteristics of the Chinese revolutionary period — are the exception rather than the rule in Africa. Most regions can support a growing population. Africa's division into separate states precluded the emergence of warlords; war has occurred (Algeria, Sudan, Nigeria), but it is not a general phenomenon. Educated men are recruited into public service by governments committed to modernization. Landlordism and village usury are not comparable to the harsh conditions of China. For these reasons, proportionately fewer

Africans than Chinese are available for recruitment into radical movements. Moreover, leaders of African opposition movements are active in a social and political environment very different from that of the CCP's early leaders.

Africa, like China in the twenties, is largely underdeveloped. Modern industry has developed in central Africa and along the Mediterranean littoral, but only South Africa has a large modern industrial sector. Even in developed regions income distribution is uneven. The Algerian war disrupted that country's economy; Egypt's economic attainments have been offset by military misadventures and rapid population growth. Some states have suffered from adverse shifts in the terms of trade. Most African states, however, have achieved a modest rate of net investment in the period since independence. Growth has exceeded the continent's 2.3 percent annual population increase. Africa is unlike China in the 1920s in that systematic moves toward economic development are being attempted throughout the continent, usually with modest success. Despite continuing achievements, the economy might prove to be a source of radical rejection of present ways, because current development rates promise no hope of escape from relative underdevelopment. The gap between per capita income in rich states and in the African states continues to widen each year.

The CCP emerged while Chinese central authority was in disorder. Although the performance of independent African governments in governing their populations is impressive by comparison with the failures of Chinese internal government in 1921–1949, neither individual governments nor the overall pattern of African states can be judged safe from future breakdown. African cultural, linguistic, racial, ethnic, and religious patterns are almost never congruent with the borders of nation-states. States are threatened by the disintegrative pressure of subnational loyalty; Biafra tragically but vividly illustrates the case. These cleavages prompt government leaders carefully and subtly to balance divergent forces and to try to build around a modern conception of nationhood; they are not always successful. Obstacles to national unity, whether regional or continental, spring from ethnic differences and the chauvinist spirit which may accompany the building of a nation.

Amid disarray, the CCP consciously exploited cleavages wherever it found them. Tales of the Long March (1934–1935) emphasize that the CCP won support from minorities traditionally hostile to the Han (ethnic Chinese) population. The distinction between city and country was not merely an administrative distinction which took on military significance in the tactic of surrounding cities; it was a social distinction as well. In the countryside, class antagonisms were commonly, but not consistently, put to political use. Where the CCP forces were opposed, they attempted to divide their foes; for example, some Japanese prisoners were treated well and returned to the Japanese lines to weaken their compatriots' will to fight. China has commented extensively on race relations in Africa and the United States since 1949. Her comments have demonstrated a capacity to note cleavages outside China and to criticize them to her own advantage. Peking seems to exaggerate cleavage in published comment and to consistently underestimate conventional solidarities.

The CCP's strongest gains were made during wartime. After Japan's invasion of China proper in 1937, the CCP enlarged its armies and harnessed patriotic sentiment. The Kuomintang proved ineffective and was unable to meet its responsibility to defend China. This element of the Chinese experience has no counterpart in Africa. Patriotism is at the disposal of existing governments even, to an extent, in white-supremacist and colonial territories; it is often unavailable to revolutionary movements. The CCP rails against neocolonialist intrusion in Africa, but, if injustice and oppression are not more direct than they are at present, they will catalyze little revolutionary resistance.

A further difference between the African and Chinese cases is the fact that African radicals may be offered attractive opportunities which do not require armed struggle. Able oppositionists have even been recruited into government posts, as happened to many in Cameroon. Abdul Rahman Mohammed Babu has held ministerial portfolios in the Tanzanian government since the merger of Zanzibar and Tanganyika. In small African countries where nationalism is strong, enemies may sublimate their differences and achieve a modus vivendi. Others have chosen exile and begun new lives abroad.

After the Shanghai Incident of 1927, in which the Kuomintang supervised the slaughter of hundreds of CCP members, the isolation of the CCP in China was much greater than that of radical oppositionists in most African situations. CCP members were unlikely to believe they would find a secure place outside the CCP ranks, and they did not always have alternative ways to find satisfaction within the system. The African exception to this rule is Pierre Mulele. As a leader of revolutionists in 1964, he posed an important challenge to the central Congolese government. In 1968 he was invited to return to the Congo, and he accepted. After dining ceremonially with Congolese leaders, he was taken away and executed.

This summary shows that Africa is not altogether like China, nor is it wholly dissimilar. In employing the Chinese model, African revolutionaries will have to exercise great skill, adopting only some elements of the model while fitting others to the changed conditions. The problem is not merely that some choice and adaptation must be made; certain fundamental characteristics of China's case — foreign invasion, internal governmental collapse, and widespread peasant discontent — are not now present in Africa. In what way is the model relevant?

Revolutionaries can copy the model, but it can also bear on African politics in more subtle ways. Its rhetoric may be borrowed by existing governments to preempt revolutionary movements. Governments (and foreign observers) may see parallels between an indigenous movement and the Chinese revolutionary movement, conclude that a revolution in the Chinese style is under way, and take repressive measures (which may actually prove to be exaggerated or inept and help bring about the conditions which will make their fears real). Governments may become frightened by the model and preclude legal contact with Chinese. Finally, governments may judge Chinese intentions from her revolutionary model, even though in practice China declined to aid revolutionaries professing to implement the model. It is important to realize that there are many levels at which a version of the model may influence the actions of persons concerned with Africa.

The CCP holds that every element of the model is mutually complementary. The adaptation which the CCP foresees will ultimately converge, in an individual state or region, on a structure and process which is similarly integral. At the present time, however, movements are at a low level of consciousness; therefore, incomplete borrowing can be accepted for it may prove better than none. As the revolutionary situation in an African country develops, China expects institutions and practices will gradually come into being to accomplish those tasks which the CCP had taken upon itself by 1949. The precise nature of the institutions and the practices which prove suitable need not be identical to those of the Chinese revolution.

Conclusion

Army, party, and united front together carry out the main tasks of a movement seeking state power. The army is the coercive arm; the party is the guarantor of purpose and orthodoxy; the united front is a symbol of broad appeal and support. Maoist strategic requirements ultimately rely upon the power of *unit acts* repeated many thousands of times: guerrilla clashes, party recruitment, intraparty criticism, and persuasive encounters with the peasantry. Instructions detailing the performance of these unit acts are an integral part of the model.

The interrelatedness of the components is illustrated by the Eight

Points of Attention of the People's Liberation Army. Instruction to soldiers in proper conduct, the eight points, if scrupulously followed, guarantee that contact between soldiers and nonsoldiers will be favorable to the political aims of the CCP. At the most elementary level of civilian fear (for dignity, life, and property), the eight points require conduct to assuage that fear. In China, where soldiers have ravaged the land and people again and again, the CCP could anticipate winning recruits to the army and civilian assistance in military operations.[30] By internalizing these instructions, members of the party and the army could sustain revolutionary initiative even when separated from the formal chain of command.

In the form revolutionary action might attain in an African state, after a period of struggle and the rise of a politically conscious Maoist leadership, the components of this model, *reduplicated again and again*, would be perfused by the doctrines of struggle, will, and persistence which distinguish the Chinese model. The authoritarian structures of the Marxist-Leninist party and the guerrilla army would be designed to resist erosion,[31] even as the stress on participation and comradeship in both would encourage voluntary commitment. Through political education, individual members of the army and party would learn to internalize both a sense of the enemy and plans for correct conduct toward "the people." The combination of organizations and doctrine should prove resilient to shock, mindful of purpose, continuously assertive, and victorious in a portion of the encounters sufficient to claim its aptness: the system would be *self-sustaining*. The unit acts are realistically adapted to personal encounters, and organization proliferates the unit acts. So long as a serious contradiction between social right and social reality is perceived by the revolutionaries and a proportion of the people among whom they live and fight, the organization can survive and expand. It is vain to imagine that quantities can be assigned to the severity of contradictions, or to the intensity and currency of perceptions, which together provide the sustaining basis for a purposive revolutionary band. Much depends on the common experience of the people and the other models for political and social action which are current among them. Nevertheless, it would be prudent to conclude that a revolutionary band can substantially increase its chances for survival and success by developing doctrines and organizations which

30. [223], pp. 341–342. The eight points are: (1) Speak politely. (2) Pay fairly for what you buy. (3) Return everything you borrow. (4) Pay for anything you damage. (5) Do not hit or swear at people. (6) Do not damage crops. (7) Do not take liberties with women. (8) Do not ill-treat captives.

31. The first of the Three Main Rules of Discipline of the People's Liberation Army is, "Obey orders in all your actions."

imitate abstract characteristics of the Chinese model, if not the components themselves. Among these characteristics are: unit acts which serve recruitment and persuasion, while forestalling the dilution of doctrine; organization against the outside which nevertheless stresses the need to enlist other people's support; action which maintains its own momentum partly because it includes strategems to prevent suppression; and emphasis on the maintenance of purpose with flexibility. The combination of broad general doctrine with insistence upon specific decisive encounters led the CCP to match its guidance to the daily life of recruits, as the eight points testify. Many of the CCP's practical procedures are consistent with modern organization theory.

Nonetheless, the context in Africa is very different from that which existed in China. Differences extend beyond the social situation to the characteristic styles of organization. The African continent is a maze of states and cultures. To cope with this diversity, China has turned to some fairly straightforward distinctions among the African regions. These have required, for most of Africa, that the problems of revolutionary organization be put to one side for the present. Peking's conception of the continent — its various states and territories — is the subject of the next chapter.

8 African States and Liberation Movements

Sensitive to strategy and organization, the Chinese Communist party won power by struggle in scattered cities and rural areas. Coordination among local operations and initiatives was dependent upon the guidance of the CCP, which viewed the effort as a *single* revolution.

Although present-day Africa has some similarities to China, it is larger in size, much more diverse in culture, and politically more self-conscious than China of the 1930s and 1940s. The states, with fixed boundaries and claims to individual sovereignty, obstruct multinational and continental schemes. Pan-Africanism itself is rigidly circumscribed because African states do not want to surrender authority.

The Chinese vision of revolution in Africa acknowledges that national revolutions must come first: national revolutions will multiply and speed the continental revolution, and the will to revolt will sweep the continent.

One should take care to see how struggle within individual nations and the continent as an entity are thought to be related in order to understand what China expects, to picture the roles allocated to the party, the army, and the united front. The *Kung-tso T'ung-hsün* [Bulletin of Activities of the People's Liberation Army] contains the least ambiguous statement of this relationship. A few of the political leaders in any newly-independent country will lean to the left. Those who lean to the right will lose the confidence of the people and will be driven from power and replaced by men who can carry through the national democratic revolution. Those who survive "must depend mainly upon their own personal experience, for foreign assistance can only come second; their victory will come eventually but no immediate results should be expected." More importantly:

> Among the independent countries in Africa, if only one or two of them complete a real national revolution, solving their own prob-

> lems of resisting imperialism and reaching an internal solution of a democratic national revolution, the effect will be very great, the time ripe for action, the revolutionary wave will be able to swallow the whole African continent, and the 200 million and more Africans will advance to the forefront of the world. We should take long-range views of this problem.[1]

However faulty the domino theory, there is evidence that Chinese believe it will prove true in the case of Africa. "If we can take the Congo, we can have all of Africa," Mao Tse-tung is supposed to have remarked.[2] Chinese repeatedly refer to the influence of a revolution on revolutionary morale in nearby territories. A *Jen-min Jih-pao* editorial claimed that "the armed struggle of the Angolan people, most of all, is exerting direct and important influence on their neighbors, the Congolese people, and both peoples encourage, influence and support each other. The struggle of the Congolese people is not an isolated one in Africa and the world."[3]

The *Kung-tso T'ung-hsün* account describes Africa as the "center of the anticolonialist struggle and the center for East and West to fight for the control of the intermediary zone." In each country the national revolution is paramount; on a continental scale, revolutionaries must strive to build a united front.

> Africa at present is mostly occupied with fighting imperialism and colonialism. Its fight against feudalism is not so important and, moreover, its role in the socialist revolution is in a dormant phase. The important part of its activities lies in its national revolution and in making the United Front spread everywhere on the continent.

Who will guide the revolution? "History and realistic life can help the Africans to take the road of healthy development." But China must point out the experience of the Chinese revolutions: "We must tell them about the Chinese revolutionary experience in order to reveal the true nature of both new and old colonialism. In Africa we do no harm to anyone, we introduce no illusions, for all we say is true." Chinese advice will suffice for some time, but indigenous Communist parties will eventually arise. The text is not wholly free of ambiguity, but it seems to envisage that such parties will appear in each African state: "According to the analysis of Marxism it is to be confirmed that the embryo of national revolution in these countries will become a genuine people's revolution, give rise to

1. [227], pp. 484–485.
2. See Chapter 3, note 106.
3. *SCMP*, no. 2332, p. 34 (*JMJP*, 30 June 1961).

Marxists, form political parties of proletariats [sic] and go towards the Socialist revolution."[4]

The *Kung-tso T'ung-hsün* projection, if we may call it that, envisions that moderate ("rightist") national leadership will be forced aside by struggle. Those who could not readily be attacked as white supremacists could be charged with complicity in neocolonial exploitation. That is the message of a *Ta Kung Pao* editorial published on the eve of the Third All-African People's Conference:

> Today, the African peoples, who have recognized even more clearly their principal enemy and the objectives of their struggle, are becoming ever more closely united. Unity is strength and unity is victory. Powerful anti-imperialist storms are sweeping the entire African continent, with a force neither the old nor the new colonialists can resist.[5]

Time and experience have not tempered China's insistence on this analysis. "We are firmly convinced," Li Hsien-nien told a visiting Guinean delegation early in 1969, "that as long as the African people unite and persist in struggle, they will certainly drive imperialism and colonialism out of Africa."

The South African Communist party (SACP), which is aligned with Moscow in the Sino-Soviet dispute, has put forth a very different projection. It is useful to compare them. The SACP foresees three successive phases: the ouster of colonialists, followed by a sweeping social revolution, and, finally, attainment of African unity. Socialism and African unity are to be reached simultaneously. The first two phases will take place inside national frontiers. The third brings into being "regional federations established by common consent, merging peacefully into a great socialist African Union." None of the phases mentions violent revolution. The plan will be carried out by "conscious patriotic organizations, by national united fronts embracing all the healthy national elements, and including in a foremost role the representatives of the working people in the towns and countryside, guided by the science of socialism, by Marxism-Leninism." Though some of the language reads like that of China's formula — the "democratic united front" under "proletarian hegemony" — it is clear that the SACP writer is proposing something quite different. He would accept much less than Communist hegemony. Noting the prevalence of one-party states in Africa, he observes:

4. [227], p. 484.
5. *SCMP*, no. 2468, p. 21 (26 March 1961).

> Certainly we are in favor of national unity, which may take the form of a single state party, or it may take the form of a united national democratic front embracing more than one party. . . . In some cases, the demand for a single party may be correct and progressive.

Continuing, he says that Ghana's Convention People's party is a "correct and progressive" single party while those in Niger, Central African Republic, and Cameroon are not. In order to qualify as correct and progressive, they should be "linked with the masses and give expression to their aspirations."[6]

The question of stages is intricate. The SACP writer does not specify at what stage of development the "representatives of the working people," guided by Marxism-Leninism, must take the "foremost role" and, by comparison, at what stage a single party — presumably something other than a Marxist-Leninist party — would be "correct and progressive." Except for this equivocation, the writer is calling for something very much like the national democratic state[7] which Moscow proposed in 1960. The national democratic state did not require proletarian hegemony.

In China's view, by comparison, armed struggle is almost certain to be needed to get from oppression to socialism. Independence granted by a colonial power is deeply suspect; where an activist leader secures his nation's independence, China explains that a concession was forced by some form of struggle — strikes, demonstrations — and the threat of still greater violence. For the SACP analyst, a progressive army is a defensive body protecting the new state from imperialism. For the CCP, the army

6. "*Phase One: Anti-Colonialist.* The replacement of colonialist governments, from Cape to Cairo, by African governments, freely chosen by the people; Africanization of the armed forces and police, the civil service; elimination of foreign monopoly-capital domination of the economy to ensure complete independence. *Phase Two: Social Revolution.* Elimination of vestiges of feudalism, tribalism, and other relics of the past deliberately preserved by the colonialists to perpetuate their rule by 'indirect government.' Massive agrarian reform, industrialization along non-capitalist lines, labor legislation against exploitation, mass participation of workers and peasants in all affairs of state to ensure that the departed colonialists are not merely replaced by a new class of indigenous exploiters and parasites. *Phase Three: African Unity and Socialism.* The artificial frontiers drawn by the rival colonialists to define 'their' respective 'possessions' are eliminated. Regional federations are established by common consent, merging peacefully into a great socialist African Union, vanquishing all the legacies and backwardness left behind by colonialism, catching up to the 'developed' countries with giant strides to win equality in status and in fact in every field, and playing a powerful part for peace and progress among the nations and continents of the world." [148], January–March 1964, pp. 7–8, 12–13.

7. In which a national army would be created, the civil service Africanized, institutions altered, and "democratic" procedures followed (which would permit a Communist party to organize legally).

is an instrument to win state control (whether from the colonizer or local rightists) and then to aid revolutionary action elsewhere (at the least by training foreign guerrillas). An army in the CCP view is an active, rather than defensive, force, limited only by a sound estimate of its own strength and the requirement that political control be foremost. The progressive state is almost analogous to a Chinese liberated area, from which revolution was carried by force to the adjacent territory. But in a continent of independent states and dependent regions, the base area exists behind legal boundaries.

The SACP calls for elimination of national boundaries only in the third phase. Although the CCP might agree to maintain their appearance over an extended time, it would eliminate the significance of national boundaries as soon as it proved useful to do so. China assumes that the phases are interwoven far more than the SACP model suggests. In general, CCP comment suggests more tension, militancy, and struggle.[8]

China has encouraged specific steps to promote revolution across national boundaries. She praised Algerian support of national liberation movements elsewhere in Africa.[9] She reportedly pledged funds for a guerrilla training center in Algeria;[10] Chinese personnel conducted guerrilla training programs in Ghana;[11] and China was in a position to train Congo (L) revolutionaries enjoying sanctuary in Congo (B) and Burundi. At the end of 1964 Chinese arms were shipped to Congolese revolutionaries via Uganda and Tanzania, and with their consent.

Although China might have commented directly on Pan-African plans and aspirations, she has chosen instead to evade the inherent doctrinal issues. Soviet spokesmen, by contrast, have put themselves forward as friendly critics. Soviet Academician I. I. Potekhin observed in 1958 that "there is much in Pan Africanism that is quite alien to our world outlook." When the Organization of African Unity was established in May 1963, *Izvestia* commentator V. Kudryavtsev welcomed it as "built on an anti-imperialist and anticolonialist foundation," but he went on to voice the fear that Pan-Africanism would lead to African isolation from "progressive" non-African forces.

8. The SACP statement is designed in part to win adherents among the non-Communists within Africa, and therefore it may not be a candid statement of the part Communist parties might play if offered opportunities. Still, it is in just such propositions as these that the contrasting revolutionary "purity" of Soviet and Chinese appeals reaches prospective African recruits.

9. *PR*, 9 November 1962, pp. 22–23.

10. [182], 13 January 1964. The report states that 1,500 guerrillas from Angola, Mozambique, Portuguese Guinea, and South Africa trained at the center in 1963.

11. [38].

China shared the Soviet predilection for judging Pan-African initiatives by whether they were progressive or not, although she defined the word in her own way. She has been loathe to alienate Pan-Africanists. Soviet commentators, on the other hand, were at one time publicly blunt in their opposition,[12] although recently they have spoken more kindly of the kindred Pan-Arab movement. China cannot ignore Pan-African ventures; she praises those specific steps which she regards as useful. At the same time, her attachment to some forms of continental cooperation does not extend to an unqualified endorsement, any more than her encouragement of nation-building amounts to a tacit approval of all national governments. As the self-selected head of a worldwide united front, China is compelled to forgo attacks on popular symbols carrying anti-imperialist and anticolonialist overtones.

The CCP has had to adopt a policy toward each separate African state and territory. Where China has been recognized and has elected to reciprocate, diplomatic relations have been established. Then the important issue has come into focus: How will revolutionary and incremental goals be reconciled?

When China carries out policy in a specific African state there is conflict between her revolutionary and incremental goals. These would be reconciled only if the individual state adopted China's world view as its own. No African state has yet done so. China has always been forced by circumstance to accept less than she wished. Every African state has taken its own particular posture toward China — and Peking in turn has practiced a different style of diplomacy toward each African state.

In her friendliest exchanges, China has extended grants and economic credits, received the chief of government in Peking, and written of the progressive steps being taken by his country. At her most hostile, she has funded dissident factions, published attacks on the leadership, and — in the heat of 1966 and 1967 — even provoked ruptures of diplomatic relations. How can this wide range of behavior be accounted for?

Four Styles of Diplomacy

Let us discuss four groups of states toward which China has practiced, or been forced to practice, different styles of diplomacy. She has spoken with special warmth of Algeria, Congo (B), Nkrumah's Ghana, Guinea, Keita's Mali, Tanzania (including Zanzibar), and the United Arab Re-

12. Compare, for example, V. Kudryavtsev's comment: "It may well be that some of the ideologists of African unity who propose the establishment of government organs on an all-Africa scale right away are running away with themselves. . . . I think that these projects are premature." [170], no. 8 (1964), p. 75.

public. She has conducted herself toward another group with proper formality and less warmth: Morocco, Mauritania, Somalia, Sudan, Uganda, and Zambia. In three cases — post-Nkrumah Ghana, Kenya, and Tunisia — her actions appear to have been designed to provoke a break in diplomatic relations. Finally, three states — Burundi, the Central African Republic, and Dahomey — have ousted the Chinese mission although China almost certainly would have preferred to stay.[13]

Chinese provocations in Africa were bizarre. Why should China decide to forfeit her embassies in spite of their usefulness? This question prompts three possible explanations. First, the designers of the provocative steps toward Ghana and Tunisia simply underestimated the readiness of the African state to break or suspend relations; that is, no break was expected. Second, the steps were consequent upon the Great Proletarian Cultural Revolution, the hasty acts of men insensitive to the usefulness of "presence" and anxious to be as revolutionary as possible. Third, the steps were calculated risks taken to make political gains even at the expense of a rupture.

Consider the cases.[14] In early 1966, once Nkrumah had fallen, China's choice of policies was hardly an easy one: Should she maintain her support of Nkrumah and the policies he symbolized, or repudiate Nkrumah by adopting a formally correct position toward the military men who removed him? The new government had pared to a minimum the operations of the Accra mission. It was restricted in size, Chinese experts had been sent home, and guerrilla training had been terminated. Moreover, China could distinguish herself from the Soviet Union by instigating a break in diplomatic relations.

Bourguiba's public denunciations of Chinese intentions and his support of the United States position on South Vietnam could have been tolerated by China if the damage done to her revolutionary image had been offset by other advantages. China had in fact tolerated Bourguiba for several years, but by late 1967 the situation was changing. Bourguiba was showing signs of age, and complaints about his party were widespread; the third Arab-Israeli War brought his vulnerability into sharp relief. Peking could easily have given undue weight to these signs. The changes coincided with repercussions of the cultural revolution on Chinese foreign policy operations that are as yet unclear.

Kenyan officials were also publicly critical of Chinese activities. The

13. Her short-lived mission in Stanleyville is not considered here, nor is the fact that union of Tanganyika and Zanzibar forced the downgrading of China's embassy in Zanzibar to a consulate.

14. They are more fully discussed in Chapter 6.

imperative governing Chinese decisions was to maintain the plausibility of Chinese radicalism in the eyes of Kenyan dissidents. If China were to abuse the Kenyatta government, plausibility could be maintained. Contacts with Kenyan dissidents were not endangered, since they could be maintained from Uganda or Tanzania.

In all three cases, therefore, China's moves protected her image as a revolutionary state, and they may have been chosen for that reason. Also, the usefulness of the mission in each case previously had been sharply reduced. The most convincing explanation of these cases is that a calculation of risks was made, rupture was judged a reasonable risk for the revolutionary benefits, and a readiness to act was catalyzed by the cultural revolution.

Dahomey and the Central African Republic did not give China time to work out a modus vivendi. Had she been less visible (thirty Chinese in Bangui, ten in Dahomey), or had Bokassa and Soglo been more confident, relations might not have been severed. If China did sponsor the Armée Populaire Centrafricaine, she acted improperly, but that charge turns on slender evidence that is unconvincing. No other charges were made. It is quite probable that China was still taking her bearings in both countries at the time she was ousted. It is also likely that she intended to maintain relations and dispense some foreign aid as long as the two governments remained hospitable. In the case of Burundi, China practiced diplomacy which was effective toward the governing faction but judged threatening by the Mwami. She could have adopted a cautious deference to the Mwami — but with costs in both short term (forgoing more assertive policies) and long term (building up the kingship at the expense of radicals). As in Kenya, China maintained good relations with a potentially viable radical group rather than appease more moderate forces (KANU, the Mwami).

If governmental changes had not occurred, if the Mwami had not asserted his authority, China's style vis-à-vis Dahomey, Centrafrica, and Burundi would probably have continued to be proper, correct, and even cordial. A modest aid program was under way in Bangui. Chinese advice to Rwandan and Congo (L) dissidents in Burundi was, at least, tolerated by that government.

In this sense, they are like those states with which China has maintained correct relations with limited cooperation. Morocco, Mauritania, Somalia, Sudan, Uganda, and Zambia are in this intermediate position. Three — Morocco, Sudan, and Uganda — are important trading partners. Zambia is a point of departure for revolutionaries seeking change in Rhodesia, Angola, South-West Africa, and South Africa; moreover, it is the inland terminal of the Tan-Zam railway. With these considerations in mind, perhaps neither the governments nor Peking have emphasized the real differences in belief and purpose which might divide them. Again, there is no opposition to the left in these states which would embrace Peking: there is now no other place to which China can turn. Somali political life has included groups which had contacts with China and which have pursued a policy toward the goal of Greater Somalia more forceful than that of the government; yet China might still conclude that a policy alienating the Somali leadership would be pointless.[15] Like Somalia, Mauritania pursues a policy of unswerving nonalignment, but she also continues a conservative tradition. By undertaking modest ties with China, Mauritania's leaders created a limited basis for rapport with the leaders of more radical African states. China's willingness to accept Mauritanian proposals for relations (once the obstacle of Moroccan claims to Mauritanian territory ceased to restrain Peking) lay in the absence of any radical alternative.

These examples suggest that, until the Great Proletarian Cultural Revolution, China was willing to tolerate any African state with which she had established relations—and that, in turn, meant any African state which had recognized Peking as the sole legitimate government of China. No revolutionary test was applied to the government, provided it was demonstrably independent. In order to coexist with some states, China was forced to contain herself, to withhold criticism she might easily have made. The case of Tunisia suggests that, before the cultural revolution, Peking even tolerated open, public criticism. The striking feature of China's diplomatic style during the cultural revolution is not that she turned against Bourguiba, but that she continued to deal with Morocco,

15. Before Somalia gained independence, China contacted leaders of the Greater Somali League and the Somali National Union, which failed to emerge as significant postindependence political forces. [123], p. 176. However, the opposition Somali Democratic Union was termed "Peking-oriented." *NYT*, 27 November 1963. An unattributed list of Communist parties and factions in [192], January 1965, p. 192, lists the Somali Democratic Union, but on p. 176, William E. Griffith writes that there is no organized Communist party in Somalia. In 1964 there was speculation that China had approached the Ogaden rebels, but the report cautioned that China and other Communist states refrained from direct aid to the rebels lest the Somali government's displeasure be incurred. Somalia was then committed to a negotiated solution of the conflicting claims to Ethiopia's neighboring Ogaden region; moreover, said this report, Somalia did not wish to acknowledge that she had no control over the rebels. *NYT*, 19 March 1964. Whatever the extent of these ties, China undertook significant aid commitments to the Somali government. The coup of 21 October 1969, which ended almost a decade of rule by the Somali Youth League, did not lead to a break in Sino-Somali relations.

Sudan, Mauritania, and other countries which pursued internal policies far different from those of China.

Peking's warmest terms, however, were reserved for the more militant African states. Peking appointed experienced and prestigious ambassadors to their capitals. The largest portion of African aid was given to these states. Nonetheless, this group — Algeria, Congo (B), Nkrumah's Ghana, Guinea, Keita's Mali, Tanzania, and the United Arab Republic — included some of Africa's most forceful and independent leaders; none of these states subordinated itself to China, or established major relations involving dependency of the kind that links, say, the United States and some Latin American states.

In what way is this group of states distinguished from those states with which China merely developed proper relations and minimal cooperation? First, each has experienced a major confrontation with indigenous moderates or Western states: Algeria's war for independence, the overthrow of Abbé Youlou in the Congo (Brazzaville), Nkrumah's conviction that his visions clashed with imperialist wishes, the precipitate French withdrawal from Guinea, Senegal's separation from the Mali Federation, the Zanzibar revolution, and the Suez crisis are cases in point. Second, they are actively committed to the overthrow of colonial and moderate regimes and have permitted national liberation movements to train on their territory or to use it as a springboard for raids (though Mali has not done so since 1961). Third, this group is given to radical language, including attacks on imperialism and the United States. Fourth, the states in this group are more willing than others to join China in political initiatives: Mali's singular support for China's position on the nuclear test ban treaty is a striking example. Also, these countries have, from time to time, pointedly emulated China. Algeria under Ben Bella began to create a militia. Guinea attempted a human investment program on the Chinese pattern. Mali organized a militia and conducted a "little cultural revolution" before the coup against Modibo Keita. Other African states might be characterized by one or two of these criteria, but not more.

How has China handled differences with these states? For the most part by selective silence, and occasionally by strong public statements carefully addressed to the issue at hand. For example, no comment was made about those who signed the test ban treaty, although many favorable responses to the Chinese circular letter were published. The United Nations operation in the Congo (L) was roundly and repeatedly attacked by China, but the African states contributing troops were largely spared from criticism.

Chinese representatives have sought to impress the local citizenry wherever possible. Therefore there are some diplomatic techniques which are common to Peking's style in all of the countries where China has had missions. Until the cultural revolution, China maintained large embassy staffs, but direct personal contact between embassy personnel and local citizens was not in proportion to the size of the staff. Favored citizens might be invited, as they were in Mogadishu, to see a movie at the Chinese embassy. Usually admission to a Chinese embassy was not casually obtained. Some ambassadors acquired reputations as effective informal representatives. Anecdotal reports mention Huang Hua's visit to the University of Ghana, where he proved to be the perfect dinner conversationalist, and Ho Ying, circulating at cocktail parties in Dar es Salaam, perfectly willing to chat with all visitors. Opposing these are reports that Chinese staff members — particularly during the cultural revolution — tended to confine themselves to the compound and avoid mixing with the local people.

The fragmentary evidence indicates that the Chinese representation included a sufficient number of people with linguistic and diplomatic abilities to maintain important political contacts, especially with national liberation movements and pivotal dissident groups. As noted earlier, contacts and impressionistic reporting of the political situation were important tasks of the New China News Agency staff. Among NCNA reporters, Kao Liang, working out of Dar es Salaam, typified the journalist who undertook political work. It is not now known whether embassy and NCNA resources remained adequate to these purposes after the cultural revolution, when there was a diminution in staff and all but one ambassador returned to Peking.

The Absence of Diplomatic Relations

China's position with independent states which have not extended recognition, or have recognized both Peking and Taipei, has depended upon whether a viable left opposition friendly to the Chinese world view was available.

Two African states delayed extending recognition, at one time or another having hinted that it would be forthcoming: Ethiopia and Nigeria. Ethiopia entertained Chou En-lai early in 1964, but Emperor Haile Selassie long postponed establishing diplomatic ties. With the rise of the Eritrean Liberation Front and Peking's decision to give it support, the prospect that Ethiopia and China might establish diplomatic ties appeared more remote. China's posture in Ethiopia was consistent with her general policy, if she believed that the Eritrean Liberation Front was an alternative to Haile Selassie's traditional government. But the Front's aims were more modest, and diplomatic relations with Ethiopia may now deter Chinese support to the Front. China's reported aid to Biafra does not appear consistent with her general line of supporting governments where no radical opposition exists, but two other arguments determined Peking's position. Some African states—Tanzania the most prominent—endorsed Biafran secession; if Biafra were independent, China could support Biafra and simultaneously maintain that her stance toward Lagos had been proper. Perhaps Soviet aid to Nigeria swayed China. In any case, once Biafra fell there was no continuing obstacle to diplomatic relations between Nigeria and China.

In a number of other countries, many of them former French colonies, either there is no viable left opposition or it is so shadowy that its existence is not well established. Many of these states recognize Taiwan.[16] For the most part, China ignores them, although she criticized French support of the late Leon M'ba of Gabon. These states are preoccupied with local issues and the tasks of nation-building; they employ moderate means to attain moderate ends. Their leaders act in concert with traditional authority (prerevolutionary Libya, Liberia) or the former colonizer, demonstrating little wish to risk their own positions. If one excludes Libya—which enjoyed sudden prosperity because of oil earnings—and Senegal,[17] these states have not evinced interest in active foreign roles. Early Sierra Leonese interest in diplomatic relations has not borne fruit.

Finally, China would almost surely like to unseat several African governments which—unlike those in the preceding group—have indigenous oppositions willing to deal with China.[18] There is little or no prospect

16. Chad, Gabon, Gambia, Ivory Coast, Liberia, Libya, Malagasy, Senegal, Togo, and Upper Volta. Senegal severed diplomatic relations with the Republic of China in September 1964, but nevertheless asserts that she recognizes both Peking and Taipei. Senegal has an identifiable left opposition, including factions which have catered to China, but the left is divided and its leaders are readily neutralized by the government. See Chapter 6. Of the others, Gambia alone does not have relations with Taipei. In July 1968 a former Liberian ambassador was convicted of treason, having been charged with planning the assassination of President Tubman and liquidation of the "Americo-Liberians"; the prosecution stated that his plan was financed by China and was to have been carried out with assistance by Chinese. In August 1968 the government of Chad called in French troops to put down a rebellion, a major ethnic conflict; whether China was in contact with the Chad National Liberation Front is unknown. See *NYT*, 29 August 1968. In late 1969 Chad officials claimed the rebellion was largely crushed, but fighting flared again in October 1970, when it was speculated that the revolutionaries might be receiving weapons from the new government of Libya.

17. See [121], on Senegal.

18. Botswana, Congo (K), Lesotho, Malawi, Niger, Rwanda, and Swaziland.

that the present governments of these states will extend recognition to China. The cases of Cameroon, Congo (K), Niger, and Rwanda demand special attention, for they have had a profound effect on the way China's revolutionary rhetoric and peaceful claims are understood.

CAMEROON

The Union des Populations du Cameroun (UPC), founded in 1947, was the Cameroon section of the Rassemblement Démocratique Africain (RDA). Houphouet-Boigny broke RDA's ties with the French Communist party in 1950, but UPC founder Ruben Um Nyobé declined to adopt Houphouet's more moderate position. In 1956, one year after it was declared illegal, the UPC initiated guerrilla activity. When China entered the picture in the late 1950s, armed conflict had begun. Ernest Ouandie, UPC vice-president, visited China in 1958, as did the president, Félix Moumié, in 1959.[19] Peking championed the cause of the UPC. Since UPC headquarters, in Cairo and later in Conakry, were located in cities where Peking maintained embassies, China could readily contact the UPC leadership.

When Ahmadou Ahidjo became prime minister, he too insisted on independence, undercutting the Moumié position. The UPC did not succeed in winning needed support beyond the two minority ethnic groups first responsive to its appeals, and it gradually forfeited the headway it had made. China continued to give nominal support, but by early 1971 was ready to establish diplomatic relations.

CONGO (K)

The Congo (K) is by far the most important African state in which China has actively supported an opposition group. Chinese awareness of developments in the Congo goes back to January 1959, when Belgian police clashed with Congolese. China's first comment on the Congo, in response to the outbreak, was that "from the very beginning it demonstrated its explicit political character [as] a movement for independence and against racial discrimination."[20] Patrice Lumumba led the largest and most militant of the forty-odd political parties active in the Congo at mid-1960.[21] His role in the First All-African People's Conference (Accra, 1958), and in the Second Afro-Asian People's Solidarity Conference (Cona-

19. Moumié succeeded to UPC leadership when Um Nyobe was killed in 1958.

20. *SCMP*, no. 1942, p. 38 (paraphrasing *JMJP*, 22 January 1959).

21. The Mouvement National Congolais (MNC) was founded in October 1958. It advocated unitary government, opposed nationalization of European property, but proposed controls to "reduce exploitation." See [75], pp. 94–105.

kry, 1960) brought him to China's attention before Congolese independence. Viewing the political scene in the Congo at that time, China saw a myriad of parties headed by men such as Antoine Gizenga, Alphonse Nguvulu, Albert Kalonji, Joseph Kasavubu, and Moise Tshombe.[22] The parties had sprung up swiftly, and they engaged in ever-shifting alliances and tactical coalitions.

Among a group of thirty diverse Congolese politicians who visited China in the spring of 1960 was Nguvulu, who had attended the Thirteenth Congress of the Belgian Communist party. In Belgium he had met Lin T'ieh, a member of the CCP Central Committee, who may have invited him to Peking.[23] Chinese interest was also evidenced by her part in the formation of a Congo-China Friendship Association in Léopoldville. Although China had quoted Lumumba as early as January 1959,[24] there is no evidence that he felt special ties to China or that China was committed to him in any way. The same disclaimer applies to Gizenga. However, China may have expected that she would, in due course, establish diplomatic relations with the newly-independent Congo.[25]

The Congolese government called for United Nations assistance soon after independence, and a United Nations force was duly dispatched. China stressed the fact that Congolese leaders intended to use the force "to get the Belgians out." She also asserted that the United States sought to replace Belgium in the Congo, especially through Ralph Bunche, the head of the United Nations operation. At the end of August 1960, Lumumba began to receive matériel from the Soviet Union; Kasavubu ousted Lumumba as premier on 5 September, provoking claims and counterclaims about which Congolese government was legitimate.[26]

22. Gizenga led the Parti Solidaire Africain (PSA), an urban party founded in Léopoldville in April 1959 that opposed "neocolonialism" and proposed Congolese attachment to the European Common Market. Nguvulu, leader of the Parti du Peuple, has been characterized as a "militant Marxist." [147], June 1960, p. 2.

23. *NYT*, 25 November 1960.

24. Lumumba stated at the First All-African People's Conference, "We want to bring a new countenance to our country, that of a people free from all yokes." *SCMP*, no. 1934, pp. 33–34 (10 January 1959).

25. The Congo did not set up relations with the Republic of China until December 1961, long after Kasavubu's ouster of Lumumba in September 1960. [147], January 1965, p. 40. In typical fashion, Chinese congratulations to the Congo (L) on its independence stated that China "had decided to recognize the Congo Republic." *SCMP*, no. 2289, p. 38 (27 June 1960). But it seems unlikely that China was even invited to attend Congolese independence celebrations.

26. See *SCMP*, no. 2304, p. 13, and Liao Ch'eng-chih's speech to a Peking rally on the Congo, 23 July 1960, in [201], pp. 70–76. The formal request for U.N. assistance was indeed based on a Congolese call for help against Belgian troops. In a telegram to the U.N., Kasavubu and Lumumba advised, "The purpose of the aid requested is

The most experienced Chinese diplomat in Africa, Ch'en Chia-k'ang, was in Léopoldville during part of this crucial period to observe a meeting of African foreign ministers which Lumumba had convened. Ch'en met with Congolese foreign minister Justin Bomboko.[27] His visit may have been the source of a later Chinese claim that "in August 1960 there came information of the formation of a Communist party" in the Congo.[28] It is possible that Ch'en met with Congolese who were well disposed to China and that some among them, perhaps from the Parti du Peuple, professed this intention. The long-term possibilities in such a development were in any case preempted by Lumumba's dismissal.

Lumumba had a plausible claim to legitimacy, one convincing to many Africans. He was identified with a strong anti-Belgian position and had sought to overcome Katangese secession. It may have been especially important to China that he had found his objectives frustrated by what he regarded as United Nations intransigence or even perfidy. Thus, on 8 September, Antoine Gizenga, Lumumba's vice-premier, sought aid from China "to permit the Government of the Republic of the Congo to assure the dangerously menaced integrity of its territory." He asked for volunteers, munitions, helicopters, food, and money. It took China only four days to place £1,000,000 "at the disposal" of the Lumumba-Gizenga government, although she declined, ostensibly for reasons of geography, to send volunteers.[29]

China's position was that the Lumumba-Gizenga government, which she supported, was the lawful Congolese government. Yet she had no established channels through which to transmit matériel or provide other effective aid to the Lumumbist center in Stanleyville. The government in Léopoldville was thus able to consolidate its position. Then, in January 1961, when Patrice Lumumba was murdered, China again made gestures of support to Stanleyville. The Stanleyville government passed certain basic tests. It was the most radical group in the Congo. Although it might

---

not to restore [the] internal situation in Congo but rather to protect the national territory against [the] act of aggression posed by Belgian metropolitan troops." They continued in language which prompted Western observers to wonder if China, among others, might not be called upon if the U.N. failed to comply: "If requested assistance is not received without delay, the Republic of Congo will be obliged to appeal to the Bandung Treaty powers." *NYT*, 14 July 1960. Kasavubu and Lumumba were reported to have cabled Soviet Premier Khrushchev, "It is possible that we may have to ask for the Soviet Union's intervention should the Western camp not stop its aggression against the sovereignty of the Republic of the Congo." *NYT*, 16 July 1960.

27. NCNA, 3 September 1960, in *SCMP*, no. 2334, p. 16.

28. [227], 27 January 1961, p. 180.

29. Texts of cables in [53].

not ultimately succeed, it was a viable group with many supporters, and it proposed itself as an alternative to the de facto government in Léopoldville. Neither China nor the Soviet Union created the Lumumba-Gizenga opposition, but they both fostered its independence when they could.

After Lumumba's death, pressure mounted on Gizenga to rejoin Léopoldville, and he abandoned his claim of leading a separate legal government. For two years following September 1961 there was no visible opposition for China to support. She did, however, maintain some contacts, notably with the late Pierre Mulele, a former Cairo representative of the Lumumba-Gizenga group.[30] Late in 1963 and in 1964, large-scale revolutionary activity took place in the Congo; it was suppressed largely by white mercenaries. Revolutionaries were driven from Stanleyville by the Belgian-American airdrop of November 1964 and a concurrent drive on that city by mercenaries. Although scattered resistance to Léopoldville's authority continued thereafter, it did not regain its former momentum.

China's tangible encouragement to the 1963–1964 revolutionaries was reported widely. Nonetheless, in a careful assessment of the revolution, Crawford Young has observed:

> Possibly the Chinese did see the Congo rebellion as a genuine peasant revolt at the mass level, but they could hardly have had any illusions about a Marxist-Leninist commitment from "national bourgeois" leaders such as Gbenye and Soumialot. . . . It seems implausible that the Chinese advised the rebels to embark upon the massive execution policy [as some reporters claimed they had] in such aimless fashion, destroying their own capacity to consolidate their rule. The Chinese were certainly keenly interested in the rebellion, but its essential dynamics seem to have been internal.[31]

China might have recognized the Gbenye government. She did not, although anti-Léopoldville forces had some freedom of movement in perhaps half the Congo at their peak. Why did China shy away from recognition? First, her experience in 1961, dispatching a chargé d'affaires to Stanleyville and then having him forced to return home, was disconcerting. Gizenga's capitulation also put China in an embarrassing situa-

30. Mulele reportedly spent some time in China during the 1961–1963 interlude. Another visitor to China was Malonga Allias, identified as general secretary of the General Union of the Confederation of Peasants' and Workers' Trade Unions of the Congo. *PR*, 9 February 1962, p. 22.

31. [147], April 1965, pp. 6–11. Young concludes that "the Congo rebellion was a social movement which had revolutionary tactics, but lacked a revolutionary strategy." For some of the more imaginative and extravagant assertions about Chinese involvement, see the article by Max Clos in [147], January 1965.

tion. Second, as Young observes, there was little ideological commitment among the leaders. China had no reason to expect that the revolutionaries would persist in implementing the purpose they avowed. Third, recognition might have burdened China with material commitments for which she was not prepared.[32] Two additional considerations may have been judged decisive by policy makers in Peking. China wished to wait and see if an anti-Léopoldville government would solidify its control. And, finally, China did not wish to appear to threaten other African states. China gave only such support as was readily and cheaply available — she remained circumspect in her commitments.

RWANDA

Rwandan opposition forces maintain an attachment to the Mwami Kigeri, who was forced into exile in Kenya by a revolution in 1959. As in the Congo in 1960–1961, Chinese support in the form of "money and encouragement"[33] went to a man who claimed to have been wrongfully removed from legitimate power in his homeland. China's ties to Rwandan dissidents are less clearly established than her links to groups in Cameroon and the Congo. Nonetheless, the Rwandan government, headed by a devout Roman Catholic who is given to anti-Communist statements and who maintains diplomatic relations with the Republic of China,[34] has no reservoir of good will in Peking. Rwanda has charged that China took part in training the exiled Tutsis who attacked her in late 1963 and early 1964.[35] China's opportunity to act was sharply curtailed when her mission was expelled from neighboring Burundi in January 1965.

NIGER

In Niger, the chief antigovernment element is the Sawaba (Freedom party), an erstwhile RDA unit which was formally expelled in 1955 when it refused to drop its ties to the French Communist party. The Niger government declared it illegal in 1959.[36] President Hamani Diori's governing party came to power with the support of chiefs and the French colonial administration, and in October 1964 an attempt to overthrow that gov-

32. Her position on material aid may have been changing, for sizable shipments had been decided upon or were already en route when Stanleyville was retaken in November 1964.

33. [120].

34. *NYT*, 6 April 1964.

35. *NYT*, 15 February 1964, reporting the comments of the Rwandan chargé d'affaires in Bonn. Captured Tutsis, he said, reported that they had foreign officers. Czechs were also implicated.

36. [52], p. 195.

ernment, attributed to Sawaba, was reported crushed by the authorities.[37] Hamani Diori later charged that "the attack [of October 1964] by commandos of the opposition Sawaba party was organized, financed, and led by Communist China and the weapons used were bought with Chinese money deposited in banks at Brussels, Geneva, and Accra."[38] Although his assertions have not been independently confirmed, Chinese support to Sawaba would conform to the pattern of Chinese support to other opposition groups in Africa. China and Niger have not cooperated. Sawaba, which opposed the Niger government before China became concerned with sub-Saharan Africa, is a radical alternative to the government of Hamani Diori. Sawaba has assumed a radical political posture and has undertaken limited armed action, which was acknowledged approvingly by the Afro-Asian Writers' Emergency Meeting in Peking in mid-1966.

OTHER INDEPENDENT STATES

In several other instances China has allegedly supported groups which oppose an existing independent African government. China supported parties in Bechuanaland (now Botswana), Basutoland (now Lesotho), and Swaziland before these three former High Commission Territories attained independence. The parties supported by China[39] have not won influential places in the newly-formed independent governments. South Africa's overwhelming influence on the three territories militated against African radicals and brought to power men who were willing to strike a

37. [147], November 1964, p. 24.

38. *Ibid.*, March 1965, p. 38.

39. *Botswana.* Chinese contacts with representatives of the Bechuanaland People's party (BPP) and a more recent opposition party, the United Front, have been reported. A BPP organization contested elections in October 1969 but won only three of thirty-one seats. In October 1964 Bobby Mack, a member of one of two BPP groups, lauded China's nuclear test. *PR*, 23 October 1964, p. 12. *Lesotho.* For example, see interview between NCNA correspondent and the Basutoland Congress party (BCP) Cairo representative in *JMJP*, 13 May 1967. Ntsu Mokhehle, leader of the BCP, said on the eve of the January 1970 elections that he did not have Communist leanings but would, if elected, "develop cooperatives in a socialist society." In the preindependence elections of 1965, the BCP fell six seats short of a majority. Mokhehle claimed that unofficial tallies gave the BCP a majority of one in the 1970 elections, but Prime Minister Leabua Jonathan declared a state of emergency, suspended the constitution, and jailed the BCP leadership. Mokhehle was subsequently released in "protective custody," and has engaged in talks with Jonathan concerning a temporary coalition government. Thus, the group with which China had contacts was on the verge of winning the government by parliamentary means, but it was prevented from doing so. *Swaziland.* A statement on China's nuclear test was made by a representative of the Ngwane National Liberatory Congress. *PR*, 23 October 1964, p. 12. In April 1965 the president and one other representative of the Swaziland Progressive party visited Peking.

bargain with that apartheid regime. China has continued to maintain at least nominal contact with the three groups.

Hastings Kamazu Banda of Malawi lodged still-unproven charges that China supported armed dissidents seeking to overthrow him.[40] The matter is confused by the sweeping audacity of the alleged plot, which seems implausible. Banda charged that China's embassy in Dar es Salaam offered economic aid if the highly-placed dissidents engineered his assassination and recognized China. Whether this is true or not, Banda's paternalistic and autocratic rule has generated opposition, and China has no special reason to refrain from aiding Banda's opponents.

From time to time Senegal has acted against members of the Parti Africain de l'Indépendence (PAI), charging it with subversive intent. In 1965, *Le Monde* (Paris) reported that a small group of pro-Chinese militants, who had been excluded from the PAI since 1960, were circulating a "Manifesto of the Senegalese Communist Party," perhaps in an effort to separate pro-Chinese rank and file in the PAI from pro-Soviet leaders of that party.[41] In mid-1968 Senegal expelled two NCNA correspondents,

40. Banda told the United Nations in 1964 that, since the People's Republic of China exercised effective authority over its territory, Malawi had no choice but to extend diplomatic recognition. *NYT*, 3 December 1964. Seven months later he charged that China was spending millions, that could better have been spent feeding China's population, to corrupt African leaders. He also accused Peking of having a hand in Ben Bella's overthrow by Boumédienne, a charge no one else has made. *NYT*, 7 July 1965. He told one correspondent that China had offered him £6,000,000 in exchange for diplomatic recognition. Kanyama Chiume, former Malawi foreign minister, was using Chinese funds to organize an invasion of Malawi by insurgents trained in Tanzania, Banda charged. [147], October 1965, p. 48. On 12 July 1966, Malawi extended de jure recognition to Taiwan.

41. [147], July 1965, p. 28, citing [176], 14 May 1965. In [33], William J. Foltz tells of the PAI splinter group that came to public attention in the spring of 1965: "The PCS [Parti Communiste Sénégalaise] . . . lined up resolutely behind the Chinese on all major issues and broke explicitly with Majmout's [Majmout Diop, PAI secretary general] 'revisionist' organization. It did not take long for the PCS leadership, whose strongest common trait seems to have been a willingness to take Chinese money and spend it on Scotch whiskey, to fall out among themselves, and their subsequent financial difficulties suggest that the Chinese were not convinced that they had found in the PCS a satisfactory agency for the spread of Chairman Mao's thought." He adds that another group, styling itself the Parti Africain de l'Indépendence Révolutionnaire and then the Nouvelle Organization du Parti Africain de l'Indépendence, was founded in August 1966; after issuing what Foltz terms a "wooly, Maoist-type manifesto," the group quietly disappeared. Foltz concludes that Soviet pressure against armed PAI excursions led to increased Chinese influence among PAI cadres, witnessed by the PCS's formation and general internal dissidence; but China, unable to supply the aid to take over the PAI, "at most . . . contributed to the final collapse of the party's organization." I am grateful to Mr. Foltz for calling this paper to my attention. The translation is his.

under circumstances which linked them to student demonstrations in Senegal.[42]

Although Colonel Odumegwu Ojukwu, the Biafran leader, appealed for help in a letter to Mao Tse-tung,[43] evidence that China actually promised aid is confined to press reports and charges by Nigerian authorities. Chief Anthony Enahoro, Nigerian federal commissioner for information, said that Chinese support reached Biafra through Tanzania. The London *Sunday Times* reported that a Chinese military expert visited Biafra, and that China offered to train Biafrans in guerrilla tactics and to supply them with small arms and sabotage equipment, aided by the Union des Populations du Cameroun.[44] Since Soviet support to crush the Biafran separatist movement was open and extensive, such Chinese involvement, if it took place, was a further projection of Sino-Soviet differences into Chinese African policy.

The Afro-Asian Writers' Emergency Meeting (27 June to 9 July 1966) resolved to give full support to the "just war of liberation of the Eritrean people for national independence and sovereignty."[45] Unconfirmed reports have been published that the Eritrean Liberation Front sent men to China for training.[46]

Casual Chinese interest in many other countries has been asserted. Justin Bomboko charged that Chinese and Cuban specialists trained nationals of the Congo (K), Cameroon, Centrafrica, Chad, and Gabon.[47] Africans from Nigeria, Gabon, Upper Volta, Niger, Cameroon, Rwanda, Zambia, Malawi, and Tanzania were on the roster of trainees at the Ghanaian camp at Obinimasi.[48]

National Liberation Movements in Colonies and Apartheid States

Colonies and apartheid states, unlike politically independent states governed by Africans, have little legitimacy except in the eyes of their own non-African populations. China readily supports nationalist and na-

42. [173], 23 June 1968, p. 27.
43. *NYT*, 30 September 1968.
44. Radio Nigeria, 10 February 1969; Colin Chapman, London *Sunday Times* dispatch, in San Francisco *Chronicle*, 30 October 1968.
45. *PR*, 15 July 1966, p. 52.
46. *NYT*, 3 March 1967, asserts that "Africans returning from China have reported that Eritreans were already in training there, but these reports have never been confirmed." [164], 11 November 1967, reports the surrender of an Eritrean Liberation Front officer and nineteen of his followers; China reportedly gave uniforms to the movement, which selected twenty men for training in China.
47. Colin Chapman, note 44.
48. *NYT*, 10 June 1966; [38].

tional liberation movements. As late as 1964 or 1965, if there were competing factions in a country China tried to keep a delicate balance among them, maintaining contacts with all.

By this policy, Peking could support the national liberation movement whose leaders' views most closely approached that of the CCP, but at the same time she could encourage nationalists to join in opposing their enemies rather than waste scarce resources in internecine strife. If any group were catapulted into power, China would be ensured entrée. Peking prepared for several alternative outcomes. Her tactically sound preference for unity among nationalist groups could not be maintained, however, in the face of Peking's worsening ideological struggle with Moscow.

After 1964, as the Sino-Soviet struggle hardened and some nationalist groups chose sides, China turned away from those who gave their support to Moscow. The most clear-cut of these cases is South Africa. China had at one time urged unity in South Africa and had taken pains to accord the Pan-Africanist Congress (PAC) and African National Congress (ANC) equal treatment, but the South African Communist party, with an important stake in the African National Congress, took the Soviet side in the dispute:

> The oppressed people of our country and all honest revolutionaries are indignant at the unprincipled backing given by the Chinese Government to certain discredited splinter groups of Southern Africa. These groups are known to all, including the Chinese Communists, for their racialism, anti-communism and disruption of the liberation struggle. By associating with them, the Chinese leaders only expose their own opportunism and lack of principle.[49]

The pattern in South Africa is approximated by competing groups in other territories. The principal organizations are shown in Table 5. These lines were most clearly seen when four probable recipients of Chinese support (PAC, ZANU, UNITA, and COREMO) issued a statement attacking the International Conference in Support of the Liberation Movements of the Portuguese Colonies and Southern Africa (Khartoum, January 1969). The conference was "calculated to control the liberation struggles of the Portuguese colonies and southern Africa in order to further Soviet cooperation with the United States for their joint domination of the world," according to the statement distributed by NCNA.[50] Representa-

49. [148], second quarter 1967, p. 17.

50. [225], no. 4008, p. 12, 23 January 1969. John Marcum brought this to my attention.

Table 5

SOVIET AND CHINESE SUPPORT OF MAJOR NATIONAL LIBERATION MOVEMENTS TO 1970

Territory	*Organization*	*Certain or Probable Recipient of Support from*			*Not Recipient of Support from China or the Soviet Union*
		China	*Soviet Union and China*	*Soviet Union*	
Angola	Movimento Popular de Libertação de Angola (MPLA)			MPLA	
	União Nacional Para a Independencia Total de Angola (UNITA)	UNITA			
	Governo Revolucionário de Angola no Exílio (GRAE)				GRAE
Mozambique	Frente de Libertação de Moçambique (FRELIMO)		FRELIMO		
	Comite Revolucionário de Moçambique (COREMO)	COREMO			
Portuguese Guinea	Partido Africano da Independencia da Guiné e Cabo Verde (PAIGC)		PAIGC		
Rhodesia	Zimbabwe African People's Union (ZAPU)			ZAPU	
	Zimbabwe African National Union (ZANU)	ZANU			
South Africa	African National Congress (ANC)			ANC	
	Pan-Africanist Congress (PAC)	PAC			
South-West Africa	South-West African People's Organization (SWAPO)			SWAPO	
	South-West African National Union (SWANU)	SWANU			

tives of the six organizations that probably received Soviet support (ANC, SWAPO, ZAPU, MPLA, FRELIMO, and PAIGC) attended the Khartoum meeting.

In Portuguese Guinea, China and the Soviet Union both extended support to PAIGC because it is the only significant group operating in that territory. It is actively engaged in armed struggle. Moreover, it is the most successful of all the groups listed, exercising control over a significant part of the territory.

In Mozambique, FRELIMO was at one time the only significant group. China probably extended some aid to it. The creation of COREMO, operating from Zambia but not from Tanzania, and in a region in which FRELIMO had not been active, offered China a second opportunity. Both groups engaged in armed struggle.

The Angolan situation is not as simple as the pattern might imply. GRAE, maintaining headquarters in Kinshasa, and MPLA, formerly in Brazzaville and later in Lusaka, were the chief nationalist groups. Both conducted some armed action in Angola. Neither was closely identified with China. Viriato da Cruz has been cited as a recipient of Chinese aid; he left MPLA in 1962 and in 1964 he was accepted into the precursor of GRAE; he has never been an effective participant in the latter. A third organization, UNITA, is led by Jonas Savimbi, who left the Kinshasa-based group of Holden Roberto in 1964. UNITA engaged in armed action in southeast Angola where — unlike the exiles of GRAE and MPLA — Savimbi maintained his headquarters. Both GRAE and MPLA were unreceptive, and UNITA became a candidate for Chinese assistance. Holden Roberto of GRAE had spoken of the need to obtain aid from China at one point, but there is no evidence that he actually solicited it.

The case of South-West Africa has unique characteristics. China has continued to give international publicity to SWANU statements, although SWANU seems to be little more than the shell of an organization, lacking an effective constituency. Because SWAPO receives Soviet support, China has chosen to help SWANU.

In describing the organizations which are members of the Conferencia das Organizaçoes Nacionalistas dos Colonias Portugesas (CONCP) and their southern African allies,[51] John Marcum says they "share a dedication to multiracialism . . . and an intellectual radicalism that seems more attuned to the permissiveness of Soviet 'revisionism' than to the rigid conformism of China's 'cultural revolution'." These groups have probably received Soviet support. Marcum believes that more movements

51. Principally FRELIMO, ANC, and ZAPU.

have been extended Chinese aid than Soviet aid, but that the former has been less extensive than the latter.[52]

Although the number of territories considered here is not large, a pattern can be discerned, and it can be expressed in a set of hypotheses.

(1) If a nationalist organization becomes friendly to the Soviet position in the Sino-Soviet dispute, China will probably aid a competing nationalist organization if a viable one exists.

(2) If two organizations are competing for influence in an exile community and one accepts Soviet aid, China will cultivate the other.

(3) If a group is the only radical nationalist movement conducting effective operations in a territory, China will give aid to that group even if the Soviet Union also gives it aid. (The case of South-West Africa suggests a qualification to this hypothesis. If China has identified herself with one group, which becomes ineffective but maintains a bare or nominal existence, and if Soviet support has gone to a competing group, China may continue to give her support to the first group).

(4) China depicts armed struggle as an outgrowth of Chinese teaching and experience, even if the nationalist movement conducting armed struggle is not a Chinese favorite.

(5) If two or more movements in a territory refuse to unite and yet refrain from mutually exclusive claims, China will attempt to maintain relations with persons or factions within both groups.

There is a dearth of data from which the extent of Chinese support might be computed, but China's visible aid to nationalist movements has never been lavish.[53] Movements continue to complain that they are short

52. [91].

53. Matthew Nkoana reportedly stated that two PAC missions to China each received $20,000. Nkoana quotes a report by the PAC treasurer general, A. B. Ngcobo, on the mishandling of the funds received: "The second grant allocated to our first mission to China was neither deposited in the Party account nor received by the Treasurer-General. This amount, like the first, was 10,000 dollars. The second mission to China, led by Mr. P. K. Leballo with Messrs. Z. B. Molete and A. B. Ebrahim as members, also realised 20,000 dollars. This was received in two lots of 10,000 dollars each. The entire amount of 20,000 [sic] was handed neither to the Treasurer-General nor deposited in the Party account." The editor, discussing Nkoana's report, comments: "I note, for example, that even Nkoana, in criticising certain misapplications of Mao's theories of armed struggle to a place like Southern Africa, feels compelled each time to stress not only the importance of the Chinese anti-imperialist policies but also the so-called 'cultural revolution' just in case he is misunderstood as criticising the whole position of the Republic of China [sic]. To accept only that part of revolutionary theory which is relevant to Southern Africa is of course proper; but one suspects that the anxiety is also to be understood against the background of the Republic of China's

of money and matériel. The reasons for China's restraint probably lie in the confined circumstances of the several liberation movements, not in China's wishes. In the strictly competitive cases — instances of a Soviet-supported group competing with a Chinese-supported group — the movements face severe obstacles which money and supplies will not overcome. Groups which have begun guerrilla operations against the Rhodesian authorities, for example, are now able to conduct no more than very limited operations. Many of their leaders are confined in camps; those in exile are few and unskilled in the intricacies of political organization; and efficient security measures are taken by the Smith regime. Access to South Africa and South-West Africa is difficult. In all three cases a combination of symbolic gifts, small sums of money, and a limited armory is as much as the movements can utilize in actual operations — although they would like additional sums to induce recruits to join them and to support international travel and publicity.

In sum, Peking may believe that it is better to harbor its favorite as a viable organization and to conduct some political training among its members than to commit the organization's personnel and prestige to large-scale operations which objective capabilities will not support. Nevertheless, China's commitment to politicization through armed struggle requires that some guerrilla operations be conducted. Political ties with China and ongoing armed struggle conducted by the liberation movement support Peking's struggle against Moscow. Peking's contributions also deny Moscow the opportunity of claiming China's favorite as an ally.

The arguments are quite different in the cases that are not strictly competitive, but the result remains the same — China's aid is limited. The clearest case is that of the PAIGC of Portuguese Guinea. The PAIGC is free to conduct guerrilla operations on a rather large scale. Members have access to their homeland; they can recruit from a large exile community; and their leadership is intact. Spared internecine quarrels (though hardly free of factionalism), they can devote more of their energies to the declared goals of liberation and nation-building. The PAIGC appears closer to its goal than, say, the groups in southern Africa; therefore it can bargain more effectively with China and the Soviet Union. Bargaining power is a safeguard against dependence on a single contributor. China may find herself a tacit partner, perhaps even an unwilling one, of the Soviet Union and other benefactors. Under such circumstances China probably would not be asked to be generous and probably would decline to be in any case.

[sic] very material assistance to the PAC." [99]. I have not seen the original document by Nkoana.

China's restraint stems from another reason, which recalls the preceding discussions of party formation and revolutionary stages. None of the liberation movements listed here is constructing an implement akin to the Chinese Communist party in its early days, nor do they place stress on ideology.[54] However, there are those in each movement who are drawn to revolutionary theory, organizational doctrine, and study of China's world view. There is no better channel to cultivate support in these territories than existing liberation movements. China's practice of granting some support to selected men and factions in them is tacit acknowledgment that the liberation movements are not perfect instruments.

China has concerned herself not only with the large dependent territories, but also with very small ones. The French-ruled Comoro Islands have generated a national liberation movement whose representatives have visited China.[55] Concerning itself with the French Territory of the Afar and Issa (French Somaliland), the Front for the Liberation of the Somali Coast, led by Abdullahi Ardiei, has also had contacts with China. China has probably given aid to both groups.

In summary, the African territories fall into the following categories:

Ruled by Africans:

(1) The territories China speaks of with special warmth.
(2) The territories toward which China is less warm but is formally proper.
(3) The territories which have terminated or suspended diplomatic relations with China, although she would almost surely have preferred to maintain them.
(4) The territories with which China has no diplomatic relations, although she maintains a correct posture.
(5) The territories China seems to have provoked in order to sever diplomatic relations.
(6) The territories with which China has no diplomatic relations,

54. PAIGC efforts to construct "alternative systems"—economic, political, and judicial structures to replace the colonial state in liberated regions—has some parallel to CCP organization of the Chinese "liberated areas." But after examining PAIGC publications, I. William Zartman concludes that "the tone that emerges is both optimistic and pragmatic, and despite the appearance of such phrases as 'our struggle of the party,' the output cannot be called doctrinaire or ideological." [147], November 1967, p. 71. See Basil Davidson, *The Liberation of Guiné*, (Baltimore: Penguin, 1969), pp. 73–90 and 135–141.

55. The Afro-Asian Writers' Emergency Meeting in Peking in mid-1966 recognized this group as the "genuine spokesman" of the Comoran people. *PR*, no. 29, 15 July 1966.

and in which an opposition group or exile movement, assertedly aided by China, seeks to bring down the present government or detach some territory from its control.

Ruled by Others:
(7) Colonial and dependent territories.
(8) Apartheid territories.

In the more complex cases, China's decisive choices turn on the answers to these questions: Is the African government ready to support some Chinese policies, and are its leaders willing to speak well of China? Is there a viable opposition group which is more radical than the present government? Other factors are considered, as the preceding discussions of specific cases show, but these questions are crucial. In apartheid and colonial territories, China's first commitment is to the prospect of an African government, but she chooses among alternative liberation forces only after learning what strategy each would be likely to pursue toward independence and how each would declare itself in the Sino-Soviet dispute.[56]

56. These considerations also apply to cases of civil war. Soviet support for the Nigerian federal government may have prompted China to support Biafra. The Sudanese civil war is not inconsistent with this analysis. The Southern Sudan forces are not distinctively radical, nor could China make a case against the Soviet Union by supporting them.

9 Prospects and Probabilities

If the political significance of China's African interests hinged solely on the likelihood that China would create a Maoist Africa, the conclusion of this inquiry could be simply stated: there is virtually no possibility that the African continent will be swept by anti-imperialist and social revolutions led by men who follow Chinese leadership. Nevertheless, China will exert an important influence on African events even if the outcome is very different from that envisaged in Peking's commentaries.

In this respect Sino-African relations resemble those between any powerful large state and distant small state. The large state wields some influence simply by virtue of its size. But, when it sets out to attain change in the political life of the small state, it finds that its instruments are ill-adapted. Its information is limited and inexact. If the large state acts covertly, this action limits the nature and degree of influence it may bring to bear. If it acts openly, its intervention may become a cause célèbre which outshadows the original political objective. In either case, whether the intentions are known by a few men among the elite or by the public, the effort to wield influence triggers unintended consequences, including local resentment. However, these hazards need not prevent the large state from changing local affairs in the direction it wishes. If skillful, it is likely to be able to effect changes, but it is unlikely to attain as much as it wished in just the form it wished, or to escape unanticipated costs.

Significance and Outcome

One reason that China's African interest is politically significant is that certain key states, including China herself, act as if it were. Peking would deny that Chinese-style revolution in Africa is virtually impossible. The most decisive event shaping CCP ideas concerning the range of possibilities in Africa is the Chinese revolution: if thoroughgoing revolution was wrought in China, some CCP leaders argue, surely it will come about in Africa. A cautious observer of China in 1924, or even 1934, would probably have considered the CCP's chances to seize state power and create a unified Chinese state to have been slim.

Peking appears not to be deterred by the fact that contemporary Africa differs in many important ways from revolutionary China. The CCP came to power while conditions were quite favorable. There were few models of effective political action competing for favor; the CCP's strict organizational form helped it to endure; and the Maoist tactical sense was appropriate to military realities. The Bolshevik Revolution and Sun Yat-sen's readiness to strike an alliance with the CCP lent it legitimacy. The Kuomintang failed to unify China and then failed to repel the Japanese. Chiang Kai-shek's Kuomintang did not achieve manifest social betterment and economic growth. The African case differs greatly from that of China, although the continent has not solved its social and economic problems nor has it built political structures which are certain to survive severe tests. The analogy between China and Africa may be inept, but there is no way to prove it wrong in advance. As long as the "Chinese path" exists as a model—and it certainly will for many decades—there is some possibility that it might be copied successfully by African revolutionaries.

In one view, China will use her "capacity for exploiting domestic instability" as a tool of foreign policy. Leaders of new African states, conscious that their rule is weak, will be "very sensitive to the threat of domestic upheaval."[1] Henry Kissinger, who advances this view, apparently believes that China will pressure African states to adopt positions they would otherwise not adopt. The record suggests, however, that the African states which have been most friendly to China are those in which China has had the least reason to provoke a "domestic upheaval." Where China is said to have supported an opposition, as in Kenya, the government has become understandably cool. China might benefit from the existence of radicals in a governing party, whom the leadership felt it had to conciliate in order to maintain party control and national cohesion. But in that case the leadership bends to domestic realities, not to any implicit Chinese threat to fund or to unleash the radical wing. Kissinger is correct: many African leaders are afraid of Chinese interference. But he is almost surely wrong if he believes China can make gains in Africa by threatening intervention.

Powers suspicious of China also tend to exaggerate the likelihood that she will successfully export her revolutionary model. This in turn breeds hostility. Peking's view of the world requires intense polarization, the

1. [64], p. 42. In 1969 Kissinger was appointed Assistant to the President of the United States for National Security Affairs.

division of the world between friends and foes, acknowledgment and celebration of hostility and struggle. Polarization is sharpened by policy makers in other states who perceive China's hostility and proceed to assert that things Chinese — whether Chinese interests, Chinese ideas, Chinese styles of organization and tactics, or even Chinese aid — are in themselves a threat to other governments and people. Upon hearing such assertions Chinese policy makers justify and reinforce their original hostility. This cycle is not readily broken. There are ample grounds for non-Chinese policy makers to remain wary: some Chinese interests do clash with those of non-Chinese; China has used coercion before and certainly will again; China insists that untrammeled discourse is wasteful; and Chinese ideology centers on struggle. The distinction between wariness and hostility is difficult to discriminate. The tragic cost of failing to make this distinction was never more strikingly illustrated than in the United States failure to discern China's intentions correctly in the early months of the Korean War. China, as Whiting has convincingly argued, acted warily; United States policy makers mistook wariness for hostility.[2]

Separation itself can be politically and economically costly. A state which chooses isolation forgoes chances for gain and risks ill-informed choices. Chinese economic aid can be beneficial. Opportunities to undo false perceptions are lost if China is excluded from normal relations. If China urged violence in gross ignorance of objective conditions, an unnecessary cost would be imposed on the revolutionaries, on China, and on the people subjected to violence. Knowledge of another society need not lead to benevolence, but contacts certainly do increase the probability that the other's institutions will be studied and understood. The retort of isolationists — that opening their societies exposes vulnerabilities and therefore threatens them — is self-condemning.

United States reaction to Lin Piao's *Long Live the Victory of People's War!*[3] illustrates the use of a document to sharpen suspicions. United States spokesmen cited Lin's pamphlet and declared that China's interest in foreign lands, including Africa, had to be countered. Hard pressed to justify United States presence in Vietnam, Dean Rusk said that ignoring Chinese avowals would be a repetition of "the catastrophic miscalculation that so many people made about the ambition of Hitler" and — from time to time — the intentions of Soviet leaders. Rusk warned that China had sought to promote "Communist coups and 'wars of liberation'" against independent African governments, as well as governments in Asia and

2. [137].
3. [216]. Originally in *JMJP*, 3 September 1965.

Latin America.[4] Lin's bold assertion about the encirclement of North America and Western Europe was much cited at that time.[5] Robert McNamara noted Lin's promise of encirclement in urging heightened NATO unity and military preparedness to the NATO Council of Ministers.[6] But some well-informed commentators have very different interpretations of Lin's pamphlet. Two RAND analysts argue that it is not Lin's brash tone, but his cautious language, that merits attention; they believe the pamphlet is directed to North Vietnam, and its author's intent is to warn North Vietnam and the National Liberation Front that Chinese military support should not be expected.[7] John K. Fairbank, testifying before the Senate Foreign Relations Committee, chided "commentators who really ought to know better" who had "overreacted to the visionary blueprint of world revolution put out by Lin Piao."[8] The Rusk-McNamara interpretation does not go undisputed.

It would be, in Rusk's own words, a "catastrophic miscalculation" to ignore Chinese statements. Yet it would be every bit as unsound to interpret a statement of wishes and long-term intentions as a program of action which China can undertake posthaste and which requires swift diplomatic and military countermeasures. Rusk failed to mention the objective constraints which limit any Chinese attempt to conduct a revolutionary program outside China. The role of misperception in making policy is illus-

4. Statement on China policy delivered 16 April 1966 before a closed session of the Far East Subcommittee of the House Foreign Affairs Committee. *NYT*, 17 April 1966.

5. The salient portion of his thesis is this: "Comrade Mao Tse-tung's theory of the establishment of rural revolutionary base areas and the encirclement of the cities from the countryside is of outstanding and universal practical importance for the present revolutionary struggles of all the oppressed nations and peoples, and particularly for the revolutionary struggles of the oppressed nations and peoples in Asia, Africa, and Latin America against imperialism and its lackeys. . . . Taking the entire globe, if North America and Western Europe can be called 'the cities of the world,' then Asia, Africa, and Latin America constitute 'the rural areas of the world.' Since World War II, the proletarian revolutionary movement has for various reasons been temporarily held back in the North American and West European capitalist countries, while the people's revolutionary movement in Asia, Africa, and Latin America has been growing vigorously. In a sense, the contemporary world revolution also presents a picture of the encirclement of cities by the rural areas. In the final analysis, the whole cause of world revolution hinges on the revolutionary struggles of the Asian, African, and Latin American peoples who make up the overwhelming majority of the world's population. The socialist countries should regard it as their internationalist duty to support the people's revolutionary struggles in Asia, Africa, and Latin America." [216], pp. 47–49.

6. *NYT*, 16 December 1965.

7. [96].

8. *NYT*, 11 March 1966. Cf. [71].

trated by the Vietnam War itself. That war seems to rest on misunderstandings of the gap between Chinese wishes and Chinese capabilities, if not a fundamental misreading of Chinese intentions themselves. China's capabilities are exaggerated, China's control of events in Vietnam is exaggerated, but, believing China's role so large, many United States policy makers cannot tolerate accommodation to Chinese influence and involvement in Southeast Asia.

China affects Africa in a second way: some elements of the Chinese model will be adopted there and China's revolutionary intentions will be partially attained. In a sense, there is contradiction in the idea of partial attainment, for the thrust of China's purist insistence is that one step without others, or a step which is incomplete, or a step which accommodates nonrevolutionary views, is evidence of error. Nonetheless, an observer can attribute a view or event to the existence of the Chinese model and China's commitment to revolution even if a Chinese policy maker would be displeased or dissatisfied by it.

China's revolutionary vision embodies many models — some purposeful, some organizational, some doctrinal, some tactical, some of international alignment — and anyone may draw whatever he wishes from these. Partial attainment may therefore take many forms. For example, a movement in a single state might endeavor to duplicate the main features of China's revolution: Marxist-Leninist-Maoist doctrine, guerrilla war, united front, seizure of state power, and creation of a socialist state. Or a movement could graft Mao's military teaching onto a popular, but non-Marxist, guerrilla endeavor. Or the leaders of a state might use fragments of Maoist teaching — "serve the people," "replace private interest by public interest" — or shadows of Chinese institutions and practices — mutual aid teams, "going down to the countryside"—in building a socialist state free of excessive coercion. Clearly, some things borrowed would hardly alter the character of political life in the recipient nation, and the CCP would be no nearer its revolutionary intention. But other things borrowed — in particular, emphasis on the role of a Communist party, the centrality of armed struggle, or the necessity for cultural revolution with control of the cultural environment and exclusion of contrary views — could stem from commitment to China's course and hasten revolution of the Chinese genre.

At the beginning of 1969 there were forty-two independent states in Africa and eight dependent territories. The multiplicity of units, each a distinct political entity, means that there are some fifty chances each year that an approximation of China's revolutionary vision might be attained in an African state. It is therefore much more likely that China's vision will be realized in one African state — if only for a limited time — than in Africa as a whole. The possibility that the Chinese model might be implemented in a region which is geographically limited — one country or a group of countries, but not the entire continent — must be seriously entertained.

Misperception and partial attainment compound each other if a suspicious power becomes frightened about a specific but limited consequence of Chinese activity. China's influence is taken by some to portend the most pessimistic outcome conceivable. Such fears do not appear to be well founded. The record of contacts prior to this writing demonstrates that China can have varying degrees of influence in several African countries without jeopardizing the indigenous character of political life. Nor can it be shown that China's commitment to extraordinary coercion has come closer to being copied in an African country because of its contacts with China. It remains to disentangle China's influence in Zanzibar from that of other states propagating taut and doctrinaire models. It remains, too, to see whether any of the movements now seeking to overturn Portuguese rule or apartheid government will adopt the CCP's techniques of governance. At this time borrowing has been controlled by African governments and movements. It does not restructure their ends, but serves existing ends. Even if China's vision were closely approximated in one African state, the possibility of its being adopted in others might not increase significantly; those indigenous forces in neighboring states which resisted adoption of elements of the Chinese model would not suddenly disappear.

The preceding discussion establishes that China's African interest will be politically significant even if her full revolutionary intent is not achieved. Moreover, it suggests that many forms of Chinese influence should be tolerable. Still, some Chinese capabilities will prompt precautions, and some Chinese initiatives may spark countermeasures. But two questions must be answered in each case: Who is to judge whether countermeasures are desirable? Who is then to parry a Chinese initiative? The easy answer may be correct: only African governments can choose and implement countermeasures. To be effective, actions must be deftly chosen and aptly undertaken. Artful moves sensitive to local uniqueness and cultural subtleties are typically unavailable to a foreign power. There may be a role for the ships, planes, and technical expertise of the United States or Soviet Union, a place for equipment, intelligence, and the arts of detection. But whether such instruments of power can prevail in a given situation is only decided in the engagement itself.

An African government's decision that it is necessary to dull the cutting edge of a Chinese initiative would be based on a judgment of both China's intentions and the likelihood that she would achieve her intentions. If the initiative were directed at the government itself, steps would be taken to prevent China's intention from being realized. If the thrust were against the government of another African state, however, the government which was deciding how to act would be placed in a position similar in some respects to that of non-African powers. It would then have to decide whether it could tolerate China's achievement of all or part of her objectives.

An African government, judging Chinese initiatives directed toward a third state, is not able to contain events in the third state simply by wishing to preserve the status quo. Any sequence of steps it might take to blunt China would involve some cost, political or economic. Assuming that it believed China's initiative would succeed, it could tolerate the outcome if it believed any one of three propositions to be true: the outcome would establish a relationship between China and the third state which would have no effect on it; the outcome would intrude, but in a way which it could manage by some political action of tolerable cost; the outcome—although intrusive and in some respects scarcely manageable—moved in a direction in which it was desirable to go or in which events would inevitably move.

The issue then hinges on whether China will acknowledge the possibility of building bilateral relations in which successive small states pay deference to China in some respects but do not commit themselves to the revolutionary enterprise, or will instead insist that each state standing in a special relationship to China devote itself to enlarging the number of committed states. Any talk of continental revolution implies the latter view and, in turn, the higher likelihood of resistance by existing African governments. Opportunity may appear only in the first form; it is possible to envision that individual African states will be governed by men who espouse revolutionary doctrine but in practice maintain cordial relations with their less radical neighbors. A strong case can be made that an African state, troubled by Chinese approaches to a third state or the rise of a group proclaiming China's world view in a third state, should devise steps to accommodate its radical neighbor rather than intervene and endeavor to shift the course of events.

Since Peking has not explained her intentions in a precise fashion, the African government confronted by this problem might choose to speculate on the most disruptive likely contingency. A careful reading of Chinese statements suggests that the most probable model of maximum Chinese engagement in world affairs that is held by Chinese policy makers turns on Chinese *hegemony*; speculation based on this model would hint at China's greatest expectations, the limits which she envisioned on her influence, and the extent to which a Chinese success could be accommodated.[9]

The main lines of this model are readily sketched. Hegemony would be attained gradually by asserting influence over states along China's borders and then in regions further away. At the maximum extent, China would have a secure capability for preventing lethal attack against her territory. She would receive material and technological resources from her client states, but she would normally provide goods or services in exchange. China would not assert sheer physical control of foreign regions, unless her very hegemony was challenged, because of the antagonism which such control customarily provokes. Rather, she would endeavor through the arts of balancing and delicate intervention, with force in reserve, to prevent the growth of hostile coalitions.

Once hegemony was attained, Chinese influence would be pervasive. Doctrinal deference would commonly be paid to Peking, even though the territorial states might pursue a variety of different paths in strictly national matters. In some territories Chinese hegemony might be strong, including a capacity to intervene in politics almost at will, though in other cases it might be weak, merely a formal deference paid for guarantees against war. But in all cases world politics would largely depend on Chinese political skill, her large share of the world's population, and, ultimately, her military power.

A *pax Sinica* in this form would hardly appeal to Washington or Moscow, but it could be compatible with the visions of radicals in an African territory who believed their nation could make its own way in an era of guaranteed peace and trade. The legitimacy of the present world order is not immune from challenge. The present order is widely con-

9. *Webster's Seventh New Collegiate Dictionary* defines hegemony as "leadership; preponderant influence or authority, esp. of a government or state." Compare E. H. Carr's observation, in 1939, that "an international order cannot be based on power alone, for the simple reason that mankind will in the long run always revolt against naked power. Any international order presupposes a substantial measure of general consent. . . . A new international order and a new international harmony can be built up only on the basis of an ascendancy which is generally accepted as tolerant and unoppressive or, at any rate, as preferable to any practicable alternative." *The Twenty Years' Crisis, 1919–1939* (New York: Harper, 1964), pp. 235–236. The notion of hegemony has three forerunners in CCP practice and doctrine. We have discussed the notion of "proletarian hegemony" in the national united front. A very "strong" hegemony has been exercised over China's national minorities, although it has gone further and involved policies of assimilation as well. Finally, the political relationship between center and periphery, especially where localism is accentuated by linguistic and ethnic differences, has demanded some concession by Peking to the power of provincial leaders.

sidered legitimate because it avoids large-scale war, guarantees a system of exchange which no major coalition has the will or power to resist, and enjoys the priority of a fait accompli. China has challenged this legitimacy, even as she contributes to it by acting in some respects in quite conventional ways. For the long term, however, Chinese hegemony would not be compatible with today's modes of international politics. Whether China or the Chinese Communist party will still exist when present-day international politics are restructured is something no one can say, but there can be no doubt that at some point in the future the present model of world politics will end and another system will be judged legitimate.

A Policy of Preparation

The discussion up to this point has included several assertions. China's objectives probably will not be attained in Africa. Her interest in Africa may nonetheless prove to be politically significant. Many forms of Chinese influence in an African state will be tolerable for other African states. Hegemony, the maximum Chinese influence which might be attained, would probably fall far short of control and would not extinguish indigenous political life in the client states. Finally, the units which are most likely to be decisive in blunting, accommodating, or adapting Chinese influence in Africa are the political systems of the African states themselves, which have very substantial assets to employ for that purpose, should they feel pressed to do so.

There is a constituency within China which believes a Chinese-style revolution will emerge in Africa sometime in the future and that China should serve as political midwife. Steps taken now by the Chinese could increase future opportunities for indigenous African radicals. These are acts of preparation. The view that preparation is an important part of Chinese African policy hinges on another notion, namely that Peking may anticipate political opportunities in Africa which cannot now be clearly seen.

The CCP asserts that the anti-imperialist revolution can be conducted in Africa, but it does not appear ready to urge social revolution. Indeed, the instruments of social revolution are virtually nonexistent. Arguing from its view of history, the CCP holds that the opportunities for revolution will increase; the future will be a better time for action than the present. But the precise opportunities—which only time, chance, growing consciousness, and inevitable progress will bring forth—are not yet discernible.

In other words, some CCP leaders believe that the general trend of human events, ebb and flow, will lead to particularly propitious moments.

This is not attributed to chance, but to the dialectical process of historical transformation. At the right time, the Chinese revolutionary model will be relevant and workable. Men armed with its vision will be able to assert themselves successfully. Revolutions compatible with the Chinese revolution will be wrought. If the speculation that China seeks hegemony is correct, each revolution would be a step toward a world order under Chinese auspices.

The CCP does not explicitly delineate the circumstances which might constitute a propitious moment. History suggests four kinds of possibilities. In the first, a major war (however begun) plays havoc with the technical apparatus and institutional structure of the present powers. The powers are severely strained; perhaps they will be reduced to ensuring their own survival. The delicate ties of interdependence in the world are severed. Willful groups, skilled in violence and techniques of persuasion, can force their way to power among peoples in disarray. This possibility is suggested by the CCP's rise in China; it gained momentum during the Japanese invasion and profited from the powers' preoccupation with World War II. When the war ended, the United States was unwilling to make further extensive commitments in Asia, although it is doubtful that United States action at that late stage could have altered the eventual outcome. In Yugoslavia, Tito also created an armed, decisive party in wartime.

A second possibility is that the ideological underpinnings of the present world order might be struck down. If no steps were taken to assure access to adequate food in all regions, or if technical and economic disadvantage became a far more potent symbolic issue than it is today, people of wealth could become outcasts from the rest of the world. Arguments about neocolonialism and imperialist aggression would take on an immediacy they do not enjoy today. In the poorer states radical revolutionaries, some of them drawn to the Chinese world view, would have a new opportunity to assert themselves.

A third possibility is that African governments might fail to meet basic needs. Even without world war or a massive challenge to the present world order, some African governments will probably be unable to provide food, security, and a better future for their people. If breakdowns are sporadic, or restricted to a handful of states at a time, remedial steps might be taken. Other African states or advanced industrial nations might assist a faltering government in weathering an economic impasse or a crisis of confidence. But if violence became the dominant mode, if belief in the efficacy of normal political and institutional means were threatened in much of Africa, breakdown could be both contagious and complete. Groups with organizational discipline and a keen sense of purpose would be able to seize power despite numerical weakness. There are many cases in recent African history of massive governmental failure which has not been accompanied by the rise of a revolutionary party. Indeed, a government may show remarkable momentum when its performance has been abominable. Nonetheless, a chronically distressed population is sure to include some desperate men who will turn to any promising model. Breakdown would almost certainly increase the likelihood that the Chinese revolutionary model will be adopted by some group.

The fourth and most likely possibility is that war might break out in Africa, threatening established governments and destroying the preconditions of evolutionist success. A clash between blacks and whites in South Africa, for example, could engulf the entire southern portion of Africa in a bloody and terrible war. Those skilled in warfare, especially guerrilla war, would be in the best position to engage proponents of apartheid and to win the allegiance of the African population. Such a war remains an ominous possibility.

Each of these four scenarios tells of opportunity for radical revolutionaries, who would be conscious of China's experience. China might provide material aid at a decisive point. The key advantage — for those who could demonstrate it — would be that combination of skill and assurance suited to the moment of disarray; existing groups, accustomed to more conventional times, would be unable to cope with unanticipated demands and new crises.

Some Chinese actions seem to be inconsistent with the policy of preparation, but on closer examination the apparent contradiction can be explained or dismissed. For example, why did China risk political assets to support the Stanleyville governments in the Congo in 1961 and 1964? Would it have been better to have waited for the growth of more reliable revolutionary groups? The answer falls in three parts: China risked little; she proceeded cautiously; and there was no way to prove that Gizenga (1961) and Gbenye et al. (1964) would not succeed. Although Peking certainly offended some African leaders and aroused the suspicion of others, there were no Chinese prospects in Léopoldville. It has been noted that China waited until the last minute to send a chargé to Stanleyville in 1961, and she did not grant recognition to the mélange of revolutionaries in 1964.

Why did Peking support anti-Kenyatta forces in Kenya? In that case, as in others where China has been implicated in supporting a minority faction or selected members of a governing party, China was indiscreet to say the least. Perhaps she erred, or perhaps she took a calculated risk.

China was not alone in having diplomats and newsmen expelled from Kenya. China's actions in Kenya can be judged careless or unwise or miscalculated, but they were not incompatible with a policy of preparation. Chinese in Nairobi could hardly have refused an approach from Oginga Odinga; it is even hard to imagine that they could have forgone approaching him on their own initiative. Such a move would have been among the most obvious available preparatory steps. A policy of preparation can never be entirely free of risks.

Why has China failed to create Marxist-Leninist-Maoist parties in Africa? A policy of preparation might seem to require their formation, but this would be deferred if Chinese leaders believed that Africa was not ready. The argument that long years of political preparation must precede party-building is wholly consistent with an emphasis on preparation.

Why has China willfully abandoned some political assets? The cases of Tunisia and post-Nkrumah Ghana, discussed in Chapter 6, appear to contradict a policy of preparation. The contradiction is real. The long-term goal of revolution intruded into the present; in the name of cultural revolution, a demand for revolutionary purity upset the orderly acquisition of assets for future action. During a part of the Great Proletarian Cultural Revolution the policy of preparation did not prevail. There is good reason to believe it returned in 1969.

If China is preparing for action at some future date, why is she not trying more vigorously to compensate for her relative ignorance of African affairs? Despite some steps — language training, employment of African cadres in China, and the relatively long tenure of office of Chinese diplomats who deal with Africa — there is no sign that China is preparing an informed body of Chinese specialists whose knowledge could be put to use at the decisive moment. Chinese intelligence probably gleans information from the press and scholarly journals; China may train men covertly to advise future guerrilla movements. It is likely that any such steps are limited in scale. There may be no value, in Peking's point of view, in training Chinese to conduct operations in Africa, precisely because revolutionary victories do go to those who know the populace and the political and geographic terrain — indigenous revolutionaries. Moreover, downgrading special knowledge about Africa would be consistent with other assertions that expertise must be subordinate to politics. If these arguments are correct, China's failure to train African specialists (save for diplomatic personnel, journalists, technicians, and a handful of students who have gained their experience inside Africa) could be perfectly in keeping with a policy of preparation.

If China wishes the downfall of existing nationalist governments, why provide them with economic and technical assistance? The breakdown of these governments is less likely to occur if they are successful in meeting economic expectations. Although China has declared her intentions (see Chou En-lai's remarks in Chapter 4), no inquiry into motives can content itself with that version. A speculative but convincing list of purposes might include these: to demonstrate China's desire to aid poor states (in part to recruit persons to a favorable view of China); to reward states which are friendly to China or refrain from hostile comment about her; to claim a place alongside the United States, Soviet Union, and other donor states; and to smooth the way to expanded trade. Economic aid probably reduces the possibility of future breakdown, although it may also raise expectations to unattainably high levels.

The policy of preparation is one element in the revolutionary aspect of China's African policy. It justifies present actions in revolutionary terms. Present actions which are plainly pragmatic or evolutionist—for example, expanding trade—can be justified in Peking on the grounds that they hasten revolution in the Chinese style. What cannot be estimated is the proportion struck between evolutionist and revolutionary goals, the extent to which immediate returns are subordinated to future returns when the two sets of goals are not complementary. But it is clear that some steps are taken which have no short- or middle-term return by conventional standards: training revolutionaries, distributing publications with an unmistakable revolutionary message, entering upon a large-scale aid program (the Tan-Zam railway), investing as much energy in contacts with national liberation movements as China has invested. These are all preparatory steps.

Countertrends

That Peking has little chance to achieve its vision in Africa, despite a policy of preparation, stems from discernible obstacles and countertrends. Failures may be interpreted and rationalized in the manner described in Chapter 5, but they remain failures.

Chinese prestige in Africa reached its zenith in 1964. As an embattled underdog, China was attractive to many Africans. China was a state of mystery, of revolutionary élan, attractive by its very distance and insularity. Newly-independent African states appeared to recognize China almost as a matter of course. Then China's support of Congolese revolutionaries frightened some moderate African leaders; when Stanleyville fell other Africans were disaffected. China announced her first nuclear test at almost the same time. Since then Peking has come under open attack in Africa much more frequently than before. The cultural revolution rendered China even more vulnerable. No one can say that China will not recoup, but future Chinese attempts to assert influence in Africa will take place against the essentially negative memories of 1964–1969.

In time African governments will probably learn how better to manage large foreign states which seek to intrude in their affairs. They have experimented, with only mixed success, with a device to check and control bilateral funding of national liberation movements, the Liberation Committee created by the Organization of African Unity. A clearer example of African precaution is the Tanzanian and Zambian management of China's participation in the Tan-Zam railway project. They entered the project step by step; had they disapproved of China's performance on one stage, they could have looked elsewhere for aid for the next step. One of the major concerns of the United Nations Conference on Trade and Development is to find ways and means by which weak states may counter the disproportionate economic leverage of rich states. African governments should learn from these and other experiences, and thus be better prepared to deal with China in the future.

If African countries continue economic development and achieve greater integration, the number of rewarding paths for socially conscious Africans to pursue should also increase. In turn, the number of men and women sufficiently disaffected to adopt the Maoist world view should be a smaller part of the populace than it would be if other paths were closed. There will always be some deeply hostile critics, but if they are few and their arguments fall on fallow ground they will not have a deciding influence. Beyond these speculations, however, one should move most cautiously. The record is mixed. Development and integration are by no means assured. Even if economic development does occur, it does not preclude disaffection; in some cases development has been accompanied by the rise of revolutionary forces. But neither breakdown nor war nor adoption of Chinese rules need occur. If none does occur, and if African peoples take satisfaction in the way in which they manage their own affairs, the required preconditions for vast changes which enhance Chinese influence will not be met.

Radical African ventures may become national in character; their authors may resist Chinese guidance. Chinese revolutionary experience embodies a precedent for autonomy which is strengthened by Chinese differences with the Soviet Union in the 1960s. Forty years earlier, Soviet organizational aid to the Kuomintang contributed to that party's cohesion and command structure, without which it might not have ousted its CCP members and survived as an important force. The pattern can be repeated.[10]

The Great Proletarian Cultural Revolution offended many who learned of its violence (sometimes exaggerated) and the simplistic views to which it was dedicated. Another counterpressure is that Chinese aid to antigovernment factions in some countries is now a matter of record. Thus, since 1964 Africans have learned more about China's internal politics and disruptive deeds abroad. Their new perspective led some Africans to limit China's freedom of action. No doubt exaggeration and fear also played a part.

It is also possible that major non-African states with a desire to contain Chinese influence will learn how to help African states which seek the same end. If they can learn to put their resources at the disposal of popular African governments without endangering indigenous political life, the United States, Soviet Union, and other states may be able to act more effectively than their present skills and dispositions permit. Little evidence is presently available that such learning is occurring, and learning is not inevitable.

In summary, there seem to be two main possibilities, both present today and both likely to persist. One turns on the prospect of severe disruption in the future. At that point radical, tightly organized, even violent actors would suddenly gain leverage. The second turns on a decline in the attraction of China's revolutionary style. Chinese moves would be dealt with prudently, national construction would preempt interest in revolution, and Africans would draw from several political models of which the Chinese model was merely one.

A third important point is whether China herself will maintain that sense of purpose which has so distinguished Maoist leadership. Never in history has so large a group striven so explicitly to maintain political purpose. But, as in so many matters, intent does not assure success.

Style

China utilized conventional means to create initial political assets in Africa. She offset her lack of contacts by contributing to new international organizations which offered entrée otherwise unavailable. As African states became politically independent, China used her first diplomatic missions and her organizational contacts to establish still more extensive rela-

10. Compare Fidel Castro's speech of 22 March 1962 attacking Anibal Escalante, who had brought his organizational skills from the Partido Socialista Popular to the post of general secretary of the new Fidelista single party in Cuba. Escalante was deported. [32].

tions. She drew from military, diplomatic, party, and university sources to staff these missions and other associated projects. Staff members were not always well prepared, but, at least until 1966, there was some emphasis on exploiting acquired experience.

China's African policy has been executed in a dualistic style. Her first style is precisely the formal, conventional model typified by diplomatic contacts. Her second is a tempered form of China's revolutionary experience, one which stresses the united front. She has not contented herself with formal diplomacy; she has also sought a range of contacts in each host community. China differs from other states, which may also attempt to reach the local public, in her persistent emphasis on contacts with prospective revolutionaries.

Many reports note the isolation of Chinese diplomatic staffs. In a conventional sense, Chinese diplomats in African capitals did choose to isolate themselves, particularly during the cultural revolution. But there is also evidence that Chinese diplomats have mingled effectively with those whom they chose to encounter.

It is more difficult to establish whether flexibility extends to a capacity to learn from mistakes. Tung Chi-p'ing testifies that Moscow's misstep in Guinea, which led to the Soviet ambassador's forced departure, was recounted in Peking as an example to be avoided. Observers tend to be less objective about events in which they are involved. Would Chinese African specialists have taken Kenya's expulsion of an NCNA correspondent as evidence of a failure? Peking could rationalize its position by arguing that the Kenyan government would not have acted had it not already been hostile; but if it was hostile, the risks taken in opposing it were justified; and so on. Since there was not merely one incident in Kenya, but a chain of incidents, either some such justification would need to have been made or, clearly, there was failure to learn from error.

Was the Great Proletarian Cultural Revolution, judged by its impact on foreign policy, a political error of massive proportions? In the infighting within the Ministry of Foreign Affairs,[11] some arguments must have turned on the foreign policy consequences of a militant and insistent diplomatic posture. We have observed that actions inconsistent with China's general African policy were taken during the cultural revolution and probably because of pressures to which it gave vent. Hostility to excesses of the cultural revolution and personal resentment by foreign ministry personnel against those who may have upset their work and careers need not result, however, in any systematic calculation of adverse consequences.

11. See [107] and [125].

The most likely alternative is that Chinese diplomats returning to African posts after the Ninth Party Congress (April 1969) will attempt to take up once again from that point they left in 1966, though their public position will be that the cultural revolution was a major success. If so, they will tacitly admit that the cultural revolution's militance was barren and unproductive in foreign policy.

The Great Proletarian Cultural Revolution was in many ways hostile to the kind of subtlety which Chou En-lai demonstrated during his 1963–1964 visit to Africa. Chou did not always persuade his hosts to share his view — some of them even chastised him — but his invocation of a reasonable image and China's selfless view of foreign aid showed sensitivity to the African audience. In a different sense, however, the tour itself was an unsubtle move: suddenly China's interest in Africa was visible to all. For that same reason large Chinese embassies may be more frightening than impressive.

The largest question mark in any study of Chinese African policy is whether Chinese concerned with Africa assess events in Africa and the statements of Africans with subtlety and sensitivity. Some members of Chinese missions and a handful of NCNA correspondents almost surely have this capability. Whether their judgments prevail in Peking, and whether they are backed up in Peking by others also well informed and sound of judgment, cannot be known. China does prize friendly comments by African spokesmen; her representatives solicit such comments and she disseminates them, in turn, within China and abroad. If her view of Africa were based solely on what Africans tell her, it would probably be a very different one than that of most systematic observers of the continent (even after allowance for the influence of ideology on perception). History includes many cases of major states which have believed what informants thought they wished to hear: witness, for example, the blunders of the United States which led her to initiate the Bay of Pigs invasion. At this point one can say only that a convincing assessment of the quality and sensitivity of the information and analysis of Chinese policy makers would be of incalculable value.

Conclusion

For the most part the short-term, pragmatic, evolutionary, and nondisruptive components of Chinese foreign policy have governed her African policy. She continues to proclaim a commitment to revolution and to take steps to enhance her position should a revolutionary opportunity present itself. The hypotheses in Chapter 1 are consistent with the diverse strains of Chinese African policy, although this study does not purport to prove them correct. The central argument is that evolutionist and revolutionary policies are pursued simultaneously: they are usually insulated from each other by the implicit guarantee that revolution is something for a later time. Diverse constituencies of the Chinese policy-making apparatus are satisfied by this view. Men whose commitments stem both from a vision of revolution and a sense of insistent practical necessity find a comfortable solution to their own personal conflicts of purpose in the simultaneous bracketing of evolutionist and revolutionary goals.

Three important exceptions have breached the insulation between the short term and long term. Chinese calls for revolution and preparatory steps are present means toward a future end; but since they rarely commit China very deeply the breach is not a serious one. A second exception lies in China's willingness to alienate an existing African government, whether she has relations with it or not, if a viable alternative to the left promises to challenge that government's authority. Two considerations must be weighed against each other: first, the likelihood that the left alternative will actually succeed (for it is never clear except in retrospect what it means to be viable) and, second, the costs which would be incurred by opposing the government. The third breach occurred during the cultural revolution and is apparently an aberration attributable to the immense pressures on foreign ministry personnel to act out their militance and revolutionary purity.

This study demonstrates that China's motives are mixed and that popular African governments, with wisdom and judicious precaution, can conduct relations with China which give play primarily to those Chinese motives which are consistent with African aims. If Africans adopt a Maoist vision, it is not likely to be because Chinese cooperate with African governments or because Africans visit China, but because African governments break down through incapacity or the ravages of war. Chinese policy appears to be sensitive to that prospect. Chinese policy makers probably believe that China could help bring to Africa that disruption in which the skills of indigenous radical revolutionaries would best fit them to seize state power. Even so, any such hopes understate the force of nationalism and the likelihood that political changes in Africa will take place within the territorial limits of existing states.

Although China subscribes to some version of a domino theory of revolution, the forces which would work against such a process appear to be very strong. On the other hand, existing African governments might enhance the prospects for unwanted Chinese influence by failure to be responsive to their people, failure to maintain effective surveillance of Chinese activities in their countries, and overdependence on foreign states hostile to China. They could best accommodate China's interests and serve their own ends by conducting normal relations with China, borrowing from Chinese models with discrimination, taking precautions where prudence appears to demand them, and increasing opportunities for Chinese to learn something of the world outside China. No policy can free African states from uncertainty and no pretence should be made that such a policy can be prescribed. Above all, no policy is merely technical and none is free of risk.

Appendix

Peking elaborated an institutional structure and recruited personnel to staff it in order to conduct increasingly complex relations with Africa. The public record contains names of organizations and personnel; in some cases an institution's creation is described, in others entire staffs are known, or the career of an individual can be traced across a decade or more. Where data on internal political processes are unavailable, regularities of structure and staffing assume a special role for they may support inferences concerning the quality of policy, its importance to the sponsoring government, and the capabilities available to carry it out. Those who have an opportunity to work with Chinese on African matters may find it useful to picture the structure within which China's policy is made and executed.

This Appendix, except as otherwise specified, describes the Chinese apparatus for Africa in the period immediately *before* the onset of the Great Proletarian Cultural Revolution. Typically, the offices named and the men and women listed as staff are those of 1964 or 1965. Chinese reports from mid-1966 until 1969 contained little data from which the maintenance or dormancy of these institutions could be discerned. The survival of personnel during the cultural revolution can only be begun to be discussed at this writing, in late 1970. In a very few instances I have discussed the situation after the cultural revolution, particularly where there are positive published reports of the continued activity of important figures. And, of course, this account must mention the downgrading of Ch'en I, though at this writing he has not been formally replaced as foreign minister. Others who are mentioned in this account have been publicly criticized or denounced. The reader would be wise to assume that many of the individuals listed here will *not* reappear in positions of responsibility, and that some of the organizations and offices will have been realigned by consolidation or simply extinguished. The extent of continuity after the cultural revolution is an important issue. A few points are made here, but for the most part that must be considered at a later time.

China must gather data, plan, and act. Some individuals engage in more than one of these tasks. Chinese personnel abroad — diplomats, newsmen, and visitors — certainly contribute information to Peking. Chinese analysts, like their counterparts elsewhere, probably study documentary sources such as press reports, official statistics, and studies by foreign Africanists. Individual Africans doubtless contribute impressions and assessments. Chinese concerned with African policy have studied Mao Tse-tung's writings with care; their approach to intelligence work and the gathering of data may be guided by this injunction:

> When we say that we are opposed to a subjective approach to problems we mean that we must oppose ideas which are not based upon or do not correspond to objective facts, because such ideas are fanciful and fallacious and will lead to failure if acted on. . . . There must be people who derive ideas, principles or views from the objective facts, and put forward plans, directives, policies, strategies and tactics.[1]

In the Chinese structure, groups of men settle disagreements and allocate tasks. The hypotheses advanced in Chapter 1 suggest how their judgments are made. Most decisive decisions are probably made by members of the Standing Committee of the Political Bureau of the Central Committee, that handful of men — seven prior to the cultural revolution — at the apex of the CCP structure. Contributions to planning doubtless are made at many levels. Embassies contribute proposals, and others are made by African governments. One purpose in displaying the array of Chinese offices and organizations concerned with African affairs is to show the many different ways data may be collected and plans advanced and selected; a hierarchy and some coordination among the offices can be reasonably inferred, although hard data on planning and decision is scarce.

Action in Africa is supported by institutions in Peking which provide personnel and guidance. Ministries, commissions, public organizations, and other groups perform specialized tasks. Some of this action is open and reported. The two most active organizations are the Ministry of Foreign Affairs and the Commission on Cultural Relations with Foreign Countries (CCRFC).

The role of the CCP is central, but the CCP does not candidly describe its structure for managing international affairs. One informant asserts that a Foreign Affairs Committee of the Central Committee of

1. [223], p. 225.

the CCP exists and oversees some operations,[2] but this is unconfirmed. It is a sound presumption that the CCP is able to control the planning and decision processes, but whether there is a party mechanism parallel to the government planning organs is unknown. Neither is it known who controls covert operations. Any organ working abroad could serve as a shield for covert activity or conduct secret work itself. In addition, there may be mechanisms expressly created to perform intelligence functions and conduct secret operations.[3]

Party Organs

How the CCP and Chinese government organs relate to one another in practice is a complex matter not yet understood.[4] Principal government offices have many ranking CCP members in leading positions. The "public organizations" profess to be guided by the CCP. For example, the All-China Student Federation (ACSF) is constitutionally bound "under the leadership of the Chinese Communist Party . . . to support the strug-

2. Interview with Tung Chi-p'ing, Cambridge, Massachusetts, 7–8 June 1965. Mr. Tung was posted to the Chinese embassy in Burundi as an assistant cultural attaché. In May 1964, shortly after his arrival, he went to the United States embassy and requested political asylum. For another interview with Mr. Tung, see [135].

3. Several reports, possibly reliant on one another, describe Africa-concerned offices and organizations which I cannot confirm, and which I doubt exist. Mention must be made of them lest this Appendix seem incomplete. Pieter Lessing declares these exist: The Chinese Institute for African Affairs, The Special Committee on Relations with Peoples of Africa, and the Special Work-Toward-Africa Committee, led respectively by Ny Yung-chen (presumably Nieh Jung-chen), Li Keh-nu (presumably Li K'o-nung, deceased 2 February 1962) and Liu Chang-sheng (presumably Liu Ch'ang-sheng). Perhaps the last is the China-Africa People's Friendship Association. [78]. Fritz Schatten, in a longer list of organizations including many dealt with in this Appendix, cites the Research Commission for African Subjects, a Special Committee for Africa formed "as part of the Political Bureau" by Mao Tse-tung in December 1960 and led by Li Keh-nu [sic], and the Commission for Social Relations with the Peoples of Africa. The first and third are under the State Council. [109], pp. 219–221. Neither the Lessing nor the Schatten assertion are documented, though Schatten otherwise uses footnotes in profusion. For similar assertions, see Madan M. Bauldie, [147], January 1965, p. 17, and [176], 9 December 1960, p. 1.

4. The 1956 CCP constitution specified in its preamble that "the Party plays the leading role in the life of the state and society." Article 47 provides that a primary party organization is to be set up in any office where there are three or more full members. Democratic centralism operates: article 19 requires that "Party decisions shall be carried out unconditionally. Individual Party members shall obey the Party organization . . . and all constituent Party organizations throughout the country shall obey the National Party Congress and the Central Committee." The "CCP Political Department for Foreign Affairs" was cited in 1965 issuing instructions to "all Party members and cadres working in foreign affairs departments." *SCMP*, no. 3645, pp. 6–7 (14 February 1965).

gle against imperialism and colonialism."[5] At least prior to the cultural revolution, leaders of the All-China Federation of Trade Unions (ACFTU) were members of the CCP Central Committee. The International Liaison Department of the China Young Communist League (CYCL) was headed by the same persons who led the International Liaison Office of the All-China Youth Federation (ACYF); in effect, the departments were identical. Such ties maintained party primacy.

In addition to the unconfirmed Foreign Affairs Committee, the Central Committee almost surely includes an International Liaison Department which maintains relations with foreign Communist parties. Tung Chi-p'ing asserts that the Investigation Department of the Central Committee sends "secret agents" abroad.[6]

Jen-min Jih-pao, the party's daily newspaper, and *Hung-ch'i*, the twice-monthly theoretical journal, are published by the Central Committee. Authoritative articles on Africa appear from time to time in *Hung-ch'i*. African coverage by *JMJP* grew to prodigious proportions during the period under study. During 1964, for example, it was customary that 8–10 percent of a day's issue was given to news accounts, commentaries, editorials, and reports about Africa and African visitors to China. On an exceptional day African items might constitute 25 percent of an issue.

Government

The State Council is the executive arm of government. At the onset of the cultural revolution, Chou En-lai was premier and Ch'en I was one of several vice-premiers. The next level of organization is the Office of Foreign Affairs,[7] established in 1958. Ch'en I was its director and its deputy directors included Central Committee members Liao Ch'eng-chih and Liu Ning-i. The five senior men appointed in 1958 still served at the end of 1965, an index of stability; Liao and Liu lost their Central Committee seats in 1969, and Ch'en was demoted from the Political Bureau. The cultural revolution has thus affected many of those who held posts in the Office of Foreign Affairs.

The principal government departments in foreign relations are the Ministry of Foreign Affairs, Commission on Cultural Relations with Foreign Countries, Commission on Economic Relations with Foreign

5. "Constitution of All-China Federation of Students," [102], Appendix H, pp. 238–239. Constitution adopted 10 February 1960.

6. [135].

7. Sometimes translated as the Office in Charge of Foreign Affairs or the Foreign Affairs Office.

Countries, Ministry of Foreign Trade, New China News Agency, Foreign Languages Publishing and Distribution Administration, and the Foreign Affairs Department of the Ministry of National Defense.

Within the Ministry of Foreign Affairs duties are allocated to geographic and functional divisions. Fission of existing departments, described in the text,[8] led in 1964 to the creation of a West Asian and North African Affairs Department and an African Affairs Department.[9] Although staff assignments in the newly-separated divisions give a clue to the way duties may have been divided before the split, reported activities of officials suggest that they were to a large degree interchangeable. The split may have made for specialization, rather than reflect a preexisting division of labor. By 1969, however, the two had been recombined.[10]

A Liaison Bureau for Cultural Relations with Foreign Countries operated under the Culture and Education Committee of the Government Administration Council (GAC). When the State Council replaced the GAC in September 1954, the liaison bureau was placed under its authority; in February 1958 it was raised to commission standing.

Until January 1964 cultural relations with Africa were carried on by an Asian and African Department of the CCRFC.[11] French-language, English-language, and Arabic-language sections dealt with Africa. Tung Chi-p'ing was one of a handful of persons in the French-language section from September 1963 until his departure for Burundi in May 1964. The number of persons directly assigned to the African sections varied, but in all three together there were as few as eight and as many as fifteen at one time, a small portion of the commission's four hundred personnel. They were supported by other CCRFC departments which performed specialized tasks, however. For example, the Propaganda Department acted jointly with the responsible African section when Chinese cinematographers went to Africa to film documentaries.

In January 1964 a separate African Department was created. Its director had been a deputy director of the former Asian and African Department, and the three sections were retained without change. As the commission grew — Tung Chi-p'ing estimated it would grow from 400

8. At pp. 26–27.

9. *JMJP*, 8, 15, and 22 September 1964. Sudan was probably a responsibility of the West Asian and North African Affairs Department, since the department's director is identified with a Sudanese guest.

10. In a West Asian and African Affairs Department again. *SCMP*, no. 4508, p. 22 (25 September 1969).

11. Also reported as the Second Department. [133], 1963.

to 500 or 600 in the year after his departure—the African Department would be assigned a larger staff.[12]

The Commission on Economic Relations with Foreign Countries (CERFC) was created as a bureau on 7 January 1960 and raised to a commission on 5 June 1964. It has had only one director, Fang I. In 1961, Fang I was appointed as an additional deputy director of the Office of Foreign Affairs. He remains prominent in 1970. The commission probably handles aid questions and the political component of trade policy.

The Ministry of Foreign Trade dealt with Africa at a very early stage and remains concerned. The minister, Yeh Chi-chuang, who died in 1967, joined Fang I in talks with high-ranking African visitors during 1964. Two of four high-level Chinese delegations dispatched in 1961–1965 to African countries were led by Lu Hsü-chang, a vice-minister of foreign trade. The Fourth Bureau of the ministry, which existed as early as December 1957, has been identified as responsible for Asian and African trade.[13]

Tung Chi-p'ing stated that CCRFC worked with special international liaison offices of thirteen ministries and commissions. The chief offices with which the commission worked were the Ministry of Education and the Ministry of Culture. When Tung worked in Peking, the CCRFC and the Ministry of Culture were in the same building.

In 1954–1964 China dispatched an increasing number of NCNA correspondents abroad, increased broadcast hours to Africa, and undertook distribution of material among African booksellers. NCNA maintains its own International Department.[14] The Foreign Languages Publishing and Distribution Administration, created 25 May 1963, coordinates and controls the work of the Foreign Languages Press, the distributor Guozi Shudian (International Bookshop), *Peking Review*, and other units which prepare and disseminate printed materials abroad.

The Ministry of National Defense includes a Foreign Affairs Department, whose mission includes dispatching military attachés abroad, maintaining liaison with resident attachés, supporting Chinese military missions traveling abroad, receiving and planning itineraries of foreign military missions to China and—important for those few African countries

12. Interview with Tung Chi-p'ing, note 2.

13. [133], 1960. Liu Hsi-wen, identified as deputy director of the bureau in December 1957, was an assistant minister of foreign trade dealing with African matters in 1969. *SCMP*, no. 4533, p. 23 (1 November 1969). See note 48.

14. Ting T'o was identified on 19 November 1961 as deputy director of that department. It is not known whether the department handles foreign news, services the NCNA correspondents abroad, distributes NCNA materials in foreign languages, or, possibly, controls political activity of NCNA correspondents.

which have requested Chinese military advisors — sending military advisors abroad.[15]

Public Organizations

The public organizations are mass organizations, more limited specialist functional organizations, and some groups created with foreign policy and foreign action as an express purpose. The mass organizations are the All-China Federation of Trade Unions (ACFTU), National Women's Federation (NWF), All-China Youth Federation (ACYF), and All-China Student Federation (ACSF).[16] Officials of all four groups have traveled to meetings abroad and visited Africa. All have been represented in the international "front" organizations.[17] The three larger groups maintain an international liaison department. The ACYF department is identical to that of CYCL, as noted above; it is not uncommon that ACSF is represented abroad by an ACYF or CYCL official with no known post in ACSF.[18] Through the mass organizations China has named persons to two roles in the international "fronts," as officers (visible at congresses and executive committee meetings) and as traveling secretaries resident in East European capitals where the "fronts" usually had headquarters. During the 1950s the "fronts" had access to African organizations and individuals whom China could not otherwise reach.

Following are the limited functional organizations, with dates of formation:

All-China Federation of Literary and Art Circles, including Union of Chinese Writers (July 1949)
All-China Athletic Association (26 October 1949)
Political Science and Law Association of China (22 April 1953)
China Islamic Association (16 May 1953)

15. [131], Appendix G, "Chinese Communist Military Organization — 1961."

16. Though smaller than the other three and a constitutional constituent of ACYF, ACSF is much larger than the specialist functional organizations. The ACSF Eighteenth Congress redefined membership to admit secondary school students as well as those getting a higher education, to whom it had originally been confined; if the change was carried out, it certainly became a mass organization. The cultural revolution, however, interrupted ACSF activities. Status of the organization after 1966 is uncertain.

17. World Federation of Trade Unions, Women's International Democratic Federation, World Federation of Democratic Youth, and International Union of Students. The latter two groups co-sponsor the World Youth Festivals, at which China had been regularly represented. China's participation in these organizations was undone during the breakdown of Sino-Soviet relations in the early 1960s.

18. The ACSF had an international liaison department in 1952, but it is not known whether it existed thereafter.

All-China Federation of Industry and Commerce (October 1953)
All-China Journalists Association (14–16 May 1957)
National Red Cross Society of China (by September 1950)
China Scientific and Technical Association (by merger 25 September 1958)

These groups too, in some cases, have ties to international "front" organizations.[19] The National Red Cross Society of China has been a member of the League of Red Cross Societies and has made financial contributions through the league to Africans in need.[20] All have sponsored visitors to Africa and have received African visitors to China.

The China Islamic Association was prominent in early contacts with Muslim countries. As early as 1951 Mohammed Makin, a graduate of Al Azhar University in Cairo teaching Arabic in Peking, spoke to a meeting of the Chinese People's Institute for Foreign Affairs (CPIFA) on political conditions in the Arab world.[21] Makin and seven others are credited with forming the China Islamic Association. In July 1952 a forty-member preparatory committee was chosen at a conference in Peking; Burhan Shahidi was named chairman.[22] The association was formally launched on 16 May 1953.[23] Its initial objectives may have been domestic, but, when China began contact with Egypt in 1955, the association spoke on international issues and sent delegations to the Middle East. Pilgrimage to Mecca has been a special concern of the association. Pilgrimages have usually included visits to Egypt and Sudan, and in one case ranged as far as Guinea.[24]

The third type of public organization has foreign action and foreign policy as prime stated goals. The chief groups are:

General Organizations
- China Peace Committee
- Chinese People's Institute of Foreign Affairs
- China Council for the Promotion of International Trade

Friendship Associations and Similar Groups Concerned with Africa
- Chinese People's Association for Cultural Relations with Foreign Countries (See note 25 for changes of name.)

19. The International Organization of Journalists, International Association of Democratic Lawyers, World Federation of Scientific Workers.

20. For example, 36,600 Swiss francs were given to support relief activities in Algeria. "Algeria Relief Action — Progress Report: September 1962," League of Red Cross Societies, 15 October 1962, p. 4.

21. *CB*, no. 195 (25 July 1952).

22. NCNA, no. 1078 (6 August 1952).

23. [133], 1960.

24. [175], May 1964.

China-U.A.R. Friendship Association
Chinese People's Committee for Aiding Egypt Against Aggression
China-Africa People's Friendship Association
Asian-African Groups
Chinese Committee for Afro-Asian Solidarity
Liaison Committee with the Permanent Bureau of the Afro-Asian Writers' Conference
China Asia-Africa Society

The general organizations were all formed between 1949 and 1952. The China Peace Committee was the Chinese affiliate of the World Peace Council, which acts internationally as a "mass" group. The Chinese People's Institute of Foreign Affairs (CPIFA) has an academic aura; each of its original trio of vice-presidents wrote on politics and foreign affairs. Its main task visible to the outside observer is to host foreign visitors to China. The China Council for the Promotion of International Trade (CCPIT) complements the work of the Ministry of Foreign Trade.

The Chinese People's Association for Cultural Relations with Foreign Countries (CPACRFC), formed on 3 May 1954, is the umbrella organization for friendship societies. Ch'u T'u-nan, newly-elected chairman, hoped that CPACRFC would encourage friendship and promote "planned development" in the field of cultural exchange.[25]

The China-Egypt Friendship Association was formed 11 November 1956, in the wake of the war in the Suez. When the United Arab Republic was created, the association merged with the China-Syria Friendship Association (February 1958). A Chinese People's Committee for Aiding Egypt Against Aggression was also formed in November 1956. Its meetings and statements were reported at that time, but there is no evidence it persisted after 1956.

Many of China's nongovernmental relations with Africa were channeled via the China-Africa People's Friendship Association (CAPFA).

25. The founding groups were the four mass organizations, plus the China Peace Committee, All-China Federation of Literary and Art Circles, China Federation of Scientific Societies, China-India Friendship Association, China-Burma Friendship Association, and the CPIFA. NCNA, 3 May 1954. Its role as umbrella is illustrated by an 11 July 1961 joint meeting between CPACRFC and "fourteen relevant associations for friendship" in Peking. The CPACRFC chairman delivered a report, the meeting discussed "the tasks of all these various associations for the future," and additional leadership personnel for the various groups were elected. *SCMP*, no. 2542, p. 28, or *JMJP*, 13 July 1961. Since the onset of the cultural revolution, CPACRFC has twice changed its name, to Chinese People's Association for Cultural Relations and Friendship with Foreign Countries and then to Chinese People's Association for Friendship with Foreign Countries (CPAFFC).

On the afternoon of 12 April 1960 representatives of seventeen "people's groups . . . decided to establish CAPFA" and a 133-member council was elected. The executive committee met the same afternoon, approved governing regulations, chose a chairman and other officers, and approved twenty groups (including the seventeen original sponsors) as members.[26] The Chinese press has mentioned CAPFA since the height of the cultural revolution, an indication of its survival.[27]

The third group of organizations is "Afro-Asian." Most active in the Chinese Committee for Afro-Asian Solidarity. It was formed in February 1956 as the Chinese Asian Solidarity Committee. The committee named Chinese personnel to the permanent secretariat of the Afro-Asian People's Solidarity Organization (see Table 8). It issues statements on political issues and receives visitors in China. It was also the acknowledged source of China's substantial funding of the Afro-Asian People's Solidarity Organization during the period that China supported that organization, and it has been the conduit for Chinese funds contributed to African national liberation movements by AAPSO's Afro-Asian Solidarity Fund.

Because the Afro-Asian Writers' Conference (Tashkent, October 1958) called for creation of liaison committees in participating countries, the Union of Chinese Writers established a committee. This was no new departure outside already existing structures, for the deputy secretary general of the Chinese Committee for Afro-Asian Solidarity, Yang Shuo, simply assumed an additional function.[28]

The China Asia-Africa Society is distinct from other groups. Its failure to become a center of action contrasts with the promise with which it began; "students of Asian and African questions" met and discussed draft regulations for the society on 30 April 1959. Leaders with links to orthodox existing structures were chosen to do the preparatory work. They stated:

26. *SCMP*, no. 2245, p. 40. Although the meeting must have been prepared in advance, it is not clear why the three nonsponsors were added. They are the All-China Federation of Industry and Commerce, All-China Student Federation, and China Cinema Workers' Association. The original seventeen sponsors were: All-China Federation of Trade Unions, All-China Youth Federation, National Women's Federation, China Peace Committee, Chinese Committee for Afro-Asian Solidarity, CPACRFC, All-China Federation of Literary and Art Circles, Union of Chinese Writers, All-China Journalists Association, China Council for the Promotion of International Trade, All-China Athletic Association, National Red Cross Society of China, Chinese People's Institute of Foreign Affairs, Chinese Scientific and Technical Association, Chinese Medical Association, and China Islamic Association. Not all 133 council members attended subsequent meetings. Only those "in Peking" attended the 12 April 1963 meeting for example. *JMJP*, 13 April 1963.

27. *SCMP*, no. 4288, p. 25 (23 October 1968).

28. *SCMP*, no. 1995, p. 42 (14 April 1959).

> [The society's founding] was prompted by an urgent desire to make a more intensive study of the social conditions, politics, economy, history, philosophy, literature and arts of the Asian and African countries so as to promote the cultural flow and mutual understanding between China and the peoples of Asian and African countries.[29]

But the society was not actually formed until almost three years later.[30] The society's tasks, more precisely defined, included increasing cultural and academic exchanges between China and Asian-African states. Ch'en I greeted the founding and linked the society's work to the growing importance of Asian and African states in world affairs.[31] The original membership of 500 consisted mostly of "professors in Chinese universities and colleges and research workers of various institutions in China." The membership of the elected council in 1959 included academicians, but there were also many officials of public organizations. On balance, however, the membership suggests that the society was intended to harness those who were relatively apolitical to political objectives. This impression is reinforced by Chou Yang's election as president of the society. Chou Yang—until his dismissal in the early days of the cultural revolution—was identified with the task of bringing intellectuals to serve party objectives.[32]

In summary, existing public organizations were utilized in the conduct of China's African policy and some new institutions were created. Their work supplemented that of the party (where it is speculated an "Africa Committee" might even have been set up) and of the government. Increasing specialization in the Ministry of Foreign Affairs and the Commission on Cultural Relations with Foreign Countries may have been matched by elaboration of such groups as the New China News Agency, which also extended its efforts in Africa. In some ways this increasing detail on organizational charts reflected innovation and substance.

29. *SCMP*, no. 2008, p. 38. Those chosen were Kuo Mo-jo, Chou Yang, Burhan Shahidi, Ch'u T'u-nan, Wu Han, and Chang T'ieh-sheng.

30. On 19 April 1962. *SCMP*, no. 2726, p. 26. This NCNA report dates preparations for the society back to 1958.

31. *PR*, 27 April 1962, p. 23: "Ch'en I noted the increasingly important role which the Asian and African countries are playing in international affairs. It is essential, he said, for us in China to have a better knowledge of these countries with their ancient cultures, and to develop cultural and academic relations between China and the other lands of the two continents."

32. *SCMP*, no. 2726, p. 26, includes a namelist in romanization and characters. On Chou Yang's fall from orthodoxy, see Merle Goldman, "Party Policies Toward the Intellectuals: The Unique Blooming and Contending of 1961–2," in John Wilson Lewis, ed., *Party Leadership and Revolutionary Power in China* (London: Cambridge University Press, 1970), pp. 268–303.

New offices and groups, though they sometimes had a flavor borrowed from Soviet experience ("friendship associations"), took up some tasks not previously performed in China. On the other hand, the stimulus for some institutional change came from outside, through the Moscow-led fronts and the Afro-Asian movement. No innovation as striking as the U.S. Peace Corps was introduced, but Chinese technical assistance personnel vowed to live abroad under conditions identical to those experienced by nationals of the host country with whom they were working. Steps which were new for China included:

(1) Creating an office to coordinate the foreign affairs work of diverse ministries, commissions, and bureaus under State Council control.
(2) Establishing foreign-aid operations.
(3) Creating sections and departments in ministries and commissions to deal with African countries with which China had previously not had relations.
(4) Creating one organization with party, government, and public members — the China-Africa People's Friendship Association — which could profess interest in many fields.
(5) Creating an institutional framework — the China Asia-Africa Society — to enlist the work of Chinese in diverse fields concerning the history and culture of other Asian and African countries.
(6) Creating new devices — especially the Chinese Committee for Afro-Asian Solidarity — which provided nongovernmental entrée to African countries.

Personnel

The names of a large number of persons occupying official roles appear in the press, on namelists, notices of appointment, and sometimes in reports of attendance at specific meetings.[33] The preceding description of institutions and their growth provides a rough index of the significance given African affairs by the Chinese Communist party; moreover, if the institutions persist it is reasonable to infer that they will gather experience and gain a momentum of their own, in addition to performing ongoing tasks. Therefore organization is a basis for rough but useful estimates of the scale of the foreign policy apparatus for Africa that exists in Peking. Identification of individual Chinese concerned with Africa serves a similar

33. Many of the facts reported in this section were made available to me by Donald W. Klein. They have proven an invaluable supplement to other materials at my disposal. Mr. Klein has also given his own observations freely, for which I am grateful. Responsibility for the accuracy of all comments in this section, of course, remains with the writer.

function. It indicates the number of Chinese who have had contact with African matters and their official positions. For even the brief period of this study, it indicates that the group of personnel concerned with Africa has had coherence and persistence. The interlocking leadership of Africa-concerned institutions is also illustrated. The most important use of this material is to identify individuals who may continue in the 1970s to be active in the Africa-concerned foreign policy apparatus. Finally, it suggests personal dimensions to a study otherwise heavily dependent on polemical documents, formal political moves and ripostes, and the skeleton of an institutional structure.

Individual Chinese who have helped to create or implement Chinese African policy can be identified in four ways. Some hold official posts which require that they deal with Africa. Some — including many of the former — have traveled to Africa. A large number are members of the China-Africa People's Friendship Association (though how deeply this involves them with African matters is not known). Finally, some are mentioned in the press as men who welcome African visitors to China. Lists of persons identified in these four ways heavily overlap. Many individuals would be on all four lists.[34] Only a few of the Chinese concerned with Africa can be mentioned here; readers wishing more detail may consult sources mentioned in the Bibliographic Note.

Mao Tse-tung has frequently received African visitors as Chairman of the Chinese Communist party, and some key statements on Africa are attributed to him. Chou En-lai, Premier of the State Council, led a large Chinese delegation to Africa from December 1963 to February 1964. In June 1965 he made two flights to Africa, one to Tanzania and another (in anticipation of the abortive Second Asian-African Conference) to the United Arab Republic. Mao and Chou are members of the Standing Committee of the Political Bureau of the CCP, the highest CCP policy-making body both before and after the cultural revolution. Moreover, Chou has maintained a special interest in foreign policy in the years since he surrendered the post of foreign minister to Ch'en I.

By the end of 1964 seven full members and two alternate members of the Central Committee had visited Africa, among them Nieh Jung-chen, who was assigned to represent China at Ghana's independence festivities in March 1957. Ch'en I and Central Committee alternate member K'ung Yüan accompanied Chou En-lai as a member of the 1963–1964 Chinese delegation. Ch'en I and Chou En-lai paid subsequent visits as well. Liu Ch'ang-sheng, Liu Ning-i, and Liao Ch'eng-chih are CAPFA members and

34. See Bibliographic Note, p. 246, for summary of lists in [70].

have visited Africa. Yeh Chi-chuang, the minister of foreign trade, led an early trade mission to Africa. The ninth visitor to Africa was Fang I, director of the Commission for Economic Relations with Foreign Countries and an alternate member of the Central Committee. Of these nine men, four survived in the Central Committee after the Ninth Party Congress of April 1969: members Chou En-lai, Ch'en I (demoted from the Political Bureau), Nieh Jung-chen, and alternate member Fang I.[35] The top CCP circles therefore have included a few men who evinced an interest in Africa and visited the continent, however briefly.

Two Central Committee employees are members of CAPFA, a clue pointing to them as possible Central Committee specialists on Africa. Central Committee staff are rarely identified as such, but Li Ch'i-hsin has been labeled a "leading official of a department of the Central Committee." He accompanied the first secretary of the Moroccan Communist party, Ali Yata, when the Moroccan spoke with Mao Tse-tung in 1959. A lesser post — "leading functionary of a department" of the Central Committee — was held by Wu Hsüeh-ch'ien, who made six trips to Africa between 1958 and 1965.

Eight of the original 133 CAPFA members were associated with the CCP's youth arm, the China Young Communist League (CYCL). Wu Hsüeh-ch'ien, who was identified as a Central Committee functionary in January 1964, had earlier been a member of the CYCL standing committee. Like most of those in CYCL leadership who visited Africa, Wu first went abroad as a representative of the All-China Youth Federation (ACYF). He was director of its International Liaison Department from 1953 to 1958.

Ch'ien Li-jen followed Wu Hsüeh-ch'ien to the concurrent posts of director of the International Liaison Departments of CYCL and ACYF, serving until 1964. He, too, traveled to Africa. In June 1965 he was listed among advisors to the Chinese delegation planning to attend the Second Asian-African Conference. Liu Hsi-yüan, CYCL secretary when CAPFA was formed, was named a CAPFA vice-president.

Jen-min Jih-pao, the party newspaper, was represented on CAPFA by a deputy chief editor, Ch'en Chün, who has been to Africa.

Four deputy directors of the Office of Foreign Affairs of the State

35. Others who have visited Africa may have been promoted in the elections of the Ninth Central Committee. One, aged Kuo Mo-jo, long involved in foreign cultural relations, is a new Central Committee member. Another, Huang Chen, ambassador to Paris before and after the cultural revolution, led a small Ministry of Foreign Affairs mission to Africa in late 1962 to explain China's case in the Indian border dispute.

Council were named CAPFA members, though none appears to be an African specialist. Of the seven senior members of the office in 1965, however, two appear to have been Asian specialists, and each of the other five had visited Africa.[36] Four of the seven are among the nine Central Committee members and alternates noted above; thus key government posts concerning Africa were held by leading CCP members, in conformance with a pattern discernible in other areas. A number of the vice-ministers of foreign affairs have been identified as participants in negotiations with prominent African visitors or events during visitors' stays in Peking, but Chi P'eng-fei and Ch'iao Kuan-hua performed these assignments rather frequently. In January 1966 two vice-ministers were added to the roster, Ch'en Chia-k'ang and Hsü I-hsin, both of whom had been ambassadors to Arab countries. Each assumed a share of concern for Africa.[37]

In the Commission on Cultural Relations with Foreign Countries (CCRFC), vice-chairmen Ting Hsi-lin and Chu Kuang appear to have borne heavy African assignments, Chu Kuang more so than his colleague.[38] Like the Ministry of Foreign Affairs, the commission structure includes specialist bureaus, but it is not clear what relationship exists between the publicly-visible vice-chairmen, quoted and photographed with African visitors or themselves visiting Africa, and the working departments of the commission.[39] According to Tung Chi-p'ing's account, the ministry is

36. Chang Yen and Li I-meng are identified with Asian affairs. The others are director Ch'en I and deputy directors Fang I, Liao Ch'eng-chih, Liu Ning-i, and K'ung Yüan.

37. Ch'en Chia k'ang served almost ten years in Cairo as ambassador and was Peking's senior diplomat in Africa, possibly responsible for coordination of work among Chinese missions on the continent. Hsü I-hsin had been ambassador to Syria. When Mao Tse-tung received the prime minister of Congo (B) in October 1967, Hsü I-hsin was present. *PR*, 13 October 1967. In 1969 the press did not mention Ch'en Chia-k'ang, and Africans were being greeted by vice-ministers Hsü I-hsin and Chi P'eng-fei. *SCMP*, no. 4515, p. 20; *SCMP*, no. 4498, p. 23.

38. Ting Hsi-lin was appointed to the CAPFA executive committee when CAPFA was formed in April 1960. In the only promotion CAPFA ever announced, he was raised to a vice-presidency in 1961. In 1969 Ting still took ceremonial roles with foreign visitors, despite his advanced years (born 1893). Chu Kuang is a veteran of the long march who was mayor of Canton from 1955 to 1960. On 22 April 1961 he was appointed a vice-chairman of the CCRFC and ten weeks later, on 12 July 1961, a member and vice-president of CAPFA. The near-simultaneity suggests that he was added to the CCRFC to cope with China's African contacts. He was removed from his CCRFC post early in 1965.

39. Tung Chi-p'ing believed that the vice-chairmen actually came to the CCRFC offices regularly. His only conversation with a vice-chairman took place shortly before his departure; ironically, the vice-chairman called Tung in to discuss his political views, possibly to quiet some doubts about his political reliability. The com-

the more prestigious and more important of the two institutions. Its concerns are broader and it supports a larger overseas establishment. The ministry and commission both were forced to staff new posts abroad as the number of embassies burgeoned, but the commission was limited to naming a handful of cultural attachés and assistants. Table 6 indicates the movement of men between the ministry African departments and foreign stations in the period 1956–1970. The roster of ambassadors in African posts appears in Table 1.

Two newcomers to the staffs of these departments, Wang Yü-t'ien and Lin Chao-nan, served in Africa before taking a department post. The remainder, with a few exceptions,[40] served in other posts in the ministry or as diplomatic personnel elsewhere abroad. The first three directors were men of considerable experience. K'o Hua had headed the Protocol Department of the ministry. Ho Ying, former ambassador in Ulan Bator, had been deputy director of the First Asian Affairs Department. Before going to Khartoum, where he was ambassador immediately preceding his appointment as director, Wang Yü-t'ien had been counselor of the Chinese embassy in Berlin. The deputy directors, too, came to their posts with experience.[41]

Not all diplomatic appointees had had unsullied careers. Chiang Yen, deputy chief of the mission in Burundi, had been expelled from Indonesia in 1960 after assiduously pressing the case of Chinese nationals with Indo-

---

mission required its staff to stay out of offices in which they had no proper business, a security precaution which severely limited Tung's ability to say much in detail about offices in the commission other than his own.

40. Prior experience in a ministry post or at a Chinese embassy abroad is recorded for all those appointed to director and deputy director posts in the departments, with the exceptions of Li Chün, Hou Yeh-feng, and Wang Jen-san. Li Chün was deputy leader of a CAPFA delegation which spent almost four months in Africa in 1961; he was first identified as a deputy director of the ministry department two months after the delegation returned. Hou Yeh-feng was named a member of the council of the China-Japan Friendship Association when it was formed in October 1963. One Wang Jen-san, who might be the same man, was identified in 1957 and 1958 as a deputy director of the propaganda department of the Kiangsu Provincial Committee of the CCP.

41. Ho Kung-k'ai was appointed on 29 May 1953 as director of the Alien Affairs Office of the Central-South Administrative Committee. Kung Ta-fei served as first secretary in Rangoon; Meng Ying served as counselor in Ulan Bator (for a time concurrently with Ambassador Ho Ying, who was later director of the Africa-concerned ministry department when Meng joined the department as a deputy director); Hsieh Feng served as counselor in Budapest. Lin Chao-nan reached Cairo as counselor before the West Asian and African Affairs Department was established, and he served there eight years before assuming a deputy directorship in Peking. Shih Ku was consul general in Damascus before his appointment in the department.

Table 6
SENIOR STAFF OF AFRICAN DEPARTMENTS IN THE MINISTRY OF FOREIGN AFFAIRS, 1956–1970*

(1) West Asian and African Affairs Department (September 1956–September 1964):

Directors	*Identified in this Post*	*Subsequent Identification*
K'o Hua	15 SEP 56	Ambassador (Guinea), 4 MAR 60
Ho Ying	19 JAN 60	Ambassador (Tanganyika), 27 FEB 62
Wang Yü-t'ien	23 JUN 62	Ambassador (Kenya), 4 FEB 64
K'o Hua	1964	Director, African Affairs Department, SEP 64
Deputy Directors		
Ho Kung-k'ai	15 SEP 56	Counselor (U.A.R.), JUN 63
Ho Ch'en	28 JUL 57	Since unreported; probably removed
Kung Ta-fei	3 JUL 59	Counselor (Morocco), 15 AUG 60
Meng Ying	12 MAR 61	Ambassador (Zanzibar), 25 MAR 64
Li Chün	30 AUG 61	Counselor (Tanganyika), arrived 24 JAN 62
Hsieh Feng	6 OCT 62	Deputy Director, African Affairs Department, SEP 64
Kung Ta-fei	26 SEP 63	Deputy Director, African Affairs Department, MAR 65
Lin Chao-nan	7 APR 64	Deputy Director, West Asian and North African Affairs Department, SEP 64
Meng Ying	1964	Deputy Director, African Affairs Department, 24 SEP 64
Assistant to the Director	*Identified in this Post*	*Subsequent Identification*
Shih Ku	JAN 61	Counselor (Tanganyika), 29 JUN 63

(2) West Asian and North African Affairs Department (from September 1964 until recombined):

Director		
Ch'en Ch'u	8 SEP 64	Ambassador (Ghana), JAN 66
Second occupant unknown		
Deputy Directors		
Lin Chao-nan	15 SEP 64	Still in post, OCT 67
Wang Jen-san	AUG 65	Still in post, NOV 65; attended CAPFA meeting in Peking, APR 66

(3) African Affairs Department (from September 1964 until recombined):

Director		
K'o Hua	22 SEP 64	Still in post, AUG 65
Deputy Directors		
Hsieh Feng	22 SEP 64	Still in post, SEP 66
Meng Ying	24 SEP 64	Ambassador (Centrafrica), announced 12 DEC 64
Kung Ta-fei	MAR 65	Still in post, OCT 67

Table 6 (Continued)

Deputy Directors	*Identified in this Post*	*Subsequent Identification*
Hou Yeh-feng	NOV 65	No further information
Ts'ao Kuei-sheng	NOV 65	No further information

(4) West Asian and African Affairs Department (recombined no earlier than October 1967 but no later than September 1969):

Director	*Identified in this Post*	*Subsequent Identification*
Ho Ying	20 AUG 70	Still in post, OCT 70
Deputy Director		
Kung Ta-fei	25 SEP 69	Identified as "leading member" of this department and as a deputy department director

* Data may be incomplete, especially for the period of the Great Proletarian Cultural Revolution.

nesian officials. Kan Mai, repeatedly cited by journalists as the chief Chinese adviser to Congolese revolutionaries in Congo (B), had served fourteen years as assistant military attaché in India and as military attaché in Nepal. He was forced to leave Nepal after charges were made that Chinese road construction in Nepal was designed to meet Chinese military specifications. His formal post in Brazzaville was second to the ambassador.

Rotation of personnel concerned with Africa from Peking to African posts, and some instances of reassignment to third and fourth posts concerned with Africa demonstrates a predilection to conserve experience systematically.[42] The pressure after 1960 to staff new and expanding African embassies was probably most easily met by appointing known personnel to foreign posts and recruiting new men into the department. Africa-concerned personnel were rarely — at least until 1965 — transferred to new assignments in other regions.

Very few ministry personnel are members of the China-Africa People's Friendship Association. The relationship of the commission to CAPFA is rather different. Tung Chi-p'ing's claim that CAPFA is really a non-

42. K'o Hua, Wang Yü-t'ien, Kung Ta-fei, and Li Chün each held three Africa-concerned posts by 1965, and Meng Ying had held four. The following Chinese diplomatic personnel, who had served in Africa before 1965 but had not held posts in the Africa-concerned department of the ministry, occupied more than one nonconcurrent post: Chang Yüeh (Egypt and Somalia) and Ku Chih-fang (Egypt, Tanganyika, and Uganda). In January 1966 Huang Hua, who had been ambassador in Accra, was named ambassador in Cairo.

existent front for commission activities appears plausible when one examines the names of CCRFC staff directly responsible for Africa, listed in Table 7.

Table 7
STAFF OF AFRICAN DEPARTMENTS, COMMISSION ON CULTURAL RELATIONS WITH FOREIGN COUNTRIES, PARTIAL LIST, 1963–1964*

(1) Asian and African Affairs Department (to January 1964)
Director: Lin Lin
Deputy Directors: Ssu-ma Wen-sen
Wu Ch'ing (f)

English-Speaking Africa Section	*French-Speaking Africa Section*	*Arabic-Speaking Africa Section*
Chief: Li Chin	Wang Ch'in-mei	Hsü Ming-chang (f)
Lin Ch'ing		
Other: Yang Wei-ho	Tung Chi-p'ing	Li Miao
	Li T'ing-hsün	Ch'en Fu
	Ting Shih-chung	Hsieh Mai-hua (f)
	Ch'en Ken-sheng	

(2) African Affairs Department (from January 1964)
Director: Ssu-ma Wen-sen
Deputy Director: Wu Ch'ing (f)
The sections remain as in (1). Wu Ch'ing was later acting director.

* Except for the identification of Lin Lin and Wu Ch'ing, the sole source for this information is Tung Chi-p'ing. [133], 1966, does not acknowledge creation of an African Affairs Department, but it lists a single Second Department (Afro-Asia), of which Lin Lin is listed as director and Wu Ch'ing, Kuo Lao-wei, and Wang I (f) are listed as deputy directors, each with "earliest" and "latest" reported date in the usual manner of the directory. Wang I is the only one for whom a notation after January 1964 is recorded.

(f) indicates a female.

The pivotal person linking CAPFA and the commission is Wu Ch'ing, who was the chief executive of CAPFA after 1960. Tung Chi-p'ing considered her to be the "only person in the commission who really knows something about Africa," although he also respected Ssu-ma Wen-sen.[43] Born about 1915, Wu Ch'ing's career has included newspaper reporting and an appointment, as early as 1953, as deputy director of the Soviet and East European Affairs Department in the Ministry of Foreign Affairs. She has visited Africa.[44] Two of the five reported CAPFA deputy chief execu-

43. Interview with Tung Chi-p'ing, note 2.

44. *Ibid.* Although Tung did not recall when she visited, she may have been a member of the CAPFA delegation which toured West Africa in 1961.

tives, Li Chin and Hsü Ming-chuang, have held full-time CCRFC posts.[45] If one turns to the CAPFA executive committee, one finds that ten of the forty-two executive members are officers, staff, or members of the commission.[46]

Tung Chi-p'ing has provided some details concerning commission staff members in the lower echelons. Foreign language competence is an important criterion in recruitment, although the standard is not high. Tung himself spoke French; Ting Shih-chung and Ch'en Ken-sheng also prepared in French. Li Miao spoke English well, Ch'en Fu spoke Arabic, and Hsieh Mai-hua, a third member of the section dealing with Arabic-speaking countries, spoke French. Of these only Ting Shih-chung, who had been a translator for *Peking Review* before coming to the commission and whom Tung considered very capable, was a CCP member. Different criteria apply in the choice of section heads. The three section heads are CCP members (see Table 7). Wang Ch'in-mei worked in the External Affairs Department in Wuhan; after four years of study, he came to the commission in 1962. Tung considered him to be ill-prepared and incapable. Hsü Ming-chuang and Lin Ch'ing had both once been in "secret work," according to Tung. Li T'ing-hsün, a CCP member who occasionally acted as executive secretary for the Africa department, came from the ministry after service in the Soviet Union and Romania. Lower-echelon personnel in the commission could anticipate foreign assignment as cultural attachés or interpreters, as had Tung Chi-p'ing.[47] Tung considered the turnover in the commission's African department to be very high.

45. *Ibid.* Since the names of commission staff are available only for the period that Tung Chi-p'ing worked there, it is possible that some or all of the four unidentified deputy chief executives also were commission employees. The full roster of CAPFA staff is: Chief Wu Ch'ing (appointed 12 April 1960), Deputy Chiefs Li Chin (12 April 1960), Shen Wen (12 April 1960), Hsü Chün-t'ing (12 July 1961), Hsü Ming-chuang (13 April 1963), and Wang Shou-jen (13 April 1963). The April 1963 appointees may have replaced Shen Wen and Hsü Chün-t'ing, who are not listed in [211], 1964. [133], 1966, lists Wu Ch'ing, Li Chin, Hsü Ming-chuang, and Wang Shou-jen. No information is given in [211], 1965, the most recently published.

46. Six commission vice-chairmen sat on the forty-two member CAPFA executive, three of them as vice-chairmen of CAPFA. Lin Lin and Wu Ch'ing were on the executive. Finally, two CCRFC "members" — it is not quite clear what that means — were also members of the CAPFA executive: Ta P'u-sheng (died 21 June 1965) and Mei I.

47. Tung stated that Ch'en Ken-sheng probably went to Morocco as an interpreter and section head Lin Ch'ing was subsequently appointed cultural attaché in Dar es Salaam. [133], 1966, shows the following persons, their titles, and their first identification with that title: Ssu-ma Wen-sen, cultural counselor (Paris), June 1964; Lin Ch'ing, third secretary (Mogadishu), August 1964; and Ting Shih-chung, attaché (Paris), June 1964. Tung may have been mistaken about Lin Ch'ing. However, it

Two officials appear to have been particularly concerned with African foreign trade, vice-minister Lu Hsü-chang and assistant minister Liu Hsi-wen.[48] Minister of foreign trade Yeh Chi-chuang and vice-minister Lei Jen-min both traveled to Africa, as did Nan Han-ch'en, chairman of the China Council for the Promotion of International Trade. Chairman Fang I of the Commission on Economic Relations with Foreign Countries, whose alternate membership on the Central Committee has already been noted, also visited Africa. Fang serves concurrently as a deputy director of the Foreign Affairs Office and a vice-chairman of the State Planning Commission.[49] Detailed information on personnel within the Commission on Economic Relations with Foreign Countries has not been published.[50]

If membership in the China-Africa People's Friendship Association can be taken to mean that the member is the official charged with a special concern for African matters in his unit, or with exercising special supervision of those within the unit who deal with African affairs, persons concerned with Africa in several key organizations can be identified. Liu Tzu-tsai, vice-minister of education, is a member. The roster includes four key persons in propaganda: the deputy-director of NCNA, Chu Mu-chih; Mei I, director of the Broadcasting Administrative Bureau; Foreign Languages Publishing and Distribution Administration director, Lo Chün; and Shao Kung-wen, the manager of Guozi Shudian.

African specialists cannot be identified in the mass organizations, but twenty-two of the 141 CAPFA members are officers or staff members of

---

does appear that five of the fourteen persons concerned with Africa whom Tung listed as staff of the commission department in January 1964, including Tung, had been appointed either to the newly-opened Paris embassy or to an African post within a very few months.

48. Lu Hsü-chang led major economic delegations to African countries in 1961 and 1964. Liu Hsi-wen was deputy director of the Fourth Bureau of the Ministry of Foreign Trade in December 1957. By September 1960 he was director of the bureau. In December 1963 he accompanied Chou En-lai's large delegation to ten African countries. He was appointed assistant minister of foreign trade in April 1964.

49. Fang I served as vice-minister of finance and for some years was Chinese economic representative in North Vietnam, a post with which he was identified as late as May 1960. On 22 April 1961 he was appointed the first director of the Commission on Economic Relations with Foreign Countries.

50. Like CCRFC, CERFC has a departmental structure. [133], 1966, lists a Second Department and a Third Department without specifying their functions. Possibly Li K'o, who heads the Third Department (identified in that post in June 1965), is the Li Ke who led a delegation of industrial and farm experts to Ghana in August–September 1964. If he is, the Third Department may be concerned with aid to Africa. Of CERFC vice-ministers, Hsieh Huai-te, a former vice-governor of Shensi Province appointed to the CERFC post in December 1964, may be responsible for African aid. He remained active in CERFC in 1969.

mass organizations.[51] Moreover, CAPFA membership does correlate with actual performance of work concerned with Africa. Ten of the twenty-two visited Africa by mid-1965. Much the same is true of the specialist functional organizations, most of which are represented in the CAPFA membership by a person who is not an African specialist. The exceptional case is the China Islamic Association. Chairman Burhan Shahidi and other leaders have made many visits to Africa and talked with numbers of Muslim visitors to China.

Individuals who specialize in African matters are readily discerned on the staffs of China's international action organizations. Wu Hsiao-ta was a CAPFA member as deputy secretary general of the Chinese People's Institute of Foreign Affairs; in January 1964 he opened the Chinese embassy in Nairobi, where he was appointed counselor. The Chinese Committee for Afro-Asian Solidarity has dispatched staff members to Cairo where, as secretaries of the Afro-Asian People's Solidarity Organization, they have traveled widely on the African continent (see Table 8).

Liu Ssu-mu, deputy secretary general of the China Asia-Africa Society, led China's delegation at the First International Congress of Africanists (Accra, December 1962). He has no credentials as an Africanist, although he has published on international matters — as early as 1951 — and he is deputy director of the Institute of International Relations of the Academy of Sciences.[52]

The organization which figures most often in receiving visitors to China is the Chinese People's Association for Cultural Relations with Foreign Countries (CPACRFC). It is the parent body of all friendship associations. Eight CPACRFC officers and staff members are members of CAPFA, but four of the eight are officers or staff members of the Commission for Cultural Relations with Foreign Countries.[53] The interlocking nature of these groups is thorough.

51. All-China Federation of Trade Unions (ACFTU), 9; National Women's Federation (NWF), 5; All-China Youth Federation (ACYF), 6; and All-China Student Federation (ACSF), 2.

52. In 1950 Liu was editor-in-chief of the Shanghai *Hsin-wen Jih-pao*. He covered the Geneva Conference of 1954 as a correspondent for that paper. See his book, [220]. Since 1950 he has been associated with the Sino-Soviet Friendship Association, China Peace Committee, Chinese People's Institute of Foreign Affairs, and other groups. In June 1965 he was named one of several advisors to the Chinese delegation to the Second Asian-African Conference.

53. See note 25. [133], 1966, shows the following held concurrent posts:

	CPACRFC	*CCRFC*
Ch'u T'u-nan	Chairman	Vice-Chairman
Ting Hsi-lin	Vice-Chairman	Vice-Chairman

Table 8

CHINESE POSTED TO THE AFRO-ASIAN PEOPLE'S SOLIDARITY ORGANIZATION, 1958–1965

Name	*Title*	*Remarks*
Yang Shuo	Secretary	Designated April 1958; elected deputy secretary general of the Chinese Afro-Asian Solidarity Committee (CAACS) in July 1958.
Chu Tzu-ch'i	Secretary	Designated September 1959; simultaneously secretary general of CAASC.
Yang Chi	Secretary	[150], no. 1–3, January–April 1963, identifies him; one of seven secretaries of CAASC; [133], 1966.
Yang Shuo	Secretary	Apparently resumed this post in 1963. Listed in *The Winneba Conference, Ghana, May 1965*, Afro-Asian Publications (14), permanent secretariat of AAPSO, as serving between the Moshi conference (February 1963) and Winneba conference.
Hsiao Chin	Assistant of Representative	Also listed in *The Winneba Conference.*
Yao Chin-jung	Assistant of Representative	Also listed in *The Winneba Conference.*
Chen Lo-min	Assistant of Representative	Also listed in *The Winneba Conference.*
Liang Keng	Assistant of Representative	Also listed in *The Winneba Conference.* One of seven secretaries of the CAASC; [133], 1966.

Of the 119 CAPFA members whose posts have been identified, seventeen are local government officials and five are local CCP officials.[54] Those in local government — mayors, cultural bureau figures, foreign trade officials, and so forth — extend hospitality to foreign visitors. The local CCP officials are in united front, propaganda, or culture and education departments.

Although several hundred Chinese concerned with Africa, up to the start of the cultural revolution, can be identified by name,[55] there are about twenty key figures. Diplomats with important ambassadorships and responsibility within the ministry for African affairs included Chi P'eng-fei,

---

	CPACRFC	*CCRFC*
Lin Lin	Deputy Sec. Gen.	Dir., Second Dept.
Ch'en Kung-ch'i	Deputy Sec. Gen.	Dir., Propaganda Dept.

54. A number of the twenty-four unidentified CAPFA members may also be local officials.

55. Listed in [70]. See Bibliographic Note, p. 246.

Hsü I-hsin, K'o Hua, Meng Ying, Ho Ying, Wang Yü-t'ien, Hsieh Feng, Kung Ta-fei, Ch'en Chia-k'ang, and Huang Hua. Ting Hsi-lin and Chu Kuang stood out among those prominent in cultural relations, but Wu Ch'ing — despite her lesser title — may have been more important than they. Yang Shuo and Chu Tzu-ch'i were important intermediaries to national liberation movements. Liu Hsi-wen and Hsieh Huai-te were central figures in trade and aid. Wu Hsüeh-ch'ien was almost surely one of the men within the central committee's staff structure who specialized in African matters. The Eighth Central Committee of the CCP included a few others who were well informed about Africa and shared in decisions made by the higher echelons: members were Liu Ch'ang-sheng, Liu Ning-i, Liao Ch'eng-chih, Ch'en I, and Chou En-lai, and alternate Fang I.

The effect of the cultural revolution on this cadre can be roughly described. Liu Ning-i and Liao Ch'eng-chih, long-standing specialists on the use of nongovernmental channels in foreign relations, have fallen. Ch'en I has been relegated to a sinecure not concerned with foreign affairs. Liu Ch'ang-sheng died in 1967. We have no information about Ch'en Chia-k'ang, K'o Hua, Meng Ying, Hsieh Feng, Wu Ch'ing, Yang Shuo, Chu Kuang, Chu Tzu-ch'i, and Wu Hsüeh-ch'ien.

Chou En-lai remains the principal figure in the State Council and the conduct of foreign affairs. Chi P'eng-fei and Hsu I-hsin continue as vice-ministers of foreign affairs. Fang I, Liu Hsi-wen, and Hsieh Huai-te retain their posts in the trade and aid apparatus. Ting Hsi-lin performs ceremonial functions. Wang Yü-t'ien was appointed to a new ambassadorship (Brazzaville); Ho Ying heads the reconsolidated ministry bureau dealing with Africa; he is assisted by Kung Ta-fei. Huang Hua, the lone ambassador to remain at his post (Cairo) during the cultural revolution, appeared in public greeting an American journalist in 1970[56] and in 1971 was named ambassador to Canada. Although some experienced personnel no longer appear to be active, a substantial portion continues to deal with African affairs.

Training of Chinese

Available biographical information does not permit a detailed assessment of the preparation of the Chinese personnel who have dealt with Africa. However, China's resources can be analyzed from another direction: consideration of the training that is available in China.

56. Edgar Snow, for whom he was interpreter in the 1930s. Huang Hua was identified only as a council member of the Chinese People's Association for Friendship with Foreign Countries. *PR*, 28 August 1970, p. 22.

Formal academic offerings in foreign affairs were instituted soon after the CCP won power in 1949. Chinese People's University, which opened on 13 March 1950, has a foreign affairs department.[57] A month after the university opened, the minister of education urged that the "scientific approach and method" be used in developing research work in the social sciences and humanities, including foreign affairs.[58]

The Peking Institute of Foreign Trade opened on 30 August 1954.[59] Two of its three departments were devoted to language study. This was a move to remedy the shortage of men with foreign language skills, something which has proven a continuing impediment to Chinese activity abroad. One department of the institute taught only Russian. A one-year course for graduates in foreign trade from other universities was set up, with provision for teaching English.[60] Arabic was taught in the Institute for Moslems, organized in late 1949,[61] and, after 1957, in the Eastern Languages Department of Peking University.[62] One report states that China's first ambassador to Khartoum was accompanied by an interpreter who spoke perfect Sudanese Arabic.[63] In 1960, an authoritative Chinese newspaper commented on the importance of language training for contacts in onetime colonial regions.[64] The most explicit coupling was made by Ch'en I in a speech to foreign language students:

> Do not consider foreign language work as very simple, and do not look upon foreign language work as a technical job. A foreign language itself is a tool for political struggle. Through mastering foreign languages, the good things of the foreign people can be introduced to China for raising the economic and cultural standard in China. Through mastering foreign languages, we can acquaint other people with our experience gained in carrying out revolutionary influence, and bringing stronger blows to bear upon imperialism.[65]

57. 16 March 1950.
58. NCNA, 16 June 1950.
59. NCNA, 1 September 1954.
60. *Ibid.*
61. NCNA, 3 December 1953. The purpose of the institute was in large measure to ensure integration of China's Muslim minority. By 1953 it had enrolled 1,400 students.
62. *SCMP*, no. 1530, p. 19.
63. Howard Boorman, "Peking in World Politics," *Pacific Affairs*, vol. 34, no. 3 (1961), p. 235, cited in [50], p. 191.
64. [203], 25 December 1960, excerpts in [128], vol. 2, pp. 198–200.
65. *SCMP*, no. 2713, p. 1 (*Kuang-ming Jih-pao* [Enlightenment Daily], 19 March 1962). The talk was first published in *Teaching and Study of Foreign Languages Quarterly*, no. 1, 1962.

Foreign language institutes were established in Peking and Shanghai. Tung Chi-p'ing was a student at the Shanghai Foreign Language Institute where, by his account, English, French, Spanish, German, Arabic, Japanese, and Russian were taught. Tung indicated that Southeast Asian languages were also taught in China and that the Chinese were "trying desperately to expand their foreign language program."[66] In September 1964 a second Institute of Foreign Languages was established in Peking. There is an unsubstantiated report that Swahili and major African dialects were taught at a large center near Nanking,[67] but Chinese emphasis has been on English and French, the chief metropolitan languages of the colonial era.[68]

Chinese could also develop language competence by study abroad. In mid-1964 France granted one hundred scholarships to Chinese for study in France.[69] In January 1965, twenty-one Chinese students began a six-month English course at England's Ealing Technical College.[70] A very few Chinese may have gone to Africa to learn African languages. Tung Chi-p'ing claims that two Chinese went to Mali for that purpose in August 1963.[71] As China approached the cultural revolution the study of foreign languages was encouraged. It is almost certain that this study was wholly interrupted during 1966–1969.

66. [135]. Tung believes that he was assigned to Burundi only because French-speaking Chinese were in short supply. His political reliability was doubted, he believed; he had failed to gain admittance to the CYCL, much less the CCP. Nonetheless, he had finished the four-year course at the Shanghai Foreign Language Institute and been assigned to work in the CCRFC. The cultural attaché to Burundi did not speak French; Tung was appointed assistant cultural attaché to serve as the attaché's interpreter.

67. [169], 28 January 1965. A North American Newspaper Alliance report from Bonn attributed the assertion to a spokesman of the West German defense ministry. This same article contains an incredible assertion that the Bundeswehr was training military assistance personnel for Africa to take countermeasures against Chinese infiltration of the ranks of African witch doctors, especially in Tanganyika. The Ministry of Defense in Bonn termed that assertion nonsense. The supposed language center may also be make-believe.

68. In November 1964 China hired thirty Britons to teach English in China at annual salaries of £800. [183], 10 January 1965. "Many students in Chinese schools and colleges have been switched from Russian to English," according to the correspondent.

69. [183], 26 July 1964. These students were reportedly withdrawn from France during the cultural revolution.

70. [183], 10 January 1965.

71. Interview with Tung Chi-p'ing, note 2. China has sent small numbers of students to countries outside Africa in which languages other than those customarily taught are spoken. For example, two Chinese students studied in Denmark in 1960–1961 and then moved to Iceland for the academic year 1961–1962, according to officials of the Studentarad Haskola Islands with whom I spoke in August 1962.

Despite Western journalists' reports that there is an Institute of African Studies and Tung Chi-p'ing's assertion that the CCP decided to create a Research Institute on Asia, Africa, and Latin America, China has made no formal declaration that these institutions exist. If they exist, they are either covert or sections of some other institutions. Moreover, no Chinese academicians are identified as African specialists who might conduct substantive programs in existing institutions. There probably are university courses in subjects such as African geography, and the Institute of Foreign Trade teaches specifics relevant to African trade opportunities, but China has no scholar comparable to the late Soviet Academician I. I. Potekhin, and she has no announced academic program in African studies.

Published material about Africa is peculiarly limited. It includes a vast number of articles of three kinds in such publications as *Jen-min Jih-pao* and *Shih-chieh Chih-shih*: feature reports by NCNA correspondents, selectively edited news reports of events in African countries, and reports about the comings and goings of Africans to China and Chinese to Africa. The tone of political articles is transparently polemical. Facts are selected to illustrate, rather than test, presuppositions about imperialism and African social organization. The *Shih-chieh Chih-shih Shou-ts'e* [Handbook of International Events] includes rather dispassionate descriptions of foreign countries, with reports in successive editions on an increasing number of African states.[72]

Some foreign book-length material about modern Africa has been published in China, as well as works on related issues of historical interest.[73] Jack Woddis's *Africa: The Roots of Revolt* was published in Chinese in March 1962.[74] Publication by China does not imply unconditional endorsement. For example, a 1959 Chinese review of one translated volume, while generally favorable, criticized the author's inadequate attention to con-

72. Later *Shih-chieh Chih-shih Nien-chien* [Yearbook of International Events]. It is probably a major source of basic information about Africa for publicists, government staff, and organization functionaries. When Tung Chi-p'ing sought to inform himself about Burundi, the only resource to which he could turn was the brief entry in this yearbook, according to his account.

73. For example, an edition of 2,000 copies of a Chinese translation of W. E. B. Du Bois's work *John Brown*, first published in 1909. [202], 1 January 1960.

74. As *Fei-chou: Feng-pao .te Ken-yuan*. Something of Woddis's position can be seen in this excerpt: "Most African people do not yet fully realize the extent to which the advances of the Soviet Union, and of China and the other people's democracies, have decisively aided the peoples fighting against colonialism. But the growing strength of the socialist camp is the strongest anti-imperialist and anti-colonial factor in the world situation." [139], p. 250.

tradictions between imperialist powers and suggested that the author's origin in the United States had made him less than fully clear on some crucial points.[75]

By contrast to Soviet specialists, who have shown considerable interest in Western scholarship on Africa, China's Africa-concerned personnel have evinced no special interest in studies of Africa made by other countries. China has not contributed to the international literature on Africa, and it is unlikely that scholarship comparable to that performed elsewhere is performed in China. Liu Ssu-mu, as if to excuse China's failure to contribute to African studies, told the First International Congress of Africanists:

> The task of [African] studies must be undertaken primarily and chiefly by the African scholars themselves.
>
> Scholars outside of Africa, if they are really just and objective and pursue truth unswervingly, can also contribute to African studies. But only the African scholars themselves, born and grown up on African soil, can best understand Africa's past and present. And it is also they who can best understand the aspirations and demands of their own people. Therefore, African scholars engaged in the study of their own continent are in a better position to arrive at the truth of the matter and reach correct conclusions.[76]

His remarks may have been intended to drive a wedge between African and Soviet scholars.[77]

China has three organizations which might sponsor or conduct work in African studies: the China Asia-Africa Society, the Research Institute of International Relations of the Academy of Sciences, and the International Relations Institute. Liu Ssu-mu is an official of the first two.[78] The third is jointly managed by the Ministry of Foreign Affairs and the Min-

75. William Alphaeus Hinton, *Decision in Africa: Sources of Current Conflict* (New York: International Publishers, 1957). The review is in [212], May 1959.

76. [219].

77. I. I. Potekhin was co-chairman of the congress.

78. He was named a deputy director of the Research Institute of International Relations when it was formed in November 1956. He was a deputy secretary general of the China Asia-Africa Society. Other links connect the two groups. Meng Yung-ch'ien, director of the research institute, is a member of the China Asia-Africa Society. He attended the Asian Countries Conference in New Delhi (April 1955) and an Afro-Asian People's Solidarity Organization conference in Conakry. If an unacknowledged African studies center does exist, it might well be part of the Research Institute of International Relations.

istry of Education,[79] and it is headed by Ch'en I.[80] Its mission includes training personnel to work in government offices.[81]

Despite the apparent lack of formal programs, a trainee could become informed if he had access to books and periodicals generally available in Africa and the West. Such material is probably not available, but Colin Mackerras testified that a daily paper containing reports from the foreign press was available in the foreigners' common room of the Peking Institute of Foreign Languages. Mackerras sensed that even students in the lower grades of the institute had a notion of its more important contents, although they did not have access to it.[82] Mackerras was also told of a more confidential publication, circulated only among very important cadres, which contained reports of events in other countries not reported in the important Western papers. "It is, then, not true," Mackerras concludes, "that China's important policy decisions are made in ignorance of the facts." But Mackerras does believe that the available facts are ideologically interpreted.[83] Henry G. Schwarz has published a detailed analysis of six issues of *Ts'an-k'ao Hsiao-hsi* [Reference Information], which may be the restricted source Mackerras encountered in the common room. Schwartz was surprised how frequently African newspaper articles were reproduced. He concludes that *Ts'an-k'ao Hsiao-hsi* does provide a more detailed image of the world than is available in the open press, but judges the resulting image to be "seriously distorted."[84] Personnel of the Commission on Cultural Relations with Foreign Countries had access to a regular report of the foreign press—probably the *Ts'an-k'ao Hsiao-hsi*—although no African periodicals were available in the section of the commission's African department in which Tung Chi-p'ing worked.[85]

Despite some such sources of information, expertise in African matters

79. Interview with Tung Chi-p'ing, note 2.

80. When Ch'en I was installed as president of the institute in 1961, the previous president, Ch'en Hsin-jen, was retained as a vice-president.

81. Wang Ch'in-mei, Tung Chi-p'ing's immediate superior in the French language section of the CCRFC's African department, had attended this institute for four years, according to Tung. Part of his program had been training in the French language, but Tung felt that Wang had not learned the language at all well.

82. Titled *For Your Information Only*, it was issued in English, Chinese, and perhaps other languages. [87], p. 184.

83. [87], p. 185. I am grateful to Jay Kajimura for calling this to my attention.

84. [113].

85. Interview with Tung Chi-p'ing, note 2. Tung believed the same material was also available to the staff of the ministry, but he did not know whether the ministry had African publications at its disposal. Tung stated that when he began work in the commission he did not have access to a map of Africa.

is acquired by Chinese primarily while holding African posts, unless training programs exist which we do not know about.[86] Typically, appointees to key posts have held more modest posts in which they were introduced to African materials. A ladder of increasing responsibility for African affairs might include the following steps:

(1) Peripheral contact with visiting foreigners while acting as a functionary of a group serving as host to foreigners; in the early 1950s, few Africans were among the visitors.
(2) Membership (rarely as a leader) in a fraternal delegation dispatched abroad.
(3) Appointment as interpreter or modest functionary in the Ministry of Foreign Affairs or the Commission on Cultural Relations with Foreign Countries, a post involving contact with foreigners and handling reports.
(4) Membership in a working delegation at an international meeting.
(5) Service in a Chinese embassy in Europe or Asia.
(6) Assignment to a responsible post in the Ministry of Foreign Affairs.
(7) Assignment as ambassador or counselor in an African embassy.

No actual biography includes every step. Many older personnel who held ambassadorships in the mid-1960s had been with the Ministry of Foreign Affairs since 1950 or 1951.

It is easy to imagine one mechanism to explain careers which conform in some respects to the hypothetical ladder. Because the candidate held a certain post he was a plausible prospect to be recruited to the next higher post; because he had then served in the next, he was recommended for an even more complex task. Language competence and service in a local organization might qualify the candidate to join a delegation to Africa; once he had served on the delegation, he had experience which commended him for other Africa-concerned appointments. Membership on a delegation did not, of course, guarantee a man any future appointment.

Some personnel were recruited mainly because of technical or professional competence. For example, a person with language competence and the standard journalistic skills might qualify to serve in a New China News Agency bureau in Africa. He would have to meet political criteria,[87]

86. Tung Chi-p'ing states that he received no formal training, either for his work in the CCRFC or his assignment in Burundi, other than the French language training at the Shanghai Institute of Foreign Languages.

87. Tung Chi-p'ing believed that all NCNA correspondents in Africa were CCP members and held a rank of Grade 17 or higher. Foreign language skill was not an essential criterion, he said, because NCNA correspondents were often supplied with interpreters.

and he might be briefed, by those with the expertise he lacked, on some aspects of his assignment. His prior knowledge of Africa would not need to be extensive.

Emphasis on in-service training is wholly consistent with Mao Tse-tung's insistence on the unity of theory and practice.[88] Chinese diplomats in Africa and the officers of Chinese public organizations remain in their posts for relatively long periods. They are pursuing careers, not merely performing public service incidental to careers as lawyers, teachers, or managers. They become specialists by the sheer accumulation of daily experience. Peking's reliance on this method of training does not generate a surfeit of knowledgeable personnel.

Learning by experience is in part learning from mistakes, but this is tolerable if decisions made by those at lower echelons do not commit China irrevocably. Experienced Chinese ambassadors in African capitals probably have authority to make many decisions of local significance (along guidelines fixed in Peking). Inexperience in Peking is mitigated, too, by the return of experienced diplomats to the African department of the ministry. Until the cultural revolution no prominent individual concerned with Africa had been cashiered in the wake of a Chinese reverse.

The fact remains that few of China's African planners know Africa well. Short of an extended tour of duty on the African continent, there seems to be no way to acquire expertise except to handle Africa-concerned material inside the ministry. Even the diplomat posted to Africa is confined by dependence on limited sources; he probably does not follow the growing literature on Africa published elsewhere.

Conclusion

Execution of Chinese African policy — and, by inference, probably its planning as well — has been carried out by a core of people with diplomatic and organizing skills. They employ diverse structures, though how their actions are orchestrated is not wholly clear. The number and complexity of institutions has grown since 1949. From 1956 to 1965 increasing elaboration forced recruitment of many new personnel to Africa-concerned programs. Replacement of personnel lost during the cultural revolution probably will require recruitment anew.

88. Consider Mao's view of the relationship between formal training and experience acquired through practice: "Reading is learning, but applying is also learning and the more important kind of learning at that. Our chief method is to learn warfare through warfare. A person who has had no opportunity to go to school can also learn warfare — he can learn through fighting in war." [223], p. 79, p. 86.

To staff this burgeoning operation, men of proven skill have been co-opted from other work and new graduates have been placed in posts of least responsibility. In-service training has been the chief device to equip both lateral entrants and new graduates for their work, but by that means Africa-concerned personnel have acquired a great deal of experience. Appointment of ambassadors to replace some chargés at African posts, retention of CAPFA and other bodies, and the continued importance of men such as Ho Ying and Wang Yü-t'ien are significant continuities in China's African policy.

Bibliographic Note

Extensive statements of Peking's position on many of the events considered in this study can be found in the Chinese press. Students dependent on English-language accounts will find the weekly *Peking Review* useful on events occurring since it commenced publication in March 1958. Key documents and speeches are often reproduced, as are reports of visits by African delegations. Some libraries hold back files of New China News Agency releases, issued regularly since 1949, under the title *Daily News Release* or *Hsinhua News Agency Release.*

Selected translations from the Chinese press prepared by the U.S. Consulate General in Hong Kong have been issued since 1950. Major research libraries often hold back files of the principal series: *Survey of China Mainland Press (SCMP), Selections from China Mainland Magazines* (entitled *Extracts from China Mainland Magazines* until 1960), and *Current Background.* Much cited in this study, *SCMP* appears each weekday with delayed translations of key Chinese articles on foreign and domestic matters. Individuals have been able to subscribe to the consulate general material since early 1970. It is described in an important bibliographic guide: Peter Berton and Eugene Wu, *Contemporary China: A Research Guide* (Stanford: Hoover Institution on War, Revolution and Peace, 1967), which also lists translations of the U.S. Joint Publications Research Service and their indices.

One publication is especially important because it was originally intended for limited distribution within China. Twenty-nine issues of the People's Liberation Army journal *Kung-tso T'ung-hsün* [Bulletin of Activities] of early 1961 are translated in J. Chester Cheng, editor, *The Politics of the Chinese Red Army* (Stanford: Hoover Institution on War, Revolution and Peace, 1966). Several articles in the *China Quarterly,* no. 18 (1964) are devoted to a description of this material. African references appear in the volume edited by Cheng, pp. 480–487 and, specifically on the Congo, pp. 398–400.

Chou En-lai's speeches during his African tour of 1963–1964 and the joint communiqués issued at the time of each visit are collected in *Afro-Asian Solidarity Against Imperialism* (Peking: Foreign Languages Press, 1964). Many are also published in *Peking Review* issues for December 1963 and January and February 1964. For one analysis of the tour, see W. A. C. Adie, "Chou En-lai on Safari," in the *China Quarterly*, no. 18 (1964).

Biographic material on Chinese involved in African affairs has been gleaned from Chinese press reports and directories published in Washington, Tokyo, and Hong Kong. *Contemporary China*, cited above, lists standard biographic directories at pp. 140 ff. The most recent available U.S. government directory, not listed there, is the *Directory of Chinese Communist Officials*, Biographic Directory A 66-8, March 1966; it displays leading officials in party, government, organizational, military, and diplomatic posts, and it includes a romanized index with the characters of names given in standard telegraphic code. Serial biographies of more important persons can be found in *Who's Who in Communist China* (Hong Kong: Union Research Institute, 1970), in two volumes. A current file of press references to individuals of interest is maintained at the U.S. Consulate General, Hong Kong; microfilm of portions of the file is available at the Hoover Institution on War, Revolution and Peace and at the Union Research Institute, Hong Kong.

On Chinese ambassadors in Africa, see Donald W. Klein, "Peking's Diplomats in Africa," *Current Scene* (Hong Kong), vol. 2, no. 36 (1 July 1964). Detailed lists of Chinese concerned with African affairs appear in the dissertation of which this study is a revision and expansion, Bruce D. Larkin, "Chinese African Policy: 1954–1964," deposited in the Archives of Harvard University Library. Appendix A of the dissertation lists all members of the China-Africa People's Friendship Association (CAPFA) announced on 12 April 1960 (with additions announced 12 July 1961 and 12 April 1963) and shows the presumed constituency of each. Appendix B is a list of CAPFA members and a partial list of other domestic officials who deal in African matters, cross-listed by institutional tie; it also indicates those on the list who were known by the author, in mid-1965, to have traveled to Africa. Appendix C is a partial register of Chinese reported to have been to Africa, divided into two lists: diplomatic personnel and others. One list shows countries to which diplomats were posted, embassy posts held, dates of appointment and removal if known, and whether the characters of the name are known; if the characters of a name are known, they appear in the Glossary. The second list shows countries which persons other than diplomats were reported to have visited, the approximate dates of the visits, whether the characters of the names are known, and in some instances the purpose of the visits.

On the Ministry of Foreign Affairs, see Donald W. Klein, "Peking's Evolving Ministry of Foreign Affairs," in the *China Quarterly*, no. 4 (1960). For discussions of the consequences of the Great Proletarian Cultural Revolution for Chinese foreign policy, see Daniel Tretiak, "The Chinese Cultural Revolution and Foreign Policy," in *Current Scene*, vol. 8, no. 7 (1 April 1970); Robert Scalapino, "The Cultural Revolution and Chinese Foreign Policy," in *The Cultural Revolution: 1967 in Review* (Ann Arbor: University of Michigan Center for Chinese Studies, 1968); and especially Melvin Gurtov, "The Foreign Ministry and Foreign Affairs during the Cultural Revolution," in the *China Quarterly*, no. 40 (1969).

New China News Agency (NCNA) offices in Africa have not been the subject of a thorough study as yet. A useful survey of NCNA work abroad is "The New China News Agency," in *Current Scene*, vol. 4, no. 7 (1 April 1967), which includes some description of Kao Liang and Wang Te-ming. A brief summary of NCNA can be found in *Communist China and Arms Control* (Stanford: Hoover Institution on War, Revolution and Peace, 1968), pp. 97–102. Information that is apparently incorrect in some respects was published in two articles in Taiwan journals: Wang Chia-yu, "Peiping's 'NCNA'," in *Issues and Studies* (Taipei), December 1965, pp. 7–16, and Ting Kuang-hua, "Peiping's Cultural Infiltration of Africa," in *Chinese Communist Affairs* (Taipei), February 1966, p. 1–11.

The author has relied heavily on African newspapers and weeklies. Among those which have been most helpful are the *East African Standard* (Nairobi), *Nationalist* (Dar es Salaam), *Standard* (Dar es Salaam), *Afrique Nouvelle* (Dakar), *Cape Times* (Cape Town), and the weekly *Jeune Afrique* (Tunis).

The first lengthy account of relations between China and one African country has just appeared: George T. Yu, *China and Tanzania: A Study in Cooperative Interaction* (Berkeley: University of California Center for Chinese Studies, 1970), China Research Monograph no. 5.

The author would also call attention to several works on Sino-African relations which he has found especially useful and which are cited in the Bibliography as items 1, 2, 72, and 83. To these can be added Joseph E. Khalili, "Communist China and the United Arab Republic," in *Asian Survey*, vol. 10 (1970).

Readers interested in the Afro-Asian People's Solidarity Organization may wish to consult Charles Neuhauser, *Third World Politics: China and the Afro-Asian People's Solidarity Organization, 1957–1967* (Cambridge: Harvard University East Asian Research Center, 1968), Harvard East Asian Monograph 27. Publications of the Afro-Asian People's Solidarity Organization are held in some research libraries, and items 7, 8, 9, and 10 listed in the Bibliography are among those used in preparing this study.

Bibliography

Non-Chinese Books and Articles

1. Adie, W.A.C. "China and Africa Today." *Race*, vol. 5, no. 4 (1964), pp. 3–25.
2. ———. "China and the Bandung Genie." *Current Scene* (Hong Kong), vol. 3, no. 19 (15 May 1965).
3. ———. "China, Russia and the Third World." *China Quarterly*, no. 11 (1962), pp. 200–213.
4. ———. "Chinese Policy Towards Africa." In Hamrell, S., and Widstrand, C. G., eds. *The Soviet Bloc, China and Africa.* Uppsala: The Scandinavian Institute of African Studies, 1964.
5. ———. "Chou En-lai on Safari," *China Quarterly*, no. 18 (1964), pp. 174–194.
6. Afro-Asian Organization for Economic Cooperation. *Proceedings of the Economic Conference for Afro-Asian Countries, Cairo, 8–11 December 1958.* Cairo: Centre of the Afro-Asian Organization for Economic Cooperation, 1959.
7. Afro-Asian People's Solidarity Organization. Permanent Secretariat. *AAPSO: Statements and Appeals of the Permanent Secretariat, 1958–1960.* Cairo: Afro-Asian People's Solidarity Organization, n.d.
8. ———. *Deuxième Congrès de Solidarité des Peuples Afro-Asiatiques, Conakry, du 11 au 15 Avril 1960.* Cairo: Afro-Asian People's Solidarity Organization, n.d.
9. ———. *International Preparatory Committee for the Afro-Asian Woman's* [*sic*] *Conference.* Cairo: Afro-Asian People's Solidarity Organization, n.d.
10. ———. *Resolutions of the Fourth Afro-Asian People's Solidarity Conference, May 1–16, 1965, Winneba, Ghana.* Cairo: Afro-Asian People's Solidarity Organization, n.d.
11. Ansprenger, Franz. "Communism in Tropical Africa." In Hamrell, S. and Widstrand, C. G., eds. *The Soviet Bloc, China and Africa.* Uppsala: The Scandinavian Institute of African Studies, 1964.
12. Attwood, William. *The Reds and the Blacks.* New York: Harper and Row, 1967.
13. Barnett, A. Doak. *Communist China and Asia.* New York: Vintage Books for the Council on Foreign Relations, 1960.
14. Bartke, Wolfgang. "Influence of China on the African Region." Translated from *Der Ostblock und die Entwicklungslaender* (Hanover), no. 15 (1964), pp. 12–31.
15. Benson, Mary. *The African Patriots.* London: Faber, 1963.
16. Black, Cyril E., and Thornton, Thomas P., eds. *Communism and Revolution: The Strategic Uses of Political Violence.* Princeton: Princeton University Press, 1964.
17. Boyd, R. G. *Communist China's Foreign Policy.* New York: Praeger, 1962.
18. Brandt, Conrad; Schwartz, B.; and Fairbank, J. K. *Documentary History of Chinese Communism.* Cambridge: Harvard University Press, 1959.
19. Brzezinski, Zbigniew, ed. *Africa and the Communist World.* Stanford: Stanford University Press, 1963.
20. ———. *The Soviet Bloc.* New York: Praeger, 1960.

21. Clews, John C. *Communist Propaganda Techniques.* New York: Praeger, 1964.
22. Cooley, John. *East Wind Over Africa.* New York: Walker, 1965.
23. Cox, Richard. *Pan-Africanism in Practice, An East African Study, PAFMECSA, 1958–1964.* London: Oxford University Press, 1964.
24. Crankshaw, Edward. *The New Cold War: Moscow v. Pekin.* Baltimore: Penguin, 1963.
25. Cremeans, Charles D. *The Arabs and the World.* New York: Praeger, 1963.
26. Crozier, Brian. *Neo-Colonialism.* London: Bodley Head, 1964.
27. Dallin, Alexander. "The Soviet Union: Political Activity." In Brzezinski, Zbigniew, ed., *Africa and the Communist World.* Stanford: Stanford University Press, 1963.
28. Dutt, Vidya Prakash. *China's Foreign Policy, 1958–1962.* New York: Asia Publishing House, 1964.
29. Eckstein, Alexander. *Communist China's Economic Growth and Foreign Trade.* New York: McGraw-Hill, 1966.
30. Emerson, Rupert. *From Empire to Nation.* Cambridge: Harvard University Press, 1960.
31. Fejto, François. "A Maoist in France: Jacques Vergès and *Revolution.*" *China Quarterly,* no. 19 (1964), pp. 120–127.
32. *Fidel Castro Denounces Bureaucracy and Sectarianism.* New York: Pioneer Publishers, 1962.
33. Foltz, William J. "Le Parti Africain de l'Indépendence: Les dilemmes d'un mouvement communiste en Afrique occidentale." *Revue Française d'Etudes Politiques Africaines,* no. 45, September 1969.
34. Ford, Harold P. "Modern Weapons and the Sino-Soviet Estrangement," *China Quarterly,* no. 17 (1964), pp. 160–173.
35. Fox, Renée C.; Craemer, W.; and Reibeaucourt, J.-M. " 'The Second Independence': A Case Study of the Kwilu Rebellion in the Congo." *Comparative Studies in History and Society,* October 1965, pp. 78–109; also in *Etudes Congolaises,* vol. 8, no. 1 (1965), pp. 1–35.
36. Friedland, William H., and Rosberg, Jr., Carl G., eds. *African Socialism.* Stanford: Stanford University Press for the Hoover Institution on War, Revolution and Peace, 1964.
37. Galeano, Eduardo. "Interview with Chou En-lai," *Marcha* (Montevideo), 13 December 1963.
38. Ghana. Ministry of Information. *Nkrumah's Subversion in Africa.* Accra-Tema: State Publishing Corporation, 1966.
39. Gologo, Mamadou. *China: A Great People, A Great Destiny.* Peking: New World Press, 1965.
40. Greenfield, Richard. *Ethiopia: A New Political History.* New York: Praeger, 1965.
41. Griffith, William E. "Africa." *Survey* (London), no. 54 (1965), pp. 168–189.
42. ———. "The November 1960 Moscow Meeting: A Preliminary Reconstruction." *China Quarterly,* no. 11 (1962), pp. 38–57.
43. ———. *The Sino-Soviet Rift.* Cambridge: M.I.T. Press, 1964.
44. Halperin, Morton. *China and the Bomb.* New York: Praeger, 1965.
45. Halpern, A. M. "The Foreign Policy Uses of the Chinese Revolutionary Model." *China Quarterly,* no. 7 (1961), pp. 1–16.
46. Hamrell, Sven, and Widstrand, Carl Gösta, eds. *The Soviet Bloc, China and Africa.* Uppsala: The Scandinavian Institute of African Studies, 1964.
47. Hassouna, Mohammed Abdel Khalek. *The First Asian-African Conference Held at Bandung, Indonesia (April 18–24, 1955).* Cairo: League of Arab States, 1955.
48. Hatch, John. *A History of Postwar Africa.* New York: Praeger, 1965.
49. Hevi, Emmanuel John. *An African Student in China.* New York: Praeger, 1963.

50. Hinton, Harold. *Communist China in World Politics*. Boston: Houghton Mifflin, 1966.
51. Ho Wei-yang. "Communist China's Policy in Africa," *Aussenpolitik* (Stuttgart) 11 (1961):162–168. Translated in U.S. Joint Publications Research Service, 8302-D. Washington: U.S. Government Printing Office, 1961.
52. Hodgkin, Thomas. *African Political Parties*. London: Penguin, 1961.
53. Houart, Pierre. *La Pénétration Communiste au Congo*. Brussels: Centre de Documentation Internationale, 1960.
54. Hsieh, Alice Langley. *Communist China's Strategy in the Nuclear Age*. Englewood Cliffs, New Jersey: Prentice-Hall, 1962.
55. Hudson, G. F. et al. *The Sino-Soviet Dispute*. New York: Praeger, 1961.
56. Humbaraci, Arslan. "Tarnished Image." *Far Eastern Economic Review*, vol. 47, no. 12 (1965), pp. 538–539.
57. Humphries, Donald H. "The East African Liberation Movement." *Adelphi Papers, No. 16*. London: Institute for Strategic Studies, 1965.
58. Indonesia. Ministry of Foreign Affairs. *Asian-African Conference Bulletin*. Djakarta, 1955.
59. Institute of Race Relations (London). *Race*, vol. 5, no. 4 (April 1964). Special issue devoted largely to Sino-African relations. Some articles are noted separately.
60. Jack, Homer A. *Bandung: An On-the-Spot Description of the Asian African Conference, Bandung, Indonesia, April 1955*. Chicago: Toward Freedom, 1955.
61. Kahin, George McT. *The Asian-African Conference*. Ithaca, New York: Cornell University Press, 1956.
62. Kautsky, John H., ed. *Political Change in Underdeveloped Countries: Nationalism and Communism*. New York: Wiley, 1962.
63. Kerr, Malcolm. "The Middle East and China." In A. M. Halpern, ed., *Policies Toward China: Views From Six Continents*. New York: McGraw-Hill for the Council on Foreign Relations, 1965.
64. Kissinger, Henry A. "Domestic Structure and Foreign Policy." In his *American Foreign Policy*. (New York: W. W. Norton, 1969). The essay first appeared in *Daedalus*, vol. 95, no. 2 (1966), pp. 503–529.
65. Klein, Donald W. "Peking's Diplomats in Africa." *Current Scene* (Hong Kong), vol. 2, no. 36 (1 July 1964).
66. ———. "Peking's Evolving Ministry of Foreign Affairs." *China Quarterly*, no. 4 (1960), pp. 28–39.
67. Kolarz, Walter. "The West African Scene." *Problems of Communism*, vol. 10, no. 6 (1961), pp. 15–23.
68. Lall, Diwan Chaman et al. *What Happened at Moshi?* A report of the Indian delegation to the Third Afro-Asian People's Solidarity Conference, 4–11 February 1963, Moshi, Tanganyika, n.d.
69. Laqueur, Walter. "Communism in North Africa." In Hamrell, S., and Widstrand, C. G., eds. *The Soviet Bloc, China and Africa*. Uppsala: The Scandinavian Institute of African Studies, 1964.
70. Larkin, Bruce D. "Chinese African Policy, 1954–1964." Ph.D. dissertation, Harvard University, 1965.
71. Lee, Oliver M. "The Myth of Chinese Aggression." *Nation* (New York), 6 November 1967, pp. 459–463.
72. Legum, Colin. "Africa." In Halpern, A. M., ed. *Policies Toward China: Views From Six Continents*. New York: McGraw-Hill for the Council on Foreign Relations, 1965.
73. ———. *Bandung, Cairo and Accra*. London: The Africa Bureau, 1958.
74. ———. "China's African Gamble." *Observer* (London), 27 September 1964.
75. ———. *Congo Disaster*. Baltimore: Penguin, 1961.

76. ———. *Pan-Africanism.* New York: Praeger, 1962.
77. ———."Pan-Africanism and Communism." In Hamrell, S., and Widstrand, C. G., eds. *The Soviet Bloc, China and Africa.* Uppsala: The Scandinavian Institute of African Studies, 1964.
78. Lessing, Pieter. *Africa's Red Harvest.* New York: John Day, 1962.
79. Le Vine, Victor T. "The Central African Republic: Insular Problems of an Inland State." *Africa Report,* November 1965, p. 19.
80. Lewin, Pauline. *Foreign Trade of Communist China.* New York: Praeger, 1964.
81. Lewis, Ida. "Black Mask of Angry Africa." *Life* (New York), 1 April 1965, pp. 111–123.
82. London, Kurt. "Communism in Africa: III — The Role of China." *Problems of Communism,* vol. 11, no. 3 (1962), pp. 22–27.
83. Lowenthal, Richard. "China." In Brzezinski, Z., ed. *Africa and the Communist World.* Stanford: Stanford University Press, 1963.
84. ———. "Communism and Nationalism." *Problems of Communism,* vol. 11, no. 6 (1962), pp. 37–44.
85. ———. " 'National Democracy' and the Post-Colonial Revolution." Paper presented at the Fourth International Conference on World Politics, Athens, Greece, 17–22 September 1962.
86. ———. "The Sino-Soviet Split and Its Repercussions in Africa." In Hamrell, S., and Widstrand, C. G., eds. *The Soviet Bloc, China and Africa.* Uppsala: The Scandinavian Institute of African Studies, 1964.
87. Mackerras, Colin, and Hunter, Neale. *China Observed.* New York: Praeger, 1968.
88. Marchand, Jean. "La République Populaire de Chine et l'Afrique Noire. *Revue de Défense Nationale* (Paris) 20 (1964):1554–1566.
89. Marco Polls. *Kenya's Little General Election: KPU vs. KANU, Public Opinion Poll No. 15.* Dar es Salaam: Marco Publishers, 1967.
90. Marcum, John. *The Angolan Revolution,* Cambridge: M.I.T. Press, 1969.
91. ———. "Three Revolutions," *Africa Report,* November 1967, pp. 8–22.
92. Medzini, Meron. "Chinese Penetration in the Middle East," *New Outlook* (Tel Aviv), vol. 6, no. 9 (1963), pp. 16–28.
93. Moore, Clement H. "One-Partyism in Mauritania." *Journal of Modern African Studies* 3 (1965):409–420.
94. Morison, David L. "Soviet Policy Towards Africa." In Hamrell, S., and Widstrand, C. G., eds. *The Soviet Bloc, China and Africa.* Uppsala: The Scandinavian Institute of African Studies, 1964.
95. ———. *The USSR and Africa.* London: Oxford University Press for the Institute of Race Relations and Central Asian Research Centre, 1964.
96. Mozingo, David P., and Robinson, Thomas W. "Lin Piao on 'People's War': China Takes a Second Look at Vietnam." RAND Memorandum RM-4814-PR. Santa Monica, California: The RAND Corporation, 1965.
97. Müller, Kurt. "Soviet and Chinese Programmes of Technical Aid to African Countries." In Hamrell, S., and Widstrand, C. G., eds. *The Soviet Bloc, China and Africa.* Uppsala: The Scandinavian Institute of African Studies, 1964.
98. Nielsen, Waldemar, A. *The Great Powers in Africa.* New York: Praeger for the Council on Foreign Relations, 1969.
99. Nkoana, Matthew. *A Special Report on the Pan-Africanist Congress of South Africa.* Not in general circulation, the report is summarized in *South Africa: Information and Analysis.* Johannesburg: Congress for Cultural Freedom, 1969.
100. Okello, John. *Revolution in Zanzibar.* Nairobi: East African Institute Press, 1967.
101. Okumu, Washington. *Lumumba's Congo: Roots of Conflict.* New York: Obolensky, 1962.

102. Orleans, Leo A. *Professional Manpower and Education in Communist China.* Washington: National Science Foundation, 1961.
103. Parti Socialiste Destourien. *La Vérité sur la Subversion à l'Université de Tunis.* Tunis: Parti Socialiste Destourien, 1968.
104. Passin, Herbert. *China's Cultural Diplomacy.* New York: Praeger, 1963.
105. "Pékin et l'Afrique." *Afrique Contemporaine,* no. 16 (1964), pp. 17–21.
106. Prybyla, Jan S. "Communist China's Economic Relations with Africa." *Asian Survey* (Berkeley) 4 (1964):1135–1143.
107. Scalapino, Robert. "The Cultural Revolution and Chinese Foreign Policy." In *The Cultural Revolution: 1967 in Review.* Ann Arbor: University of Michigan Center for Chinese Studies, 1968. Michigan Papers in Chinese Studies no. 2.
108. ———. "Sino-Soviet Competition in Africa." *Foreign Affairs* 42 (1964):640–654.
109. Schatten, Fritz. *Communism in Africa.* New York: Praeger, 1966.
110. ———. "Peking's Growing Influence in Africa." *Swiss Review of World Affairs* (Zurich), August 1960, pp. 8–11.
111. Schram, Stuart. *Mao Tse-tung.* Baltimore: Penguin, 1966.
112. Schwartz, Benjamin. "The Polemics as Seen by a Non-Polemicist." *Problems of Communism,* vol. 12, no. 2 (1964), pp. 102–106.
113. Schwartz, Harry G. "The Ts'an-k'ao Hsiao-hsi: How Well Informed Are Chinese Officials about the Outside World?", *China Quarterly,* no. 27 (1966), pp. 54–83.
114. Seale, Patrick, "The Anarchist from Notting Hill Gate." *Observer* (London), 8 March 1964. An interview with Abdul Rahman Mohammed Babu.
115. Segal, Aaron. "Havana's Tricontinental Conference." *Africa Report,* April 1966, p. 51.
116. Segal, Ronald. *African Profiles.* Baltimore: Penguin, 1963.
117. Slawecki, Leon M. S. "The Two Chinas in Africa." *Foreign Affairs* 41 (1963):398–409.
118. Snow, Edgar. *Red Star Over China.* New York: Grove Press, 1961.
119. Sonnenfeldt, Helmut. "Soviet Strategy in Africa: Lessons Learned in the Congo?" *Africa Report,* November 1960, p. 5.
120. Sterling, Claire. "Chou En-lai and the Watusi." *Reporter,* 12 March 1964, pp. 22–23.
121. Thiam, Doudou. *The Foreign Policy of African States.* London: Phoenix House, 1965. The unrevised version is *La Politique Etrangère des Etats Africains.* Paris: Presses Universitaires de France, 1963.
122. Thompson, W. Scott. *Ghana's Foreign Policy* 1957–1966. Princeton: Princeton University Press, 1969.
123. Touval, Saadia. *Somali Nationalism.* Cambridge: Harvard University Press, 1963.
124. Townsend, James R. "Communist China: The New Protracted War." *Asian Survey* 5 (1965):1–11.
125. Tretiak, Donald. "The Chinese Cultural Revolution and Foreign Policy." *Current Scene,* vol. 8, no. 7, 1 April 1970.
126. Tsou, Tang, and Halperin, Morton H. "Mao Tse-tung's Revolutionary Strategy and Peking's International Behavior." *American Political Science Review* 59 (1965): 80–99.
127. Tung Chi-p'ing, and Evans, Humphrey. *The Thought Revolution.* New York: Coward-McCann, 1966.
128. Union Research Institute. *Communist China 1961.* Hong Kong: Union Research Institute, 1962.
129. ———. *Who's Who in Communist China.* Hong Kong: Union Research Institute, 1966.
130. United Nations. *Yearbook of International Trade Statistics.* New York: United Nations, 1958, 1961–1963.
131. U.S. Department of the Army. "Communist China: Ruthless Enemy or Paper Tiger? A Bibliographic Survey." DA PAM 20-61. Washington: Department of the Army, 1966.

132. U.S. Department of State. Division of Russian Affairs. *The Second Congress of the Communist International as Reported and Interpreted by the Official Newspapers of Soviet Russia.* Washington: U.S. Government Printing Office, 1920.

133. U.S. Government. *Biographic Directory: Party and Government Leaders of Mainland China.* Washington: U.S. Government, 1960 (BD271), 1963 (63-7), and 1966 (A 66-8).

134. U.S. Senate. Committee on Government Operations. *National Policy Machinery in Communist China.* Washington: U.S. Government Printing Office, 1960.

135. U.S. Senate. Committee on the Judiciary. Subcommittee to Investigate the Administration of the Internal Security Act and Other Internal Security Laws. "Chinese and Russian Communists Compete for Foreign Support: Testimony of Tung Chi-p'ing, 20 August 1964." Pamphlet. Washington: U.S. Government Printing Office, 1964.

136. Wallerstein, Immanuel. *Africa: The Politics of Independence.* New York: Vintage Books, 1961.

137. Whiting, Allen S. *China Crosses the Yalu: The Decision to Enter the Korean War.* New York: Macmillan, 1960.

138. Wilson, Dick. "China's Economic Relations with Africa." *Race,* vol. 5, no. 4 (1964), pp. 61–71.

139. Woddis, Jack. *Africa: The Roots of Revolt.* New York: Citadel Press, 1962.

140. Wu Yuan-li. *The Economic Potential of Communist China.* Menlo Park, California: Stanford Research Institute, 1963.

141. Young, Merwin Crawford. "The Congo Rebellion." *Africa Report,* April 1965, pp. 6–11.

142. ———. *Politics in the Congo.* Princeton: Princeton University Press, 1965.

143. Yu, George T. "China's Failure in Africa." *Asian Survey* 6 (1966):461–468.

144. ———. "Chinese Rivalry in Africa." *Race,* vol. 5, no. 4 (1964), pp. 35–47.

145. ———. "Dragon in the Bush: Peking's Presence in Africa." *Asian Survey* 8 (1968): 1018–1026.

146. Zagoria, Donald. *The Sino-Soviet Conflict 1956–1961.* Princeton: Princeton University Press, 1962.

Non-Chinese Serials (Including Translations of Chinese Periodicals)

147. *Africa Report.* Previously *Africa Special Report.* Washington: African-American Institute.

148. *African Communist.* London: South African Communist Party.

149. *Afrique Nouvelle.* Dakar.

150. *Afro-Asian Bulletin.* Cairo: Afro-Asian People's Solidarity Organization. Permanent Secretariat. Irreg.

151. *Afro-Asian Quarterly.* Cairo: Afro-Asian People's Solidarity Organization. Permanent Secretariat. Irreg.

152. *L'Aube Nouvelle.* Porto-Novo.

153. *Cahiers du Communisme.* Paris: Parti Communiste Français.

154. *Cape Times.* Capetown.

155. *Central Asian Review.* London: Central Asian Research Centre.

156. *China Quarterly.* London.

157. *Le Courrier d'Afrique.* Léopoldville (Kinshasa).

158. *Current Background.* Hong Kong: U.S. Consulate General.

159. *Current Digest of the Soviet Press.* New York: Joint Committee on Slavic Studies.

160. *Daily Telegraph.* London.

161. *Direction of Trade Annual.* Washington: International Monetary Fund.

162. *East African Standard.* Nairobi.

163. *Egyptian Gazette.* Cairo.

164. *Ethiopian Herald*. Addis Ababa.
165. *Extracts from China Mainland Magazines*. Hong Kong: U.S. Consulate General.
166. *Far Eastern Economic Review*. Hong Kong.
167. *Financial Times*. London.
168. *Ghanaian Times*. Accra.
169. *Globe*. Boston.
170. *International Affairs*. Moscow: All-Union Society "Knowledge."
171. *I.U.S. News Service*. Prague: International Union of Students.
172. *Japan Times*. Tokyo.
173. *Jeune Afrique*. Tunis.
174. *Kenya Weekly News*. Nakuru.
175. *Mizan Newsletter*. London: Central Asian Research Centre.
176. *Le Monde*. Paris.
177. *Le Moniteur Africain du Commerce et de l'Industrie*. Dakar.
178. *National Observer*. Silver Spring, Maryland.
179. *Nationalist*. Dar es Salaam.
180. *New Times*. Moscow: Trud.
181. *New York Times*. New York.
182. *Newsweek*. New York.
183. *Observer*. London.
184. *Pravda*. Moscow.
185. *Réalités*. Paris.
186. *Révolution: Africa-Latin America-Asia*. Paris and Lausanne: Nouvelles Editions Internationales.
187. *La Semaine*. Brazzaville.
188. *Somali News*. Mogadishu.
189. *Soviet News Booklet*. London: Soviet News. Irreg.
190. *Standard*. Dar es Salaam.
191. *Sunday Telegraph*. London.
192. *Survey*. London.
193. *Survey of the China Mainland Press*. Hong Kong: U.S. Consulate General.
194. *Uganda Argus*. Kampala.
195. *West Africa*. London.
196. *World Strength of Communist Party Organizations*. U.S. Department of State. Bureau of Intelligence and Research. Washington: U.S. Government Printing Office.
197. *World Student News*. Prague: International Union of Students.

Chinese Works, Documents, and Serials

198. *Afro-Asian Solidarity Against Imperialism*. Peking: Foreign Languages Press, 1964. A collection of documents, speeches, and press interviews from the visits of Chinese leaders to thirteen African and Asian countries.
199. *China and the Asian-African Conference (Documents)*. Peking: Foreign Languages Press, 1955.
200. *China Reconstructs*. Peking.
201. *Chinese People Resolutely Support the Just Struggle of the African People*. Peking: Foreign Languages Press, 1961.
202. *Ch'üan-kuo hsin shu-mu* [National Bibliography of New Publications] Peking: Ministry of Culture. Publications Control Bureau. Publications Acquisitions Library.
203. *Chung-kuo Ch'ing-nien Pao* [China Youth]. Peking.
204. Editorial Department of *Hung-ch'i* [Red Flag]. *Long Live Leninism!* Peking: Foreign Languages Press, 1960.
205. *Eighth National Congress of the Communist Party of China*. Peking: Foreign Languages Press, 1956.

206. Feng Chih-tan. *Glimpses of West Africa.* Peking: Foreign Languages Press, 1963.
207. *Hsüeh-hsi* [Study]. Peking.
208. *Hung-ch'i* [Red Flag]. Peking: Chinese Communist Party Central Committee.
209. *In Support of the People of the Congo (Léopoldville) Against U.S. Aggression.* Peking: Foreign Languages Press, 1965.
210. *Jen-min Jih-pao* [People's Daily]. Peking.
211. *Jen-min Shou-ts'e* [People's Handbook]. Peking: Ta Kung Pao She.
212. *Kuo-chi Wen-t'i Yen-chiu* [Research in International Problems]. Peking: International Problems Research Committee.
213. Li Huang, Chang Feng-yi, Lin Yin-wu, and Chu Tsu-yi of the Drama Group of the Political Department of the Navy of the Chinese People's Liberation Army. *War Drums on the Equator.* Peking: Foreign Languages Press, 1966.
214. Li Wei-han. "The Struggle for Proletarian Leadership in the Period of the New-Democratic Revolution in China, Part 1." *Peking Review,* 23 February 1962. Parts 2–5 appear in the four subsequent issues.
215. ———. "The Chinese People's Democratic United Front: Its Special Features," *Peking Review,* 18 August 1961.
216. Lin Piao. *Long Live the Victory of People's War!* Peking: Foreign Languages Press, 1965.
217. Liu Shao-ch'i. *Internationalism and Nationalism.* Peking: Foreign Languages Press, n.d.
218. ———. *Report on the Draft Constitution of the People's Republic of China. Constitution of the People's Republic of China.* Peking: Foreign Languages Press, 1962.
219. Liu Ssu-mu. "Tasks and Outlooks of African Studies." Speech delivered at the International Congress of Africanists, Legon, Accra, Ghana, December 1962.
220. ———. *Tzen-yang Hsüeh-hsi Kuo-chi Shih-shih* [How to Study International Events]. Peking: *Shih-chieh Chih-shih Ch'u-pan She* [World Knowledge Publishing House], 1951.
221. Mao Tse-tung. *On Contradiction.* Peking: Foreign Languages Press, 1960.
222. ———. *On New Democracy.* Peking: Foreign Languages Press, 1960.
223. ———. *Selected Military Writings of Mao Tse-tung.* Peking: Foreign Languages Press, 1963.
224. ———. *Selected Works.* Four volumes. Peking: Foreign Languages Press, 1961, 1964, and 1965.
225. New China News Agency English Language Service. *Daily News Releases.*
226. *Peking Review.* Peking.
227. People's Liberation Army. *Kung-tso T'ung-hsün* [Bulletin of Activities]. Issues of early 1961. Translated as *The Politics of the Chinese Red Army.* J. Chester Cheng, ed. Stanford: Hoover Institution on War, Revolution and Peace, 1966.
228. *Shih-chieh Chih-shih* [World Knowledge]. Peking: *Shih-chieh Chih-shih Ch'u-pan She.*
229. *Shih-chieh Chih-shih Ch'u-pan She. Ti-san chieh Ya-fei Jen-min T'uan-chieh Ta-hui Wen-chien Hui-pien* [Collected Documents of the Third Afro-Asian People's Solidarity Conference]. Peking: *Shih-chieh Chih-shih Ch'u-pan She,* 1963.
230. *Shih-chieh Chih-shih Nien-chien* [World Knowledge Yearbook]. 1958, 1961. Peking: *Shih-chieh Chih-shih Ch'u-pan She.*
231. *Shih-chieh Chih-shih Shou-ts'e* [World Knowledge Handbook]. 1954, 1957. Peking: *Shih-chieh Chih-shih Ch'u-pan She.*
232. *Ten Glorious Years.* Peking: Foreign Languages Press, 1960.

Index